Braude's
Source Book for
Speakers and Writers

Jacob M. Braude

Braude's
Source Book for
Speakers and Writers

Prentice-Hall, Inc.   Englewood Cliffs, N. J.

DEDICATION

With deep and profound affection
I dedicate this volume
to the revered and cherished memory
of my dear mother and father
Anna and Emil Braude

WHAT THIS BOOK CAN DO FOR YOU

This is essentially a reference book. It is intended to save you countless hours of reading and library research. It contains illustrative anecdotes; overall themes; countless aphorisms and bon mots and philosophical tidbits—some original, others not. It provides a handy source of adrenalin for any speech or paper which appears a little weak-in-the-knees at spots.

Used in this fashion, this book will enable you to complete a manuscript, speech or outline with a minimum of effort and a maximum of result. If whatever it is you are preparing requires buoying up, you have but to select the weak spots and then turn these pages until you come to the most likely categories where you will be sure to find just the material you need.

Or better still, why not make use of the several indexes which are done elaborately and in minute detail. It has been said that nothing is more important in determining the value of a good reference book than its Index. And this volume has three of them! Lord Campbell once wrote, "So essential did I consider an index to be to every book that I proposed to bring a bill into Parliament to deprive an author who publishes a book without an index of the privilege of copyright, and, moreover to subject him for his offense to a pecuniary penalty." And he was backed up by Horace Binney who declaimed," I certainly think that the best book in the world would owe the most to a good index, and the worst book, if it had but a good single thought in it, might be kept alive by it."

Any key word, thought, idea or broad classification can put you on the trail of what you are looking for in the Subject Index and by a process of triangulation you can put your finger on the desired item in the fraction of a minute. And should you know the name of an author or the place where some special piece of wisdom or some factual or philosophical material has appeared, you have but to turn to the Author and Source Index to track it down. In similar fashion, if it is an anecdote about a specific person which you are seeking, you will have no difficulty pinpointing where it can be found in the book by simply referring to the third index entitled Index of Names and Personalities.

Once you have determined the subject of your manuscript or speech, you have your starting point which you may use together with allied or associated topics as your several reference points. And thus go forward to the completed thoughts, comments, stories, using quotations of outstanding personalities in their respective fields as a sort of cement which will firmly hold together all the material you have assembled. Much of this "cement" you will find in the pages that follow.

This book may even do more than all this for you. It may provide the very idea or thought which could evolve into the principal theme of your ultimate product. Among the hundreds of categories available for you to choose from are: Advertising, Aging, Americanism, Ancestry, Atheism, Automation, Business, Capital-Labor, Child Guidance, Christianity, Church Attendance, Cooperation, etc., etc., on through the rest of the alphabet.

There is yet one other way in which this book can be used and that is for purposes of entertainment—simple and pure. Nowadays there are very few who are never called upon to make some sort of speech, write an article, submit a business report, present an idea at a club meeting or serve as chairman or toastmaster. But if you should never chance to find yourself in such a delightful vacuum, the contents of this book, you will find, will make for just plain good reading.

Altogether I have in my files as of today a total collection of more than 100,000 cards which I have accumulated over the past half century and in which I still find pleasurable joy and entertainment as I riffle through them and again taste the collective wisdom and wit of great minds both past and present.

Jacob M. Braude

September 1968

Contents

Braude's
Source Book for
Speakers and Writers

Ability—Abilities

1.   Abilities not used are abilities wasted.

2.   There is only one proof of ability—results. Men with ability in action get results.

—HARRY F. BANKS

3.   To develop ease and confidence in doing, you must develop abilities and then develop excellence in the use of these abilities.

—RHODA LACHAR

Abnormal—Abnormality

4.   To study the abnormal is the best way of understanding the normal.

—WILLIAM JAMES

Absence

5.   Absence increases fondness—and ends in forgetfulness.

—DAGOBERT D. RUNES

Absolutism

6.   Nothing is more certain in modern society than the principle that there are no absolutes; that a name, a phrase, a standard has meaning only when associated with the considerations which gave birth to the nomenclature.

—PERCIVAL E. JACKSON

Accomplishment—Accomplishments

7.   Every worthwhile accomplishment big or little, has its stages of drudgery and triumph; a beginning, a struggle, and a victory.

Accord

8.   In the United States, to an unprecedented degree, the individual's social role has come to be determined not by *who he is* but by *what he can accomplish.*

Accord

9.   If a conference last a long time, it must end in peace; no one can keep on defying his enemies all day.

—ALFRED DUGGAN

10.   Underlying practically all our attempts to bring agreement is the assumption that agreement is brought about by changing people's minds—other people's.

—S. I. HAYAKAWA

Achievement—Achievements

11.   When you're trying to get something done, don't worry too much about stepping on someone else's toes. Nobody gets his toes stepped on unless he is standing still or sitting down on the job.

12.   The world judges you by what you have done, not by what you have started out to do; by what you have completed, not by what you have begun. The bulldog wins by the simple expedient of holding on to the finish.

—BALTASAR GRACIÁN

13.   When your work speaks for itself, don't interrupt.

—HENRY J. KAISER

14.   The first principle of achievement is mental attitude. Man begins to achieve when he begins to believe.

—J. C. ROBERTS

15.   The TWINS of achievement are HEADWORK and HARDWORK. They go together, for neither can do the job alone. Anyone who thinks otherwise quickly learns how wrong he is.

The importance of HEADWORK is more appreciated today than at any other time in our history. Today the choice jobs in every field of endeavor are being offered to those whose education qualifies them for the opportunity. It is no secret that most business leaders accept college degrees as indicating HEADWORK achievement.

This does not mean that formal education is the sole qualifier for HEADWORK. There always have been and always will be individuals whose HEADWORK on the job moves them toward the top.

And there is the accompanying recognition that HARDWORK is also vital to achievement. Not only must those who want to move up have the brains and the training, but they must have the capacity for and the willingness to work; for HEADWORK gets nowhere without its twin HARDWORK. One complements the other. The potential for HEAD-WORK means little in a lazy individual, for sheer brilliance can be self-defeating when it has contempt for work. And it might be added that HARDWORK often fails its goal when not directed by the head.

Put the two together, HEADWORK and HARDWORK, and there is no limit to what may be achieved.

—*Nuggets*

Acquiescence

16. Most people prefer a blunt "Yes" to a polite and gracious "No."

17. Always fall in with what you're asked to accept. Take what is given, and make it over your way. My aim in life has always been to hold my own with whatever's going. Not against-with.

—Robert Frost

Action—Actions

18. In the performance of a good action, a man not only benefits himself, but he confers a blessing upon others.

—Sir Philip Sidney

19. A man who has to be convinced to act before he acts is *not* a man of action.

—Georges Clemenceau

20. To know what to do is wisdom. To know how to do it is skill. But doing it, as it should be done, tops the other two virtues.

21. To do an evil action is base; to do a good action, without incurring danger, is common enough; but it is the part of a good man to do great and noble deeds, though he risks everything.

—PLUTARCH

22. Life was not given for indolent contemplation and study of self, nor for brooding over emotions of piety: Action and actions only determine the worth.

—IMMANUEL FICHTE

23. The sincerest satisfactions in life come in doing and not in dodging duty; in meeting and solving problems, in facing facts, in being a dependable person.

—RICHARD L. EVANS

24. Existence was given us for action, rather than indolent and aimless contemplation; our worth is determined by the good deeds we do, rather than by the fine emotions we feel. They greatly mistake, who suppose that God cares for no other pursuit than devotion.

25. It is no use for one to stand in the shade and complain that the sun does not shine upon him. He must come out resolutely on the hot and dusty field where all are compelled to antagonize with stubborn difficulties, and pertinaciously strive until he conquers, if he would deserve to be crowned.

—E. L. MAGOON

26. Napoleon was the most effective man in modern times—some will say of all times. The secret of his character was, that while his plans were more vast, more various, and, of course, more difficult than those of other men, he had the talent at the same time, to fill them up with perfect promptness and precision, in every particular of execution.

—HORACE BUSHNELL

27.   The only things in which we can be said to have any property are our actions. Our thoughts may be bad, yet produce no poison; they may be good, yet produce no fruit. Our riches may be taken away by misfortune, our reputation by malice, our spirits by calamity, our health by disease, our friends by death. But our actions must follow us beyond the grave; with respect to them alone, we cannot say that we shall carry nothing with us when we die, neither that we shall go naked out of the world.

—CHARLES C. COLTON

28.
1. Do more than exist, live.
2. Do more than touch, feel.
3. Do more than look, observe.
4. Do more than read, absorb.
5. Do more than hear, listen.
6. Do more than listen, understand.
7. Do more than think, ponder.
8. Do more than talk, say something.

—JOHN H. RHOADES

Adaptability

29.   It seems to me that the key to our future can be summed up in one word—adaptability. In a rapidly changing world it is often a matter of survival to change one's mind—one's attitude—one's way of thinking and doing things. Even when survival is not at issue, we should all know how to adjust to changed circumstances in order to capitalize on new opportunities.

—DUDLEY DOWELL

Adoration

30.   Whoever you are, there is some younger person who thinks you are perfect. There is some work that will never be done if you don't do it. There is someone who would miss you if you were gone. There is a good reason for becoming better than you are. There is a place that you alone can fill.

Adulthood

31. Labeling literature and movies as "adult" would be all right if "adult" meant the maturing of judgment instead of just the passage of years.

Adversity—Adversities

32. Prosperity is a great teacher; adversity is a greater. Possession pampers the mind; privation trains and strengthens it.

—WILLIAM HAZLITT

33. In the day of prosperity we have many refuges to resort to; in the day of adversity, only one.

—HORATIUS BONAR

34. As the valley gives height to the mountain, so can sorrow give meaning to pleasure; as the well is the source of the fountain, deep adversity can be a treasure.

—DR. WILLIAM ARTHUR WARD

35. The truly great and good, in affliction, bear a countenance more princely than they are wont; for it is the temper of the highest hearts, like the palm tree, to strive upwards when it is most burdened.

—SIR PHILIP SIDNEY

Advertising

36. Nothing except the Mint can make money without advertising.

—THOMAS B. MACAULAY

37. Advertising is an aggressively creative force that makes music at the cash registers by stimulating the public's desire to acquire goods.

38. Those who say advertising sells people things they don't need remind us of the salesman who once sold two hats to a man with only one head.

6

39. During the panic of 1907, William Wrigley, Jr., the famous chewing-gum manufacturer, did the opposite of what everyone else was doing. He invested the then unheard of sum of $1 million in advertising and practically doubled his sales within a year. Twice he mailed free gum to every name listed in every telephone book in the country. His outdoor sign along the Trenton-Atlantic City railway tracks was nearly a mile long!

40. Advertising is as vital to the preservation of freedom as free exercise of publishing a newspaper or the free exercise of building a church or the free exercise of the right of trial by jury. Advertising is not only the practical source of advocating to the people of this country the economic choices they have before them. It is practically the sole support of the only communication system that is not under the control of the state.

41. Advertising is like fire. Fire can broil a steak for you, nice and charred on the outside and pink and rare and juicy on the inside—or, uncontrolled, fire can burn your house down for you—and the fire doesn't care. And so it is with advertising. Advertising is an instrument in the hands of the people who use it. If evil men use advertising for base purposes, then evil can result. If honest men use advertising to sell an honest product with honest enthusiasm, then positive good for our kind of capitalistic society can result.

—JOHN W. CRAWFORD

42. This crazy, mixed-up world . . .
DO YOU KNOW JOHN X. MUGWUMP?

John gets up every morning to the ring of an advertised clock radio . . . cleans his teeth with an advertised brush and toothpaste; washes and shaves with an advertised soap and razor . . . puts on advertised underwear, hose, shoes, shirt and suit . . . eats an advertised breakfast food and bread; drinks an advertised cup of coffee, puts on an advertised hat.

John drives an advertised car to the station, smokes an advertised cigarette, gets to his office where his secretary is ready to work on an advertised typewriter, using advertised bond and carbon paper for a letter which John will sign with an advertised pen and an advertised ink . . . to turn down a proposal to advertise on the ground that advertising does not pay!

Advice

43. In the multitude of counselors there is safety.

—OLD TESTAMENT

44. Advice from an old carpenter: Measure twice and saw once.

45. To ask for advice is in nine cases out of ten to tout for flattery.

—JOHN CHURTON COLLINS

46. Friendship will not stand the strain of very much good advice for very long.

—ROBERT LYND

47. Appraise the spring before you drink the water;
Observe the mother ere you wed the daughter.

—FROM THE CHINESE

48. Advice is not disliked because it is advice, but because so few people know how to give it.

—LEIGH HUNT

49. One good thing about people who ignore your existence is that they do not give you any bad advice.

50. No one is more confusing than the fellow who gives good advice while setting a bad example.

51. Don't give advice, even if people ask for it; they don't want it, they only want to be told that what they are doing is all right.

52. Sometimes it takes more judgment to separate the good advice from the bad than is needed to make your own decision.

53. A man takes contradiction and advice much more easily than people think, only he will not bear it when violently given, even though it is well founded. Hearts are flowers; they remain open to the softly falling dew, but shut up in the violent downpour of rain.

—JEAN PAUL RICHTER

54.   Taking counsel is worthwhile; not for the sake of the counsel, which is not worth a button to you in any case, but for the sake of seeing in your counselor's eyes the flame of gladness at being important to somebody.

—HENRY S. HASKINS

Age

55.   The beauty of old men is the grey head.

—OLD TESTAMENT, *Proverbs*

56.   Mature men generally look younger than mature women because a woman of 40 is usually 50.

57.   With the ancient is wisdom; and in length of years understanding.

—OLD TESTAMENT, *Job*

58.   You can judge your age by your attitude toward a vacation: Is it a time to play or a time to rest?

59.   Women have a natural antipathy to their right age—the years they lop off before 60 they often add on after 80.

60.   You are as young as your faith, as old as your doubt; as young as your self-confidence, as old as your fear; as young as your hope, as old as your despair.

61.
Though gray be your hair
With little to part
This does not denote
The age of your heart.

—MICHAEL FRANKLIN ELLIS

Aging

62. How amusing are the answers people of different ages give to "How old are you?" A youngster will say: "I'm five-and-a-half and three months." A teenager: "I'm almost sixteen" (when she is actually just fifteen). A woman nearing middle-age: I'm in my forties." While Grandma proudly answers: "Eighty next birthday."

It seems you have to be young enough or old enough not to be age conscious!

Aging

63. To stay youthful, stay useful!

64. Everyone has talent at twenty-five. The difficulty is to have it at fifty.

—Edgar Degas

65. By the time a man gets to greener pastures, he can't climb the fence.

66. As people grow older they often confuse being careful with being wise.

67. *Husband to friend:* "It's terrible to grow old alone—my wife hasn't had a brithday in six years."

68. Part of the wisdom of age is to realize that youth will insist upon making its own mistakes.

69. No man is so old as to believe he cannot live one more year.

—Sean O'Casey

70. There is no way of living a long time without growing old, and yet everyone hates to grow old.

—Ruth Smeltzer

71. Growing old is no cause for hysteria. The rose bush does not scream when the petals begin to fall.

—DOUGLAS MEADOR

72. If wrinkles must be written upon our brows, let them not be written upon the heart. The spirit should not grow old.

—JAMES GARFIELD

73. You can tell that a child is growing up when he stops asking where he came from and starts refusing to tell you where he is going.

74. Wrinkles are only the by-paths of many smiles, and some tears; gray hair is the silver-dust of the stars; and growing gracefully slower of step is only walking nearer to God.

—LAVETTA HUMMEL

75. Childhood must pass away, and then youth, as surely as age approaches. The true wisdom is to be always seasonable, and to change with a good grace in changing circumstances.

—ROBERT LOUIS STEVENSON

76.
No man should fret in case his hair
   Turns silver in his prime
He's fortunate that some was there
   To turn at turning time.

—WILLIAM W. PRATT

Alertness

77. If you want to be well heeled you've got to be on your toes.

78. You can stay alive as long as you live by keeping your mind alert, by feeding yourself new ideas, by exploring the world of ideas with the help of the books in your own public library.

Alibi—Alibis

79.　After inspecting a branch plant that wasn't doing so well, the president said to the personnel manager, "You ought to hire a few ballet dancers."

"Ballet dancers?" exclaimed the startled personnel manager.

"Yes," said the president. "We need someone on their toes around here."

Alibi—Alibis

80.　There are plenty of alibis for failure because success doesn't need them.

Alimony

81.　Alimony: a system by which one pays for the mistake of two.
　　　　　　　　　　　　—JOHN GARLAND POLLARD

82.　Alimony has one advantage in that a husband no longer need bring his pay check home to his wife. He can mail it to her.

Ally—Allies

83.　An ally is not necessarily your friend—he is an enemy of your enemy.

Ambition—Ambitions

84.　Ambition is but avarice on stilts.
　　　　　　　　　　　　—WALTER SAVAGE LANDOR

85.　There is a loftier ambition than merely to stand high in the world. It is to stoop down and lift mankind a little higher.
　　　　　　　　　　　　—HENRY VAN DYKE

86. The ambitious man climbs up high and perilous stairs, and never cares how to come down; the desire of rising hath swallowed up his fear of a fall.

—Thomas Adams

87. The amount of ambition a man possesses determines his place in the auditorium of life; whether he will be in the audience or on the stage.

—Douglas Meador

88. Ambition is the mainspring of nearly all progress, yet uncontrolled, unbridled ambition can spur men into cruel, selfish, despicable deeds. To be without ambition is to be mentally dead. But supreme caution must be taken that ambition is not such as to kill us morally and spiritually. Ambition may be likened to a spirited, speedy horse; it can carry us quickly over much ground if we keep a proper rein on it and guide it along the right road, but if given too much rein, it is in danger of landing us in the ditch. Ambition should be akin to ideals.

—B. C. Forbes

America—American—Americanism

89. Be glad you're living in a land where you can say what you think without thinking.

90. When the spirit and fiber of Washington fail to appear in each American generation, then, indeed, things will go ill with us.

—Nathan Wright Stevenson

91. If a man is going to be an American at all let him be so without any qualifying adjectives; and if he is going to be something else, let him drop the word American from his personal description.

—Henry Cabot Lodge

92. It is doubtful if American institutions and the American character could ever have evolved in Europe. The seed came from there but it took the sum of freedom and American soil to produce the fruit.

Amusement

93. It is probably a pity that every citizen of each state cannot visit all the others, to see the differences, to learn what we have in common, and to come back with a richer, fuller understanding of America—in all its beauty, in all its dignity, in all its strength, in support of moral principle.

—Dwight D. Eisenhower

94. You have to travel around over the country to discover that Americans are not all alike, after all. For instance, in Kentucky fresh green beans are cooked with bacon, whereas in Maine they are prepared with milk. House ceilings are calcimined in Massachusetts, but papered in Iowa. New Englanders cool off on the piazza on a warm summer evening, but Alabamans seek relief on the gallery and Westerners on the porch. Hot breads are considered wholesome in Arkansas, but slow poison in Wisconsin.

95. When God made the oyster, he guaranteed his absolute economic and social security. He built the oyster a house, his shell, to shelter and protect him from his enemies. When hungry, the oyster simply opens his shell, and food rushes in for him. He has Freedom from Want. But when God made the Eagle, He declared, "The blue sky is the limit—build your own house!" So the Eagle built on the highest mountain. Storms threaten him every day. For food, he flies through miles of rain and snow and wind. The Eagle, not the oyster, is the emblem of America.

Amusement

96. You can't live on amusement. It is the froth on water, an inch deep, and then the mud!

—George Macdonald

97. Amusements are to religion like breezes of air to the flame; gentle ones will fan it, but strong ones will put it out.

—David Thomas

Ancestry

98. The cheapest way to have your family tree traced is to run for public office.

99. A million years from now the earth may be filled with creatures who stoutly deny that they ever descended from man.

100. It is better to be the builder of our own name than to be indebted by descent for the proudest gifts known to the books of heraldry.
—HOSEA BALLOU

101. Don Marquis was exchanging mock insults with a friend. "Do you realize, sir," the friend said, "that you are vilifying one who is descended from royalty? Which reminds me, who are *you* descended from?"
"I am not a descendant," replied Marquis. "I am an ancestor!"
—EDWARD ANTHONY

Anger

102. An angry man stirreth up strife.
—OLD TESTAMENT

103. Let not the sun go down upon your wrath.
—NEW TESTAMENT

104. He that is slow to wrath is of great understanding.
—OLD TESTAMENT

105. Anger is the sinew of the soul; without it a man would be lame.
—SHELAGH DELANEY

106. No one ever makes us mad. We grow angry as a result of our own choice.

107. Violence in the voice is often only the death rattle of reason in the throat.
—J. F. BOYES

108. When anger snuffs out the lamp of reason, delay is your only safeguard.

109.   The torrid sun melts mountain snows.
When anger comes, then wisdom goes.
—From the Chinese

110.   Anger is often a substitute for knowledge; violence, a defense against truth.
—Dr. William Arthur Ward

111.   Whenever someone or something irritates you or makes you angry, take a moment before reacting and acting. Consider what has really been said to make you angry and then decide whether it will only serve the person's purpose if you show your anger—or whether it is better to ignore the remark and serve your own purpose.

112.   Anger is a common sin. It is one of the most dangerous and injurious sins of them all. It ruins health. It destroys peace at home. It leads to violence. It turns love to hatred. It leads to open crime. Friendships are blasted by it. All that one has been building for years can be destroyed in a moment's anger. No man can be a real and vital force until he has learned to control his temper, or until he has brought it under control of a greater power than himself. To master one's temper is one of life's greatest problems, and when done, one of life's greatest victories.

Antagonism

113.   Men are not against you; they are merely for themselves.
—Gene Fowler

Antique—Antiques

114.   One way to become rich would be to develop the ability to tell exactly when a piece of junk becomes an antique.

115.   An antiquarian displayed in his window five wooden statues, which he titled: "The Five Senses." When a customer bought one of the statues, the antiquarian calmly relettered the title card: "The Four Seasons." Upon selling another, the remaining group became: "The Three Graces." Then they became: "Night and Day." When all but one had been sold, he titled the remaining statue: "Solitude."

Apology—Apologies

116.   Swallowing angry words is better than choking on an apology.

117.   Sometimes one wishes the people who are so quick to apologize wouldn't do some of the things they have to apologize for.

Apparel

118.   No matter what new styles are, the women first to wear them are the ones who shouldn't.

119.   Women will wear anything new, no matter how uncomfortable; and men will wear anything comfortable, no matter how old.

120.   All women's dresses are merely variations on the eternal struggle between the admitted desire to dress and the unadmitted desire to undress.

—LIN YUTANG

Appreciation

121.   By appreciation we make excellence in others our own property.

—VOLTAIRE

122.   The most difficult thing in the world is to appreciate what we have—until we lose it.

Architect—Architecture

123. We must never undervalue any person. The workman loves not that this work should be despised in his presence. Now God is present everywhere, and every person is his work.

—St. Francis de Sales

124. No human being can be genuinely happy unless he or she stands well in the esteem of fellow mortals. Who would deal successfully with us must never forget that we possess and are possessed by this ego. A word of appreciation often can accomplish what nothing else could accomplish.

—B. C. Forbes

Architect—Architecture

125. The architect should seek opportunities to be of constructive service in civic affairs, and to the best of his ability, advance the safety, health and well-being of the community in which he resides by promoting therein the appreciation of good design, the value of good construction, and the proper placement of structures, and the adequate development and adornment of the areas about them.

Argument—Arguments

126. The strongest words are often used in the weakest arguments.

127. The more arguments you win the fewer friends you will have.

—Ruth Smeltzer

128. A man who cannot discuss a point without quarreling had better refrain from argument altogether.

—St. John Ervine

129. Be calm in arguing; for fierceness makes error a fault, and truth discourtesy.

—George Herbert

130. An argument is a collision between two trains of thought in which both are derailed.

—CHARLES L. LAPP

131. Gratuitous violence in arguments betrays a conscious weakness of the cause, and is usually a signal of despair.

—JUNIUS

132. Before any man begins arguing he ought to be sure he knows the definitions of the words he uses.

133. *How to Win an Argument*
The way to convince another is to state your case moderately and accurately. Then scratch your head, or shake it a little and say that is the way it seems to you, but that of course you may be mistaken about it; which causes your listener to receive what you have to say, and as like as not, turn about and try to convince you of it, since you are in doubt. But if you go at him in a tone of positiveness and arrogance, you only make an opponent of him.

—BENJAMIN FRANKLIN

Armistice Day

134. The Armistice was signed on November 11, 1918, and since then every year there have been two minutes of peace.

135. **Armistice Day Prayer**
Our Father who art in heaven—
We thank you for this Armistice Day . . . and beseech you to give to all men's hearts, hands and minds the capacity to work for continued peace. Let us not through greed and false values permit the destruction of all the beauty which has been wrought since first you created our world. Help us turn swords into ploughshares that all may have enough to eat. Help us turn atomic energy into life saving use that will lengthen man's span rather than blow him to dust. Let us hold in affection and respect all those made in your image around the world—whatever their race, color or creed. Then we will not sadden you with more warring; then this Armistice date will truly signify peace at last—to last.

Arrogance

136.   If we must condemn, let us first condemn our own imperfections and shortcomings; if we must fight, let us first fight our own complacency and unconcern; if we must destroy, let us first destroy our own ignorance and prejudice; if we must kill, let us first kill our own false pride and arrogance.

—Dr. William Arthur Ward

137.   When Diogenes came to Olympia and perceived some Rhodian youths dressed with great splendor and magnificence, he said with a smile of contempt, "This is all arrogance." Afterwards some Lacedaemonians came in his way, as mean and as sordid in their attire as the dress of the others was rich. "This," said he, "is also arrogance."

—Ælian

Art

138.   Copy nature and you infringe on the work of our Lord. Interpret nature and you are an artist.

—Jacques Lipchitz

139.   The object of art is to crystallize emotion into thought, and then to fix it in form.

—François Delsarte

140.   Excellence in art, as in everything else, can only be achieved by dint of painstaking labor. There is nothing less accidental than the painting of a fine picture or the chiselling of a noble statue. Every skilled touch of the artist's brush or chisel, though guided by genius, is the product of unremitting study.

—Samuel Smiles

141.   Art is always the index of social vitality, the moving finger that records the destiny of a civilization. A wise statesman should keep an anxious eye on this graph, for it is more significant than a decline in exports or a fall in the value of a nation's currency.

—Sir Herbert Read

142.　In the creative state a man is taken out of himself. He lets down as it were a bucket into his subconscious, and draws up something which is normally beyond his reach. He mixes this thing with his normal experiences, and out of the mixture he makes a work of art.

—E. M. FORSTER

Artist—Artists

143.　A man who works with his hands is a laborer. A man who works with his hands and his brain is a craftsman. But a man who works with his hands and his brain and his heart is an artist.

144.　A firm which produces painting boxes for amateur landscapists encloses the following instructions with every kit. "Take the palette from the box, squeeze some paint on it from the tubes, dip your brush into the paint and daub the canvas with it." Rembrandt, Titian and all other great painters used this method.

145.　One day while the great Hindu poet and educator, Sir Rabindranath Tagore, was writing, an ink blot marred the sheet of paper near the bottom. His first impulse was to tear up the sheet and throw it away, but paper was not as plentiful in India then as it is in America today. The stain was too deep to erase and no chemical eradicator was available. There was only one thing left to do—change the bolt from a blemish into a decoration. It was in his efforts to do this that Rabindranath Tagore discovered a latent talent for art. Of course, there were many hours of hard, and often frustrating, work between the blot on the paper and the exhibition of his drawings in London.

Assistance

146.　The man who needs no one's help is a lonely man indeed.

—DAGOBERT D. RUNES

147.　The only way to help people is to give them a chance to help themselves.

—ELBERT HUBBARD

148. Any man who lives to help other people will soon have other people living to help him.

149. If the life of a river depended only on the rainfall within the confines of its own banks, it would soon be dry. If the life of an individual depended solely on his own resources, he would soon fall. Be grateful for your tributaries.

—Dr. William Arthur Ward

150. Help others solve their problems; standing farther away, you can often see matters more clearly than they do. . . . The greatest service you can render someone else is helping him help himself. . . . If you see an opportunity in his path, point it out, but let your hand guide, not push, him. Remember that the risk is his, and that he who takes it must make the decision.

—Baltasar Gracián

Atheism

151. An atheist cannot find God for the same reason a thief cannot find a policeman.

152. The worst moment for an atheist is when he feels grateful and has no one to thank.

—Samuel McCrea Cavert

153. Religion assures us that our afflictions shall have an end; she comforts us, she dries our tears, she promises us another life. On the contrary, in the abominable worship of atheism, human woes are the incense, death is the priest, a coffin the altar, and annihilation the Deity.

—François Auguste de Châteaubriand

154. The atheist does not deny God so much as he denies himself. A book is more enjoyable when we know its author. A symphony is more stirring when we know its composer. A painting is more meaningful when we know the artist. A poem is more personal when we know the poet. Life is more purposeful when we know the Creator.

—Dr. William Arthur Ward

155.   Atheism can benefit no class of people; neither the unfortunate, whom it bereaves of hope, nor the prosperous, whose joys it renders insipid, nor the soldier, of whom it makes a coward, nor the woman whose beauty and sensibility it mars, nor the mother, who has a son to lose, nor the rulers of men, who have no surer pledge of the fidelity of their subjects than religion.

—François Auguste de Châteaubriand

Atomic Age

156.   We who live in the shadow of the atom sometimes forget the dangers which confronted our forefathers when they began building a nation. The atom can do no more to any individual today than the tomahawk and the scalping knife could do to those pioneers. They willingly risked everything hoping to gain some security from hunger and want and to make for their children a better place in life than they had themselves enjoyed.

Nor did all the dangers of the frontiers come from the violence of the Indians. Nature, too, was a worthy foe. The diseases incident to harsh winters and hot summers took their toll when such medical care as there was did not reach out into the distant settlements. And crop failures, floods and fires could be equally deadly.

The atom may be awesome today because it can threaten wholesale destruction, but so far as each individual life is concerned it is no worse than the dangers our ancestors faced with courage and faith.

Today, perhaps, we need equal faith and courage.

—*Nuggets*

Attire

157.   A fashion is nothing but an induced epidemic.

—George Bernard Shaw

158.   The secret of fashion is to surprise and never to disappoint.

—Edward Bulwer-Lytton

159.   When no one can remember what you wore you are well dressed.

160. There is only one proper way to wear a beautiful dress: to forget you are wearing it.

MME. DE GIRARDIN

161. Your necktie betrays you! One can tell the kind of man you are by the tie you wear.

According to the British magazine, *Tailor and Cutter.*:

Neat patterns are chosen by men modest and careful in thought and action.

Stripes are selected by men overwhelmingly conscious of fashion, decisive, and reluctant to take no for an answer.

A single motif is chosen by those who are studious, attentive to detail, and efficient.

Knitted ties are for the flamboyant, with an eye for color.

A plain or single color indicates one who is upright, conservative, and careful with money.

The bow tie is for the extrovert.

Authorship

162. To expect an author to speak as he writes is ridiculous; or even if he did you would find fault with him as a pedant.

—WILLIAM HAZLITT

163. Writing a book was an adventure. To begin with, it was a toy, an amusement; then it became a mistress, and then a master, and then a tyrant.

—WINSTON CHURCHILL

164. Abuse is often of service. There is nothing so dangerous to an author as silence. His name, like a shuttlecock, must be beat backward and forward, or it falls to the ground.

—DR. SAMUEL JOHNSON

165. In a very real sense, the writer writes in order to teach himself, to understand himself, to satisfy himself; the publishing of his ideas, though it brings gratifications, is a curious anticlimax.

—ALFRED KAZIN

166. There is nothing more dreadful to an author than neglect; compared with which, reproach, hatred, and opposition are names of happiness; yet this worst, this meanest fate, everyone who dares to write has reason to fear.

—DR. SAMUEL JOHNSON

167. A young writer seeking advice from the aged English author, W. Somerset Maugham, said; "Mr. Maugham, I've just written a novel, but I haven't been able to come up with a suitable title. You seem to have such a knack for titles, sir, *Cakes and Ale, The Razor's Edge,* I wonder if you would read my novel and help me."

"Don't need to read your novel," the old man said "Are there drums in it?"

"No, it's not that sort of story. You see it deals with the alienation of . . ."

"Are there any bugles in it?"

"No, sir."

"Call it, 'No Drums, No Bugles.' "

Automation

168. Automation does not cut red tape—it perforates it.

169. The greatest danger in modern technology isn't that machines will begin to think like men, but that men will begin to think like machines.

—EDWARD H. WEISS

170. The glory of man, the human being, is that he can't be dispensed with. The more automation we get, the more indispensable becomes the man who controls it.

171. According to *Planes* it takes 25 men on the ground to control an electronically guided aircraft that could be flown by *one man* in the pilot's seat. The science of automatic controls is a long way from push-button replacement of the human brain.

172. It is important to think of automation as replacing human muscle rather than brain power. We know the brain operates as part of a self-conscious, feeling, willful creature with a unique life-experience. To *build a brain one would have to build a man.* . . . We know the computer can never reach man's power to abstract thought nor have a new thought.

—Lucy R. Goodwin

173. The computer-minded who think that logic is always superior to common sense may be interested to hear of the man who had two wristwatches. One gained two seconds a day and the other had no works—just a dial.

After programming the latest computer to decide which he should discard, he got the answer that he should keep the empty watch since it would tell him the correct time twice a day, whereas the one that gained two seconds would give him the exact time only once every 120 years!

174. The era in which we live is unlike any in our history. Automation is changing the lives of our people. It is creating a need for more skills and it is making it increasingly difficult for the unskilled to find employment. That's why we must do everything in our power to place the tools of knowledge in the hands of America's youngsters and their parents. School alone is not enough; it is the extra help that children get at home that makes the difference between mediocrity and success.

—Charles W. Lockyer

Automobile—Automobiles

175. Back in 1968, just resting in the garage, your car cost you $2.17 a day. This was the fixed cost of owning an average 8-cylinder, four-door sedan, according to the American Automobile Association. It figured to $792 a year, including $30 for fire and theft insurance, $117 for property damage and liability, $24 for licensing and registration—and $621 in depreciation. Once on the highway, the cost was increased by 3.7 cents a mile—2.61 cents for gas and oil, .68 cents for maintenance, and .41 cents for tires.

176. There is no longer a "motoring public": the automobile has become so universal that "motorists" are simply the public in cars. So far people have made few if any concessions towards living with the motor car; the car is hitched on to normal social occasions, and inevitable restrictions on complete freedom to do what one likes with a car are grumbled at. Yet the car is bringing such vast changes in day-to-day affairs that urban society must either learn to live with it, or run a real risk of being destroyed by it. The car itself is a blessing, not an evil. It is among the most valuable tools of living that man has ever invented, and its capacity for fertilizing social life is vast. But people have still to learn to use the car—to drive it properly, to adapt their own habits to the speed and ease of transport that the car makes possible.

Bank—Banks—Banking

177. Banking: lending out other people's money and keeping the interest for yourself.

178. Some 300 years ago, when a man put money in an English bank, his deposit was recorded by notching a stick. The stick was then split, the bank keeping one half, the depositor the other half. Before the money could be withdrawn, the two pieces had to be matched. The depositor's half was called "Bank stock," whereas the part kept by the bank was the "Check."

Beard—Beards

179. Alexander the Great, tradition has it, was beardless, and he forbade his soldiers to grow beards. Caesar, too, wore no beard. In fact, the majority of the ancient Greeks and Romans frowned on beards.

The word "barbarous," which today means savage or wild, originally meant beard-wearing, for most of Rome's enemies, as a rule, wore beards.

Beauty

180. The beauty seen is partly in him who sees it.
—CHRISTIAN NEVELL BOVEE

27

181. Beauty without grace is a hook without bait.

—Ninon de Leclos

182. If the nose of Cleopatra had been a little shorter, it would have changed the history of the world.

—Blaise Pascal

183. It's a commonplace that the prettiest girl is not necessarily the most popular. The usual explanation is that a homely girl cultivates her personality, has wider interests, and is more likely to be a good sport.

At the risk of riducule, I venture another opinion. Man's modesty tells him that a truly beautiful girl is beyond his reach. Being conservative by nature, most men recognize their limitations and invest their time and money in girls who might appreciate such attention.

Appreciation is an important element in romance. Many a homely girl is happily married because her lone suitor was overwhelmed with gratitude.

—William Feather

Beginning—Beginnings

184. The beginning is half of the whole, and we all praise a good beginning.

—Plato

Behavior

185. Rudeness is a weak man's imitation of strength.

186. Act well at the moment, and you have performed a good action for all eternity.

—Johann Kaspar Lavater

187. The excessive desire of pleasing goes along almost always with the apprehension of not being liked.

—Thomas Fuller

188. What changes there would be in the world, if people lived up to their religious beliefs as fully as they live up to their incomes.

Belief—Beliefs

189. To believe is to be strong. Doubt cramps energy. Belief is power.

—FREDERICK W. ROBERTSON

190. Modern man has tried the suspense of believing nothing, and because suspense is soon unbearable, he has ended by believing almost anything.

—GEORGE ARTHUR BUTTRICK

Bequest—Bequests

191. What you leave at your death, let it be without controversy, else the lawyers will be your heirs.

—F. OSBORN

192. Robert Louis Stevenson, dying a slow death on a Pacific island, bequeathed his birthday as a legacy to a young friend because she had complained to him that hers fell on Christmas Day, and as a result she felt she had been deprived of presents all her life. A clause runs: "If, however, she fails to use this bequest properly, all rights shall pass to the President of the United States."

Betrayal

193. People don't mind if you betray humanity, but if you betray your club, you are considered a renegade.

—ARTHUR KOESTLER

Bible, The

194. The Old and New Testaments contain but one scheme of religion. Neither part of this scheme can be understood without the other.

—RICHARD CECIL

195. Be less concerned about the number of books you read, and more about the good use you make of them. The best of books is the *Bible*.

—CHRISTIAN SCRIVER

196. Do you know a book that you are willing to put under your head for a pillow when you lie dying? Very well; that is the book you want to study while you are living. There is but one such book in the world.

—JOSEPH COOK

197. It is not enough to own a *Bible;* we must read it.
It is not enough to read it; we must let it speak to us.
It is not enough to let it speak to us; we must believe it.
It is not enough to believe it; we must live it.

—DR. WILLIAM ARTHUR WARD

198. The Bible should have as important a place as the TV set in our American homes. Our future progress may well depend not so much on our productive and technological genius as upon our moral awareness.

—CLIFFORD F. HOOD

199. How fast we learn in the day of sorrow! Scripture shines out out in a new effulgence; every verse seems to contain a sunbeam, every promise stands out in illuminated splendor; things hard to be understood become in a moment plain.

—HORATIUS BONAR, D. D.

200. There is something in the *Bible* to fit every devotional mood and to fill every spiritual need. There are passages that express joy and thanksgiving when we are elated, hope when we are discouraged, consolation when we are bereaved, forgiveness when we have fallen.

—DON F. NEUFELD

201. The *Bible*, as a revelation from God, was not designed to give us all the information we might desire, nor to solve all the questions about which the human soul is perplexed, but to impart enough to be a safe guide to the haven of eternal rest.

—ALBERT BARNES

202.   The *Bible* is not only the revealer of the unknown God to man, but His grand interpreter as the God of nature. In revealing God, it has given us the key that unlocks the profoundest mysteries of creation, the clew by which to thread the labyrinth of the universe, the glass through which to look from Nature up to Nature's God.

—L. J. Halsey

203.   If you are ever tempted to speak lightly or think lightly of it, just sit down and imagine what this world would be without it. No *Bible*! A wound and no cure, a storm and no covert, a condemnation and no shrift, a lost eternity and no ransom! Alas for us if this were all; alas for us if the ladder of science were the only stair to lead us up to God!

—R. R. Meredith

204.   The *Bible* is the treasure of the poor, the solace of the sick, and the support of the dying; and while other books may amuse and instruct in a leisure hour, it is the peculiar triumph of that book to create light in the midst of darkness, to alleviate the sorrow which admits of no other alleviation, to direct a beam of hope to the heart which no other topic of consolation can reach; while guilt, despair, and death vanish at the touch of its holy inspiration.

—Robert Hall

205.   Now you wonder if man has much to learn from the *Bible* and I answer "A great deal." I believe that the *Bible* is almost unknown today. It isn't a book about God, though that's how it's generally considered, but a book about man. The *Bible* offers a sublime answer, but unless we know the question to which it responds, we can hardly understand it. The *Bible* is an answer to the question, "What does God require of man?"

—Rabbi Abraham Joshua Henschel

206.   Parents, I urge you to make the *Bible* the sweetest, the dearest book to *your children*; not by *compelling* them to read so many chapters each day, which will have the effect of making them hate the *Bible*, but by reading its pages *with* them, and by your tender parental love, so showing them the beauty of its wondrous incidents, from the story of Adam and Eve to the story of Bethlehem and Calvary, that no book in the home will be so dear to your children as the *Bible*; and thus you will be strengthening their minds with the sublimest truths, storing their hearts with the purest love, and sinking deep in their souls solid principles of righteousness, whose divine stones no waves of temptation can ever move.

—A. E. Kittredge

Bigotry

207.   He that will not reason is a bigot; he that cannot reason is a fool; he that dares not reason is a slave.

—William Drummond

Birthday—Birthdays

208.
BIRTHDAYS
Count your garden by the flowers
Never by the leaves that fall;
Count your days by the golden hours,
Don't remember clouds at all.
Count the nights by stars, not shadows,
Count your life by smiles, not tears,
And with joy on every birthday
Count your age by friends, not years.

—Author unknown

Birth control

209.   Most of the people favoring birth control have already been born.

Blame

210.   Those whom fate spared or favored are inclined to condemn in haste the one who drew a bad lot.

—Dagobert D. Runes

Blessing—Blessings

211.   One should not only count his blessings—he should also check the addition once in a while.

Book—Books

212. A book may be as great a thing as a battle.
—BENJAMIN DISRAELI

213. Each age, it is found, must write its own books; or rather, each generation for the next succeeding.
—RALPH WALDO EMERSON

214. A book may be compared to the life of your neighbor. If it be good, it cannot last too long; if bad, you cannot get rid of it too early.
—HENRY BROOKE

215. Books are the food which develops the intellect, character and personality, for in all good literature there is truth, wisdom, and imagination.
—GERTRUDE GILL

216. Many times the reading of a book has made the fortune of the man—has decided his way of life. . . . 'Tis a tie between men to have been delighted with the same book.
—RALPH WALDO EMERSON

217. The world of books is the most remarkable creation of man. Nothing else that he builds ever lasts. Monuments fall, nations perish, civilizations grow old and die out and after an era of darkness new races build others. But in the world of books are volumes that have seen this happen again and again and yet live on, still young, still as fresh as the day they were written, still telling men's hearts of the hearts of men centuries dead.
—CLARENCE DAY

218. Consider the book. Is it just a few pennies worth of paper, ink, glue, cloth, and boards? Or is it a record of man's best—a mirror to life?

In five hundred years we have not fully grasped the significance of books. Books are a part of every invention and discovery, religion, philosophy, and ideology, aids to every kind of enterprise.

Books enhance freedom, save time, increase our chances of success. They are indispensable to civilization. Who says that books have not shaped his life? What would any of us be had we read not a single book?

—WILLIAM EMERSON HINCHLIFF

Boredom

219. Highly educated bores are by far the worst; they know so much, in such fiendish detail, to be boring about.

—LOUIS KRONENBERGER

Borrow—Borrower—Borrowing

220. He who borrows and never repays is too great a coward to steal.

221. The fellow who is too proud to beg and too honest to steal can still borrow and forget to pay.

Bravery

222. It is easy to appear brave if there is no place to run.

Brevity

223. No speech can be entirely bad if it is short enough.

—IRVIN S. COBB

224. If you can't keep your mouth shut, be brief; if you can't be brief, then you are no worse than the average speaker.

225. Much wisdom can be crowded into but four words, as witness the following:

In God we trust; this, too, shall pass; live and let live; still waters run deep; bad news travels fast; love laughs at locksmiths; nothing succeeds like success; charity begins at home; politics makes strange bed-fellows; nothing ventured, nothing gained; man proposes, God disposes; let sleeping dogs lie.

The moral may be: If you can't say it in four words, don't say it.

Bribery

226.   One is never sure of those who sell themselves.

—Haitian proverb

Brotherhood

227.   Whoever in prayer can say, "Our Father," acknowledges and should feel the brotherhood of the whole race of makind.

—C. L. Thompson

228.   Through our scientific genius we have made of this world a neighborhood; and now we are challenged, through our moral genius, to make of it a brotherhood.

—Martin Luther King

229.   As for the great truth of universal brotherhood, we can never bring about its practical realization by asking others to be brotherly to us. All progress starts within ourselves; it is the only progress we can achieve, and in achieving it we help the world towards brotherhood.

230.   We are all brothers—by the laws of nature, of birth, of death, as also by the laws of our utter helplessness from birth to death, in this world of sorrow and deceptive illusions. Let us then love, help and mutually defend each other against the spirit of deception; and while holding to that which each of us accepts as his ideal of truth and unity—i.e., to the religion which suits us—let us unite to form a nucleus of a Universal Brotherhood of Humanity without distinction of race, creed or color.

—B. P. Blavatsky

231.   *Some Presidential Thoughts on Brotherhood*
George Washington: Happily the Government of the U. S.,

which gives to bigotry no sanction, to persecution no assistance, requires only that they who live under its protection should demean themselves as good citizens.

Abraham Lincoln: As I would not be a slave, so I would not be a master. This expresses my idea of Democracy. Whatever differs from this, to the extent of the difference, is no Democracy.

Franklin D. Roosevelt: All men are children of one Father and brothers in the human family. Brotherhood dedicates us to the practice of understanding and justice through which freedom and equality flourish in human society.

Harry S. Truman: The true foundation of the brotherhood of man is belief in the knowledge that God is the Father of mankind. For us, therefore, brotherhood is not only a generous impulse but also a divine command.

Dwight D. Eisenhower: Our abundant plains and mountains would yield little if it were not for the applied skill and energy of Americans working together as fellow citizens bound up in common destiny. The achievement of brotherhood is the crowning objective of our society.

John F. Kennedy: Without brotherhood there can only be chaos; with brotherhood we may look forward to reaching the ultimate goal of mankind—peace with freedom and justice.

Lyndon B. Johnson: Democracy cannot live in hate and fear. Prejudice and bigotry are the advance guard of failure.... Let us hear again the faith of our forebears; let us listen again to the inspired hopes of our national conscience; let us obey again the word of our religions.

Budget—Budgets

232. A budget is like a girdle—take care of a bulge one place and it pops out another.

233. Living on a budget can be the same as living beyond your means, if you plan it that way.

Burden—Burdens—Burdensome

234. When the wheel creaks, it's moving.

—RUTH SMELTZER

235.　It is not the load that weighs us down; it's the way we carry it.

236.　There is no better way to take the irk out of work than to put love into it.

Bureaucracy

237.　We must beware of trying to build a society in which nobody counts for anything except the politician or an official, a society where enterprise gains no reward and thrift no privileges.

—Winston Churchill

Business

238.　"Waiting for times to get normal" means never doing anything.

239.　Business is like an automobile. It will not run itself except downhill.

240.　Business is a lot like a game of tennis ... those who don't serve well end up losing.

241.　In business, yesterday's formula for success is often tomorrow's recipe for trouble.

242.　When there are two men in a business who always agree, one of them is unnecessary.

—William Wrigley, Jr.

243.　Most of us never recognize opportunity until it goes to work in our competitor's business.

—P. L. Andarr

244. It isn't the number of people employed in a business that makes it successful, it's the number working.

245. Markets as well as mobs respond to human emotions; markets as well as mobs can be inflamed to their own destruction.

—OWEN D. YOUNG

246. Too many executives tend to follow the road proved safe, rather than the dynamic approach of self-reliance, individualism and initiative.

—LOUIS E. WOLFSON

247. A man begins to grow in business when he stops worrying about putting his own ideas over and keeps his mind open for the best ideas, no matter whose they are.

248. All too much of the wage structure has been based on the time workers put in, rather than upon the product put out. The consumer dollar has no interest in how much time it buys—only in the character and quality of the product itself.

—WHEELER MCMILLEN

249. "Women have a better business sense than men," said the after-dinner speaker. "When her business is to catch a man, she doesn't sit around criticizing the government. She spends half her time in beauty parlors and the other half out where eligible men can be found.

250. Every successful business in the world is in existence because its founder recognized in a problem or need an opportunity to be of service to others. Every problem or need in your life is in reality an opportunity to call forth inner resources of wisdom, love, strength and ability.

—J. SIG PAULSON

251. Just as there are 3 R's there are also 3 A's of business life. They are: Ability, Ambition and Attitude. Ability establishes what a worker does and will bring him a pay ckeck. Ambition determines how much he does and will get him a raise. Attitude guarantees how well he does.

—WILBERT E. SHEER

252. Business is the very soul of an American. He pursues it not as a means of procuring for himself and his family the necessary comforts of life but as the fountain of all human felicity; and shows as much enthusiastic ardor in his application to it as any crusader ever evinced for the conquest of the Holy Land, or the followers of Mohammed for the spreading of the Koran.

—Francis J. Grun

253. John T. Connor, when Secretary of Commerce, pointed out the importance of business in the United States when he said: "The business organization is the very heart of the system that provides the goods and services which enable man to devote more of himself to higher attainments. Thus, the business system is the essential material means to an ultimately spiritual goal."

254. The most successful highest-up executives carefully select understudies. They don't strive to do everything themselves. They train and trust others. This leaves them foot-free, mind-free, with time to think. They have time to receive important callers, to pay worthwhile visits. They have time for their families. No matter how able, any employer or executive who insists on running a one-man enterprise courts unhappy circumstances when his powers dwindle.

—B. C. Forbes

255. I like business because it is competitive, because it rewards deeds rather than words . . . compels earnestness and does not permit me to neglect today's task while thinking about tomorrow . . . it undertakes to please, not reform . . . is honestly selfish, thereby avoiding hypocrisy and sentimentality . . . it promptly penalizes inefficiency, while rewarding well those who give it the best they have in them. Lastly, I like business because each day is a fresh adventure.

—R. H. Cabell

256. One of the great weaknesses of the American executive has been his indifference to those who misrepresent Business. The average man is too busily engaged to reply to those who malign Business. He seems to accept the misrepresentation, libel and calumny as one of the necessary evils of Business, and silently submits until finally the undenied lies grow

into general beliefs, with the result that both the public in general and
Business in particular suffer.

—CHARLES E. CARPENTER

257. Findings about human personality and how it functions often
arouse skepticism. The term "social sciences" raises questions of doubt.
Yet as businessmen we should be as willing to accept the aid of the social
sciences as we do the physical sciences. Social scientists are constantly discovering new facts about our greatest business asset—people. We should
be as willing to adopt such findings as we are the newest chemical or elec-
tronic discovery.

—LOUIS E. WOLFSON

258. O Lord, in these days when anybody can sell anything, help
me to remember—that it will not always be thus; that Humility is still the
hallmark of the successful firm; that the seller is always the servant of the
buyer; that arrogance costs as many orders as ignorance of line; that I have
too short a memory to tell a lie, and that buyers have too long a memory
to forget a wrong. Above all, help me to remember that no one ever lost a
customer because the quality was too high, or the service too good.

—ANON.

259.   A BUSINESS MAN'S PRAYER
          Teach me that sixty minutes make an hour, sixteen ounces
a pound, and one hundred cents a dollar. Help me so to live that I can lie
down at night with a clear conscience, without a gun under my pillow, and
unhaunted by the faces of those to whom I have brought pain. Grant that
I may earn my meal ticket on the square, and in earning it I may do unto
others as I would have others do unto me. Deafen me to the jingle of
tainted money and to the rustle of unholy skirts.
          Blind me to the faults of the other fellow, but reveal to me my
own. Guide me so that each night when I look across the dinner table at
my wife, who has been a blessing to me, I shall have nothing to conceal.
Keep me young enough to laugh with little children and sympathetic
enough to be considerate of old age. And when comes the day of darkening
shades and the smell of flowers, the tread of soft footsteps and the crunching
wheels in the yard—make the ceremony short and the epitaph simple—
"Here lies a man."

—AUTHOR UNKNOWN

Calmness

260. To act coolly, intelligently and prudently in perilous circumstances is the test of a man and also a nation.

—ADLAI E. STEVENSON

261. If you can keep your head while all others about you are losing theirs, you'll be the tallest one in the crowd.

Capability—Capabilities

262. A man never really knows what he can do until he tries to undo what he has done.

263. All the discontented people I know are trying sedulously to be something they are not, to do something they cannot do.

—DAVID GRAYSON

264. There is no upper limit to what individuals are capable of doing with their minds. There is no age limit that bars them from beginning. There is no obstacle that cannot be overcome if they persist and believe.

—E. F. WELLS

Capacity—Capacities

265. No man ever lived who became all he was capable of being.

266. The main thing is to be honest with yourself, know and recognize your limits and attain maximum achievement within them. I would for example get more satisfaction from climbing Snowdon, which I know I could, than from attempting Everest, which I couldn't.

—STIRLING MOSS

Capital

267. A businessman who came up the hard way makes the observation that about all one can do on a shoestring these days is trip.

Capitalism

268.   And the word is capitalism. We are too mealy-mouthed. We fear the word capitalism is unpopular. So we talk about the "free enterprise system" and run to cover in the folds of the flag and talk about the American Way of Life.

—ERIC A. JOHNSTON

Capital—Labor

269.   The worst crime against working people is a company which fails to operate at a profit.

—SAMUEL L. GOMPERS

270.   In every instance where capital is so employed to produce a profit, it arises either from supplanting a portion of labor, which would otherwise be performed by the hand of man, or from performing a portion of labor beyond the reach of man to accomplish.

—LORD LAUDERDALE

Career—Careers

271.   People don't choose their careers; They are engulfed by them.

—JOHN DOS PASSOS

272.   "I hear you have a boy in college. Is he going to become a doctor, an engineer, or a lawyer, perhaps?"

The slow, quizzical answer was: "That I do not know. Right now the big question is: Is he going to become a sophomore?"

Carelessness

273.   Carelessness does more harm than a want of knowledge.

—BENJAMIN FRANKLIN

274.   A man who is turning out careless, imperfect work is turning out a careless, imperfect character for himself. He is touching deceit every moment, and this unseen thing rises up from his work like a subtle essence and enters and poisons his soul.

275.   How long do you think you have left to live? Here's how you can figure out approximately how many years you have left: first, subtract your present age from 80. Now take what you get and multiply by seven. Then take that answer and divide it by ten. According to life insurance actuarial tables, this system will give you a pretty good idea of your remaining time. CAUTION: if you're a careless worker, don't bother to work this out—your last day could come any time!

Cause and effect

276.   It is not the weapon that causes the crime any more than weapons cause the wars in which they are used. In both cases the cause is in the minds and hearts of men, and that is where the improving must be done.

277.   In a tax case which involved substantial concealment of income, the defendant's lawyer told the court that his client became confused from taking too many tranquilizers. That raises the question: Would he have needed the tranquilizers if he had been honest about his tax report?

Caution

278.   The timid way is safer, but they are slaves who take it.
—Publilius Syrus

279.   It's a good thing to get in and dig, but be careful which way you throw the dirt.

280.   It's paradoxical, but cold feet are often the direct result of burned fingers.

281.   Live every day as if it were your last. Do every job as if you were the boss. Drive as if all other vehicles were police cars. Treat everybody else as if he were you.

Certainty

282. I am inclined to believe that much of our economy is based upon the feelings of people rather than upon reality. And therefore the primary belief I have is never to be too sure about anything.

—NORTON SIMON

Chain reaction

283. If you would be interesting, be interested; if you would be pleased, be pleasing; if you would be loved, be lovable; if you would be helped, be helpful.

284. Love is the great transformer, turning ambition into aspiration, selfishness into service, greed into gratitude, getting into giving and demands into dedication.

285. Where there is love, there is concern. Where there is concern, there is kindness. Where there is kindness, there is harmony. Where there is harmony, there is helpfulness. Where there is helpfulness, there is Christ. Where there is Christ, there is love.

—DR. WILLIAM ARTHUR WARD

286. Love is the spark that kindles the spark of compassion. Compassion is the fire that flames the candle of service. Service is the candle that ignites the torch of hope. Hope is the torch that lights the beacon of faith. Faith is the beacon that reflects the power of God. God is the power that creates the miracle of love.

—DR. WILLIAM ARTHUR WARD

Chance

287. Chance favors the prepared mind.

—LOUIS PASTEUR

Change

288. In prosperity prepare for a change; in adversity hope for one.

289. The world is a scene of changes, and to be constant in nature is inconstancy.

—ABRAHAM COWLEY

290. You must change with the times unless you are big enough to change the times.

291. One must never lose time in vainly regretting the past or in complaining against the changes which cause us discomfort, for change is the essence of life.

—ANATOLE FRANCE

292. Change does not necessarily assure progress, but progress implacably requires change. . . . Education is essential to change, for education creates both new wants and the ability to satisfy them.

—HENRY STEELE COMMAGER

293. There are no new girls, no new women. Your greatgrandmother was a devil of a clip half a century before you were born. You knew her only when she was wrinkled and hobbling, reading the Epistle to the Thessalonians in a lace cap and saying she didn't know what the world was coming to. The young have always been young, and the old always old; men and women don't change. The changes that you think you see lie just on the surface. You could wash them away with soap and hot water.

—STEPHEN LEACOCK

Changelessness

294. There is no sadder or more frequent obituary on the pages of time than "We have always done it this way."

Character

295. Character is destiny.

—HERACLITUS

296. Character is more easily kept than recovered.

—THOMAS PAINE

297. Character, like a rifle, cannot shoot higher than it is aimed.

298. If you're good just because it pays to be good, you'll be bad for bigger wages.

299. Strength of character consists of two things—power of will and power of self-restraint.

300. A college diploma may be used to hide cracks in the wall, but it can't conceal defects in character.

301. The world may take the liberty of making our reputations for us, but we alone can build our own character.

302. The measure of a man is not the number of servants he has but the number of people he serves.

303. I believe in the sacredness of a promise, that a man's word should be as good as his bond; that character—not wealth or power or position—is of supreme worth.

—John D. Rockefeller, Jr.

304. Above all other things in the world, character has supreme value. A man can never be more than what his character—intellectual, moral, spiritual—make him. . . . Nothing valuable can come out of a man that is not in him, embodied in his character.

—Josiah G. Holland

305. That character is power, is true in a much higher sense than that knowledge is power. Mind without heart, intelligence without conduct, cleverness without goodness, are powers in their way, but they may be powers only for mischief.

—Samuel Smiles

306. We sometimes say that "money talks." To be sure it does. Get to know two things about a man—how he earns his money and how he spends it—and you have the clue to his character, for you have a searchlight that shows up the innermost recesses of his soul.

—The Rev. Robert J. McCracken

307. Though the reputation of men of genuine character may be slow of growth, their true qualities cannot be wholly concealed. They may be misrepresented by some, and misunderstood by others; misfortune and adversity may for a time overtake them; but, with patience and endurance, they will eventually inspire the respect and command the confidence which they really deserve.

—Samuel Smiles

308. Every man sets himself a certain standard. The hard thing is to live up to it. In my line of work, the temptation to serve something other than the public interest is constant. The human instinct to protect friends, the natural desire to escape criticism, the direct or indirect pressure from business and editorial associates, always raise ethical issues. Without some guiding principle it is not easy to know what to do. The simplest way out is to yield to pressure. But that undermines character and makes it more difficult to resist the next demand.

—Hans V. Kaltenborn

Charity

309. Real charity doesn't care if it's tax-deductible or not.

310. A rich man without charity is a rogue; and perhaps it would be no difficult matter to prove that he is also a fool.

—Henry Fielding

311. True charity is not just giving a man a dime when he is hungry, but giving a man a dime when you are as hungry as he is, and need the dime just as much.

Cheerfulness

312. The cheerful loser is the winner.

313. If you'll sing a song as you go along,
In the face of the real or the fancied wrong,
In spite of the doubt if you'll fight it out,
And show a heart that is brave and stout;
If you'll laugh at the jeers and refuse the tears,
You'll force the ever-reluctant cheers
That the world denies when a coward cries,
To give to the man who bravely tries.
And you'll win sucess with a little song—
If you'll sing the song as you go along!
If you'll sing a song as you trudge along,
You'll see that the singing will make you strong.
And the heavy load and the rugged road
And the sting and the stripe of the tortuous goad
Will soar with the note that you set afloat;
That the beam will change to a trifling mote;
That the world is bad when you are sad,
And bright and beautiful when glad.
That all you need is a little song—
If you sing the song as you trudge along!
        —R. McCLAIN FIELDS
        From *The Value of Cheerfulness*, by
        MARY M. BARROWS (H. M. CALDWELL Co.)
                BY PERMISSION

Child—Children

314. Badgered, snubbed and scolded on the one hand; petted, flattered and indulged on the other—it is astonishing how many children work their way up to an honest manhood in spite of parents and friends.
        —HENRY WARD BEECHER

✓ **315.** WHAT IS A CHILD

A child is a person who is going to carry on what you have started. He is going to sit where you are sitting and, when you are gone, attend to those things which you think are important. You may adopt all the policies you please, but how they will be carried out depends on him. He will assume control of your cities, states and nations. He is going to move in and take over your churches, schools, universities and corporations. All your books are going to be judged, praised or condemned by him. The fate of humanity is in his hands. So it might be well to pay him some attention.

Child discipline

316.   Often what a child learns over his father's knee is worth as much as what he learns at his mother's knee.

—RUTH SMELTZER

317.   While getting her things together for a visit with her grand-mother, little six-year-old Susie ran to the bookcase and brought back three books—*Peter Rabbit, Little Red Riding Hood* and *Child Guidance.* "Susie," said her mother, "you won't need that *Child Guidance.*"

"Oh, yes, I will," replied the child. "Grandma still believes in spanking."

Child guidance

318.   It would seem that much of the difficulty with young people today is due to the fact that many parents attempt to shield their children from the challenges of life, rather than teach them how to meet and cope with their daily experiences. . . . To take the struggle out of life is to remove the absolutely necessary opportunities for experience which are the only means we have of gaining wisdom that nourishes the spirit.

—EDITH WILKINSON

319.   Perhaps democracy is being forced upon children when they are too young. To saddle a child or adolescent with freedom beyond his demonstrated capability of judgment is not fair, even though it be done under some high-sounding name. The privilege of developing children little by little up to the point where they can cope with the bewildering world into which they have been launched is the reward and crown of parenthood. It is popular to blame influences outside the home when a boy goes wrong, or to rail against television, radio, newspapers and magazines. But all these enter as a second influence, and if the first—the ingraining of a sense of decency by parents—has been effectively done, then all these lose their power to debase.

Child training

320. The best thing parents can spend on their children is time—not money.

321. There is no future for any country that neglects the training of its children.

322. When a child is allowed to do absolutely as he pleases, it will not be long until nothing pleases him.

323. Your son at five is your master, at ten your slave, at fifteen your double, and after that your friend or foe, depending on his bringing up.

324. Our greatest obligation to our children is to prepare them to understand and to deal effectively with the world in which they will live and not with the world we have known or the world we would prefer to have.

—GRAYSON KIRK

325. It always grieves me to contemplate the initiation of children into the ways of life when they are scarcely more than infants; it checks their confidence and simplicity, two of the best qualities that heaven gives them, and demands that they share our sorrows before they are capable of entering into our enjoyments.

—CHARLES DICKENS

326. I have noticed that many women tend to be overprotective, smothering rather than mothering their children. I think it unfair to any young person to raise him in this way, and then expect him to cope successfully with life's problems when he is on his own. The finest legacy any parent can leave his child is the ability to do his own thinking when the parent is no longer around to make decisions.

—BERNICE CLIFTON

327.   A child who knows there is a system of reward and punishment gradually develops a well-founded feeling of security. . . . He becomes insecure if he has to make all his decisions. He needs someone who will direct him. Discipline produces security. Discipline will not cause your child to love you less. The child will first associate pain with bad acts. Eventually, the bad act is associated with punishment. The punisher tends to fade in the background and is replaced by the conscience. Then the child will take the discipline in stride. . . . The goal of discipline is to produce an adult who is strict with himself. If the child or adult persistently strives to do what he must do, some day he will discover that he wants to do what he must do.

—PETER G. CRANFORD

Choice

328.   If you must choose between two evils, forget it.

329.   Whenever two ways lie before us, one of which is easy and the other hard, one of which requires no exertion while the other calls for resolution and endurance, happy is the man who chooses the mountain path and scorns the thought of resting in the valley. These are the men and women who are destined in the end to conquer and succeed.

Christianity

330.   Christ would never hear of negative morality; *thou shalt* was ever His word, with which He superseded *thou shalt not*.

—ROBERT LOUIS STEVENSON

331.   The word of God is the Christian soul's best weapon, and it is essential to have it with him always. In doubt it decides, in consultation it directs; in anxiety it reassures; in sorrow it comforts; in failure it encourages; in defense it protects; in offense it is mightier than the mighty.

—WILFRED T. GRENFELL

332.   "Praising we plow, and singing we sail," wrote Clement, one of the early Church fathers. . . That is the true spirit of Christian living; not something that is assumed or that is on the surface only, but that grows out of the very nature of the life within.

333. Christianity means: In the home, kindness; in business, honesty; in society, courtesy; in work, thoroughness; in play, fairness; to the unfortunate, pity; to the fortunate, congratulations; to sin, resistance; to the strong, trust and good will; to the weak, help; to the penitent, forgiveness; to all, reverence and love; to God, worship and service.

—CHARLES F. BANNING

334. We Christians are part of the oldest and most radical revolution in human history. It is so old that some of us have forgotten how radical it is, so misshapen that some people are actually shocked to be told that Jesus was a rebel, a revolutionist. So long have they accepted the false picture of a gentle Jesus, meek and mild, that they have forgotten the central fact of our faith: He was executed as an insurrectionist, regarded as an agitator too dangerous to live, and put to death as a public menace. In His heart was a deep protest against the evils that blight man, and in His mind was a great thought-out plan for man's salvation.

—J. WALLACE HAMILTON

Christmas

335. The truly poor at Christmas are those who have no one with whom to share its spiritual joys and its material happiness.

336. Christmas customs are based on the myths of many countries. Each has its own traditions dear to the hearts of its people.

The beautiful story of the Christmas Tree comes from Germany. Santa Claus as Father Christmas first appeared in Austria. The mistletoe had an aura of magic in the ancient days when the Scandinavians worshipped the Norse gods. The Druids used it in their ceremonies, and honored it with a golden sickle.

The poinsettia came from Mexico.

The Yule log was a European rite. In our own South of plantation days, it was a much loved custom, for as long as it burned, the slaves had a holiday.

Boxing Day, celebrated in England of old, was the day when the serfs came to the Manor House to receive gifts. A similar custom prevailed in the Old South. Early on Christmas morn, the plantation workers appeared at the Big House calling out "Christmas Gift." The custom has "gone with the wind," but their cry is still the Southern greeting on that day.

Carols were sung first in Bethlehem by the angels over the manger where the Christ Child lay. Each land has its own carols which have been sung for almost 2000 years.

337. MERRY CHRISTMAS IN 27 LANGUAGES
God Jul (Swedish).
Glaedelig Jul (Danish).
Gledelig Jul (Norwegian).
Froehliche Weihnachten (German).
Hartelijke Kerst Groeten (Dutch).
Hauskaa Joulua (Finnish).
Joyeux Noël (French).
Buon Natale (Italian).
Felices Navidades (Spanish).
Boas Festas (Portuguese.)
Wesolych Swiat (Polish).
S Rozhdestvom Christova (Russian).
Crystas Rozdzajetsia, Slawyte Jeho (Ukrainian).
Befele Vanebhi (Bohemian).
Boldog Karacsonyt (Hungarian).
Sretan Bozic (Croatian).
Sretan Bozic (Serbian).
Linksmu Kaledu (Lithuanian).
Vesele Vanoce (Czech).
Kala Christougenia (Greek).
Nodlaig Nait Cugat (Irish).
Ge Chenorhavorem St. Zenount (Armenian).
Mele Kaliki maga (Hawaiian).
Chuk-syong takn (Korean).
Yasu Suntel Kowa (Chinese).
Shin-nen omedito (Japanese).
Gajan Kristnask (Esperanto.)

Church—Churches

338. Churches should be schools of friendship.
—HENRY WARD BEECHER

339. A church is a hospital for sinners; not a club for saints.
—RUSSELL BLOWERS

340.   Who builds a Church within his heart, and takes it with him everywhere, is holier far than he whose church is but a one-day house of prayer.

341.   Horace Greeley once received a letter from a woman stating that her church was in distressing financial straits. They had tried every device they could think of—fairs, strawberry festivals, oyster banquets, Japanese weddings, poverty sociables, mock marriages, grab bags, box sociables and necktie sociables. Would Mr. Greeley be so kind as to suggest some new device to keep the struggling church from disbanding? The editor replied: "Try religion."

342.   Long ago a hurricane swept down on the English coast and destroyed, among other things, a little church. The people of the congregation felt that they were unable to rebuild, but one day a representative of the government came to ask if the chruch would be reconstructed.

   When the pastor of the little church explained why they could not do it, the man from the Royal Navy said, "Then we will rebuild it for you. Your church spire is on all our charts and maps. It is a landmark by which ships from the world over steer their course."

—Paul L. Swauger

Church attendance

343.   The most expensive piece of furniture in the church is the empty pew.

344.   A hearse is a poor thing to go to church in for the first time.

345.   The fastest growing sect in America—"The Seventh Day Absentists."

346.   Every time we are absent from church we are voting that it shall be closed.

—Roy L. Smith

347.   *Notice posted outside a church:*
If your trouble is deep-seated and of long standing, try kneeling.

348.   The finest Easter parades in the land will be from the homes of the faithful to the churches of their choice.

349.   One of America's basic troubles is revealed in the fact that many parents are willing to *take* their children to the circus but *send* them to Sunday school.

350.   They who go to church out of vanity and curiosity, and not for pure devotion, should not value themselves for their religion, for it is not worth a straw.

—Samuel Croxall, D. D.

351.   The retiring usher was instructing his youthful successor in the details of his office. "And remember, my boy, that we have nothing but good, kind Christians in this church—until you try to put someone else in their pew."

352.   Let no one be critical of those who go to church on Easter because it is fashionable; rather let everyone find inspiration in the fact that in this country it is the fashion to go to church on Easter.

353.   In theory the automobile should have proved a blessing to the church because it provided an easy means of attending services. The problem began when drivers discovered the ease with which they could reach a lot of other places.

354.
"Whenever I go past our
   church,
I stop and make a visit,
For fear that, when I'm carried
   in,
The Lord might say, 'Who
   is it?'"

—Author unknown

55

355.   Once upon a time, long long ago, in a land far away, a pastor preached a sermon on Christians recognizing one another in heaven. As they left the church a good lady said to the preacher, "I wish you'd preach on Christians recognizing one another on earth; I've been a member of this church for six months and not a soul has spoken to me yet!"

356.   The time was way back, when the frontier church burnt down. The town saloon keeper offered his place for Sunday services. As the preacher was covering up the bar and bottles with sheets, the saloon's parrot spoke up and said: "Ah-ha! A new bartender!"

Then the women of the choir came in and the parrot said: "Hey! A new floor show!"

But then, when the congregation arrived for service, the parrot lamented: "Heck. The same old customers!"

357.   *Don't Stay Away From Church*

—Because you are poor. There is no admission charge.

—Because you are rich. The church can help you cure that.

—Because it rains. You go to work in the rain.

—Because it is hot. So is the golf course.

—Because it is cold. It's warm and friendly inside.

—Because no one invited you. People go to the movies without being asked.

—Because churches have emotional religion. How about the ball game?

—Because you have little children. What if you didn't any longer have them? Churches welcome children.

—Because you don't like the preacher. He's human like you.

—Because there are hypocrites. You associate with them daily.

—Because you have company. They will admire your loyalty if you bring them along or tell them to wait 'til you get back.

—Because you need a little week-end vacation occasionally. If your soul takes a vacation from God, it's not good.

—Because your clothes are not expensive. Church isn't supposed to be a fashion show anyway.

—Because church standards are too high. Take a look at the *Bible* standards if you think the church's are too high!

—Because the church always wants money. So does your grocer.

56

Church collections

358. No church would have a financial problem if more people gave in proportion to the blessings they receive.

359. A little tot in church for the first time watched the ushers pass the collection plates. When they neared his pew, the little fellow piped up so that all the congregation could hear, "Don't pay for me, Daddy, I'm under five."

360. A revival was underway at a church . . . and the entire community was being uplifted spiritually by the visiting preacher. Included in the lot was an old man more noted for his miserly nature than for his church attendance. When the meeting was in the last week, a group of young brethren sallied forth to collect donations to pay the preacher. Their first call was on the old tightwad.

"That preacher has made me aware of how good the Lord has been to me," he said before they could explain their visit. . . . The leader of the group announced . . . they were there to collect money to pay the preacher and he could show his thanks to the Lord with a sizable donation.

"Boys, I'll tell you," the old man said, "I'm gettin' to be old, and you fellers is young. I imagine I'll be seein' the Lord before any of you, so I just think I'll wait and hand my donation to Him in person."

Civilization

361. Civilization is just a slow process of learning to be kind.
—Charles L. Lucas

362. Civilization is a stream with banks. The stream is sometimes filled with blood from people killing, stealing, shouting and doing the things historians usually record, while on the banks, unnoticed, people build homes, make love, raise children, sing songs, write poetry and even whittle statues. The story of civilization is the story of what happened on the banks. Historians are pessimists becauses they ignore the banks for the river.
—Will Durant

Civil rights

363.   Susan B. Anthony stood up in the prisoners' dock. "Yes, Your Honor," she snapped, "I have many things to say; for in your ordered verdict of guilty, you have trampled under foot every vital principle of our government. My natural rights, my civil rights, my political rights, my judicial rights, are all alike ignored. Robbed of the fundamental privilege of citizenship, I am degraded from the status of a citizen to that of a subject; and not only myself individually, but all my sex are, by Your Honor's verdict, doomed to political subjection. . . ."

Nevertheless she was fined $100.

364.   "The very purpose of a Bill of Rights was to withdraw certain subjects from the vicissitudes of political controversy, to place them beyond the reach of majorities and officials and to establish them as legal principles to be applied by the courts. One's right to life, liberty, and property, to free speech, a free press, freedom of worship and assembly, and other fundamental rights may not be submitted to vote; they depend on the outcome of no elections."

> *—Jackson, J., in West Virginia State*
> *Board of Education v Barnette, 319*
> *U S 624, 87 L ed 1628, 63 S Ct 1178*

Clergy—Clergyman

365.   A British clergyman commented: "People expect the clergy to have the grace of a swan, the friendliness of a sparrow, the strength of an eagle and the night hours of an owl—and some people expect such a bird to live on the food of a canary."

366.   Many young ministers are poor men, but that is no reason why they should be poor ministers.

What is ministerial success? Crowded churches, full aisles, attentive congregations, the approval of the religious world, much impression produced? Elijah thought so; and when he discovered his mistake, and found out that the Carmel applause subsided into hideous stillness, his heart well-nigh broke with disappointment. Ministerial success lies in altered lives, and obedient, humble hearts, unseen worth recognized in the judgment-day.

> —F. W. ROBERTSON

Coexistence

367. A Western visitor to the Moscow Zoo was amazed to see a cage labeled "Coexistence," containing a lion and some lambs.

"How in the world do you do it?" he asked the zoo keeper.

"Nothing to it," replied the Russian. "You just add a fresh lamb now and then."

Coffee break—Coffee breaks

368. The number of unemployed people is deplorably high, but it would be far higher if the employed didn't take coffee breaks.

369. The coffee break is a fairly well-established practice in many business organizations. It is a term loosely used for a brief rest period whether the people stop for coffee, a soft drink, or a glass of milk.

But there was one historic coffee break which stands out for two reasons. It occurred under most trying circumstances, and the man who served the coffee later became President of the United States.

On the afternoon of September 17, 1862, Federal troops crossed Antietam Creek and were pressing toward Sharpsburg against fierce resistance. The sergeant in charge of the Commissary Department for an Ohio regiment voluntarily carried a bucket of hot coffee and a box of cooked rations to the men of his regiment along the firing line. He ladled the coffee into a tin cup and let each man have his fill. He also served the warm food from the ration box.

The sergeant who instituted this historic coffee break and later became President of the United States was named William McKinley.

A tall granite monument can be seen today on the site of this historic engagement in western Maryland. It bears an inscription citing this thoughtful and considerate action voluntarily undertaken in the face of grave danger.

College—Colleges

370. Helping your eldest son pick a college is one of the great educational experiences of life—for the parents. Next to trying to pick his bride, it is the best way to learn that your authority, if not enitrely gone, is slipping fast.

—SALLY AND JAMES RESTON

371. A college should feel alarmed rather than pleased if it graduates nothing but good citizens. For when the body politic is composed of nothing but submissive individuals, half of its health and all of its vigor have disappeared.

—George Boas

372. The proper function of the college is not education at all, but de-education. It is, however, an inclination due to no logical process, but to individual experience. When I entered college at the age of 17 I knew everything. When I emerged, just short of 21, I had begun to doubt that I knew anything; and the subsequent fifty years have been one long confirmation of the doubt.

—Gerald W. Johnson

373. College education is more than a mastery of tricks which bring early success; more than a secret magic, knowledge of which will transform one's personality and confer fame and fortune. Shoddiness is the result when shortcuts are sought in matters of mental growth. The only time wasted in education is that spent trying to save time. There should be no haste or crowding or cramming. Mastery of any subject requires years of familiarity with it. The formal training one receives at college is but the introduction.

—Joseph L. Lennon

Committee—Committees

374. Having served on various committees, I have drawn up a list of rules: Never arrive on time; this stamps you as a beginner. Don't say anything until the meeting is half over; this stamps you as being wise. Be as vague as possible; this avoids irritating the others. When in doubt, suggest that a subcommittee be appointed. Be the first to move for adjournment; this will make you popular; it's what everyone is waiting for.

—Harry Chapman

Communism

375. Communism is the cult of those who think man created God, and not the other way around.

—Dorothy Thompson

376. Communism is the opiate of the intellectuals, but it isn't a cure—except as the guillotine might be called a cure for dandruff.

—Clare Booth Luce

377. Any Communist worth his salt is dedicated to the proposition that Communism must rule the world. Communists accept delays and setbacks but they never lose sight of their ultimate goal. Communism is an aggressive foe that is constantly challenging its enemies and is not above sacrificing its friends.

Companionship

378. The story is told of a weary traveler who was passing along a lonely roadway and noticed in his path a dry, shrivelled leaf. Picking it up, he was amazed at the lovely perfume it exuded.

"Oh, you poor withered leaf," he exclaimed, "whence comes this exquisite perfume?"

The leaf replied, "I have lain for a long time in the company of a rose."

Compensation

379. The trouble with some people is if they do an honest day's work, they want a week's pay.

380. A man doesn't always get paid for what he knows, but seldom escapes paying for what he doesn't know.

381. No evil is without its compensation. The less money, the less trouble; the less favor, the less envy. Even in those cases which put us out of wits, it is not the loss itself, but the estimate of the loss that troubles us.

—Seneca

Competition—Competitiveness

382. The way to kill competition is to create something too good for competition to imitate.

Complacency

383. Today's competitiveness, so much imposed from without, is exhausting, not exhilarating; is unending—a part of one's social life, one's solitude, one's sleep, one's sleeplessness.

—Louis Kronenberger

384. There is little economic competition in an impoverished country. When there are few customers and little money to spend, there is scant incentive to produce goods for sale. There is little competition in a rigidly controlled economy, and with good reason. When the state controls the source and flow of raw materials, and dictates the price, amount and product design, there is little room for competition.

Complacency

385. Live and *let* live is not enough; live and *help* live is not too much.

—Orin E. Madison

386. A reasonable number of fleas is good for a dog. They keep him busy. In much the same fashion, psychologists agree that a reasonable number of anxieties and personal conflicts is often good for people. Tension can keep men from getting complacent, from feeling so secure in their jobs that they forget to look for ways to improve themselves.

Complaint—Complaints

387. Instead of crying over spilt milk go milk another cow.

388. It is usually not so much the greatness of our trouble as the littleness of our spirit which makes people complain.

—J. Taylor

Compromise—Compromises

389. People are usually willing to meet each other half way but their judgment of distances varies considerably.

390.   You may either win your peace, or buy it:—win it, by resistance to evil;—buy it, by compromise with evil.

—JOHN RUSKIN

391.   Compromise is not evil *per se*. In political situations the citizen rarely confronts compromise between sheer good and sheer evil. Compromise is often an effort to achieve several goals partially, acknowledging that none of them may be attainable entirely. It is compromise between varying degrees of good for various groups in the society. Compromise is difficult to reach without accepting the fact that men are neither perfect nor perfectible, and that men are not going to be able to eliminate evil from the face of the earth or the hearts of men.

—BRUCE L. FELKNOR

Conceit

392.   No man was ever so much deceived by another as by himself.

—LORD GREVILLE

393.   A limited amount of conceit gives a man the confidence he needs; too much conceit gives him the overconfidence he is better off without.

Conformity

394.   Beaten paths are symbols for beaten men and beaten organizations.

395.   The surest way to corrupt a young man is to teach him to esteem more highly those who think alike than those who think differently.

—FRIEDRICH WILHELM NIETZSCHE

396.   The perils of conformity are well known, among them being a loss of individuality. But what remains to be pointed out is that if we keep on conforming, the day will come when we will have nothing to say to one another.

Conscience

397. We fuss about the pressures for conformity: but the pressures on us are much less than those on a medieval serf, a Greek slave or a Neolithic villager. Elizabethan England and fifth-century Athens sound exciting, but this was so for only a very limited section of the population. In days long past, when man was close to nature, it was simply unthinkable to depart from the customs of the tribe. There was only one way of life, and everyone followed it.

—MARSTON BATES

Conscience

398. Before I can live with other folks I've got to live with myself. The one thing that doesn't abide by majority rule is a person's conscience.

—HARPER LEE

399. The voice of conscience is so delicate that it is easy to stifle it; but it is also so clear that it is impossible to mistake it.

—MADAME DE STAËL

400. The conscience is a built-in feature.
That haunts the sinner, helps the preacher.
Some sins it makes us turn and run from,
But most it simply takes the fun from.

—RICHARD ARMOUR

Consecration

401. "Will you please tell me in a word," said a woman to her minister, "what your idea of consecration is?"

Holding out a blank sheet of paper, the pastor replied. "It is to sign your name to the bottom of this blank sheet, and let God fill in as He wills."

Contentment

402. Drink the water as you find it; don't stir up the mud.

—OLD SAYING

403. If you can't be the locomotive, isn't it better to be the caboose than not on the train at all?

404. Contentment preserves one from catching cold. Has a woman who knew that she was well dressed ever caught a cold? No, not even when she has scarcely a rag on her back.
—Friedrich Wlihelm Nietzsche

405. When we look at what we want and then compare that with what we have, we shall be unhappy. When we think of what we deserve, then of what we have, we shall thank God.

Conversation

406. Getting a word in edgewise with some women is like threading a sewing machine with the motor running.

407. When we talk in company we lose our unique tone of voice, and this leads us to make statements which in no way correspond to our real thoughts.
—Friedrich Wilhelm Nietzsche

408. Conversation is but carving!
Give no more to every guest
Than he's able to digest.
Give him always of the prime,
And but little at a time.
Carve to all but just enough,
Let them neither starve nor stuff,
And that you may have your due,
Let your neighbor carve for you.
—Jonathan Swift

409. The noted Harvard scholar Charles T. Copeland was once approached by a student who asked: "Why are there no courses in conversation? How can I learn the art of conversation? Is there anything I can do to learn the art of conversation?"

Corruption

"Of course, there is," answered Copeland, "and if you'll just listen, I'll tell you what it is."

There ensued a long and awkward silence which the student finally interrupted with:

"Well, I'm listening."

"You see," said Copeland triumphantly, "you are learning already!"

Corruption

410.   Money is an amoral instrument, and like science serves good and evil alike. There's no such thing as dirty money: the stain is only on the hand that holds it as giver or taker.

411.   The time to guard against corruption and tyranny is before they have gotten hold of us. It is better to keep the wolf out of the fold than to trust to drawing his teeth and talons after he shall have entered.

—THOMAS JEFFERSON

Courage

412.   There is a wide difference between true courage and mere contempt of life.

—CATO

413.   A great part of courage is the courage of having done the thing before.

—RALPH WALDO EMERSON

414.   Courage is what it takes to stand up and speak; it is also what it takes, on occasion, to sit down and listen.

415.   Courage is more than standing for a firm conviction. It includes the risk of *questioning* that conviction.

—JULIA WEBER GORDON

416. Courage is a good word. It has a ring. It is a substance that other people, who have none, urge you to have when all is lost.

—JIM BISHOP

417. Courage is poorly housed that dwells in numbers; the lion never counts the herd that are about him; nor weighs how many flocks he has to scatter.

—AARON HILL

418. Courage, it would seem, is nothing less than the power to overcome danger, misfortune, fear, injustice, while continuing to affirm inwardly that life with all its sorrows and good is meaningful even if in a sense beyond our understanding, and that there is always tomorrow.

—DOROTHY THOMPSON

419. Courage! What if the snows are deep,
And what if the hills are long and steep
And the days are short and the nights are long
And the good are weak and the bad are strong.
Courage! The snow is a field of play.
And the longest hill has a well-worn way,
There are songs that shorten the longest night,
There's a day when wrong shall be ruled by right,
So Courage! Courage! 'Tis never so far
From a plodded path to a shining star.

—ANON.

Courtesy

420. No man is too big to be courteous, but some are too little.

421. Be courteous—treat the other fellow as though he is as important as he thinks he is.

422. Courtesy is the Gulf Stream in business that melts the mountains of icy indifference and sends the old ship safely into the harbor of success.

Credit

423.   As the sword of the best tempered metal is most flexible, so the truly generous are most pliant and courteous in their behavior to their inferiors.

—THOMAS FULLER

424.   Courtesy is the one medium of exchange which is accepted at par value by the best people of every country on the globe. It is sentiment, cloaked in reasonable and businesslike expression. It is the embellishment which adds tone and harmony to matter-of-fact routine. It is the oil which lubricates the machinery of commercial good-fellowship, and promotes the smooth running of the many units of an organization. . . . Life is not too short, and we are never too busy to be courteous. No man is too big to be courteous, but some are too little.

Credit

425.   Credit was a word with meaning to the earliest civilizations of the New World. The Inca in Peru, who built aqueducts and roads and knew a great deal about such complex matters as textiles, medicine and even surgery, made credit a part of their lives. When newly-weds picked the site for their homes the Inca government extended a helping hand and advanced credit allowing them to buy the land and erect a house. Helped by the advanced Inca systems of agriculture and irrigation, the young people would produce good crops and repay their loans.

Credo—Credos

426.   If I can live in simple comfort and owe no man, sharing intimateley with loved ones life's varied experiences; if I can bring a touch of healing and a clearer outlook into the trials and problems of those with whom I mingle; if I can humbly undertake public service when the public calls me, caring neither too much nor too little for popular approval; if I can give spiritual values always the first place, and gladly sink from sight, like a bit of leaven, that others might be elevated—then will this experiment of living yield in full measure the true wealth of contentment and happiness.

—ALFRED OSBORNE

427.   To live in the affections; not to dwell in pride. To cultivate courtesy, which is the manner of the heart. To be considerate of those who serve, since they are not free to resent. To avoid arrogance, which corrodes the man and estranges his friends. To mingle freely with all classes, and thus to know mankind. To be mastered by no habit or prejudice, no triumph or misfortune. To promise cautiously, and perform faithfully. To choose hobbies with care, and pursue them with diligence. To value people above thoughts, and thoughts above things. To curb personal wants, which expand easily but shrink with difficulty. To be just, man's supreme virtue, which requires the best of head and heart. These are the things I ask of life!

—ANON.

428.   I believe that in moments of dire distress, charitable people come to relieve; that there is everywhere more helpfulness than selfishness; more sincerity than deceitfulness; more bravery than cowardice; more love than hate; more liberality than economy; more cheerfulness than dejection.

I believe that the invalided are not wholly forgotten and that, although unseen, they are cheered by the sympathetic, the kind-hearted; that strangers in cities and towns are ever met by cordiality and guided into rightful ways.

I believe in the brotherhood of man; that friendship is just as vital an element in commercial marts as between one individual and another; that each day is filled with opportunities, with fellowship, with common affection; that sentiment lives, thrives, exists, and is a reality.

I believe in the goodness and greatness of human nature; that joy and happiness are secured by personal conquest; that there are times when sorrow and misfortune come to every life, and, in such hours, men and women by patient suffering become heroic; that little children by innocence and simplicity preach masterful sermons.

I believe in the good, great, broad, beautiful world, and I love it; I love and believe in man, and the call of the soul that is in it, and yet above it—I believe in the God who made it all.

—LOUIS VARNUM WOULFE

Criticism

429.   Criticism is most effective when it sounds like praise.

—ARNOLD H. GLASOW

430.   Brief review of a new book: "The covers are too far apart."

431.   Today's compliments are often the fruit of yesterday's criticism.

432.   If you are not big enough to stand criticism, you are too small to be praised.

433.   A smile in giving honest criticism can make the difference between resentment and reform.

—PHILIP STEINMETZ

434.   Never fear criticism when you are right; never ignore criticism when you are wrong.

435.   Criticism should not be querulous and wasting, but guiding, instructive, inspiring.

—RALPH WALDO EMERSON

436.   The man who points out what is wrong renders only half a service unless he can point out what is right.

437.   A stout heart never went with a thin skin. Anyone who has the courage to act must find the courage to face his critics.

—BURTON HILLIS

438.   Knock no man behind his back, lest he turn about and praise thee to thy face, in the presence of thine enemies.

439.   It is one of the signs of maturity to be able both to give and to receive criticism in a spirit of charity. If the criticism is surrounded by bonds of mutual concern and love, it need not be destructive, but can actually be creative.

—ROBERT MCAFEE BROWN

440.   A true critic, in the perusal of a book, is like a dog at a feast, whose thoughts and stomach are wholly set upon what the guests fling away, and consequently is apt to snarl most when there are the fewest bones.

—JONATHAN SWIFT

441. A very able minister, preaching on criticism, admitted that criticism can sometimes prove infinitely more valuable than the fair words of friends, and cautioned against shutting one's ears and mind to adverse comments, advising the adoption of a calm, philosophic attitude. Only the shallow are moved by applause from without, and only the shallow allow unjustified criticism to wreck their peace of mind. Stand right with yourself and you can stand criticism.

—B. C. FORBES

442. No one should take lightly criticism that might prove helpful; no one should take to heart criticism that could be unwarranted. The opinions of others ought never discourage anyone from doing something which he feels in his heart he can do and should do. In such things, each person's decision should be his own.

When the great Polish pianist, Ignace Paderewski, first chose the piano, he was told by a music teacher that his hands were too small to master the keyboard.

When the great Italian tenor, Enrico Caruso, first applied for instruction, the teacher told him his voice was like "wind whistling through a window."

When the great statesman of Victorian England, Benjamin Disraeli, attempted to speak in Parliament for the first time, the members hissed him into silence and laughed when he said, "Though I sit down now, the time will come when you will hear me!"

When the great electrical engineer, Guglielmo Marconi said that the discoveries of the German scientist, Henrich Hertz, could be applied to world-wide wireless communication, he was told his ideas were contrary to the laws of physics.

All of these men knew what they wanted to do, or what they wanted to be. Criticism did not discourage them; it proved to be a challenge. They simply worked harder until they achieved success.

Curiosity

443. Curiosity is free-wheeling intelligence. It endows the people who have it with a generosity in argument and a serenity in their own mode of life which spring from the cheerful willingness to let life take the forms it will.

—ALISTAIR COOKE

444. Curiosity deserves credit for most of the progress humanity has made. It has pulled a good portion of the race out of caves and skin tents into homes with electric lights, comfortable heat, sanitation, and TV. It has given us a greater variety of food, and clothing that is attractive as well as useful.

Franklin's curiosity helped to open the door to the miraculous world of electricity.

Gutenberg's curiosity led directly to the invention and development of the printing arts, and the low-priced abundant literature of every variety we have today.

Burbank's curiosity to know what would happen if he performed certain experiments with plants, resulted in improvements which will benefit the race until the end of time.

We live in a scientific age and science is nothing more than the curiosity of trained minds intent upon discovering the secrets of nature.

We also live in a time of religious reawakening. Curiosity is a tremendously important factor in the development of our spiritual life, as moral and religious ideas are also the subject of human speculation. The quest for divine truths is as old as the race itself.

Custom—Customs

445. Custom is the great leveller; it corrects the inequality of fortune by lessening equally the pleasures of the prince and the pains of the peasant.
—Lord Kames

446. Be not too rash in the breaking of an inconvenient custom; as it was gotten, so leave it by degrees. Danger attends upon too sudden alterations; he that pulls down a bad building by the bulk may be ruined by the fall, but he that takes it down brick by brick may live to build a better.
—Francis Quarles

447. New Year has been celebrated as a holy festival from early times. The Jews kept the Feast of Trumpets; the Druids made sacrifices, sometimes human, to their gods. In many countries gifts were exchanged on New Year, and in Scotland it used to be allowable to *ask* for a gift on that day. The lovely "open house" custom is English. The doors of all houses were opened at midnight, on New Year's Eve, so that the spirit of the Old Year might go out, taking with him old habits and foolish mistakes, and the spirit of the New Year might come in with bright new resolutions.

448.　Tradition still governs most of the world's wedding customs, and romantic couples prefer the traditional month of brides (June). . . . The color of the bride's costume is also a matter of tradition. In the U. S., the bride wears white; but in China, where white is reserved for mourning, she dresses in red. Superstitious Norwegian girls often choose green for luck. The colors most popular in Rumania are red and gold.

449.　The custom of standing when the national anthem is played is believed to have originated with Daniel Webster during a concert by the famous Swedish artist, Jenny Lind. She was singing "The Star Spangled Banner" in Castle Garden in New York City when the great statesman rose to his feet and stood until she had finished. Most of the audience rose and stood with him. However, it was not until March 3, 1931, that this song became the official national anthem by Act of Congress.

450.　Most of our wedding customs have come down to us through the centuries. In nearly every wedding at least some of the customs are observed. However, not many people know, for instance, why a bride wears a veil. Or, who started the use of wedding rings? Why is the ring placed on the fourth finger of the left hand? Why do friends throw rice, or sometimes old shoes? What about the wedding cake?

It is said that the bridal veil is nothing more than the continuance of the ancient Eastern rule that no man should see a woman's face except her husband, and not even he until after the ceremony. Today's veil is used more to add a touch of distinction to the bridal costume than to conceal the bride's face.

No one can be sure when the ring became a symbol of marriage. One theory goes back into a trade practice of ancient times. When few people could read or write, merchants needed a way to accomplish what we do today with a person's signature. Individual seals, or signets, were devised to authenticate documents and to serve as symbols of authority. The simplest and safest way to carry such a signet was in a ring, so the signet ring came into widespread use. Then when a man married it was perfectly logical for him to give his wife a signet ring to show merchants that she had his authority to buy for the household and to act for him in his absence.

The choice of the fourth finger of the left hand for the wedding ring is an old custom from pagan Rome. There was a time when people believed that a nerve went directly from that finger to the heart.

Rice-throwing is another custom from the East. Rice is the

staple food in the East, and throwing it symbolizes a wish for a prosperous life.

Shoe-throwing is a little more modern, but also another Eastern custom which has changed slightly from the original. In the older days the bride's father handed the bridegroom an old shoe as a symbol of the parental right of chastising the daughter. A shoe or slipper was the usual instrument employed. Giving the shoe transferred the parent's right to the bridegroom.

The wedding cake came down from the Romans, A part of their marriage rites was the eating of a cake made of flour, salt, and water in the presence of the priest. Some of the wedding cakes baked today would certainly pop the eyes of any young Roman couple.

The question, "Who giveth this woman to be married to this man?" probably comes from the old concept of woman as a "chattel." The owner had to identify himself and confirm the surrender of his "property" to another.

Cynicism

451.   Watch what people are cynical about, and one can often discover what they lack, and subconsciously, beneath their touchy condescension, deeply wish they had.

—Harry Emerson Fosdick

Death

452.   Wise men know death to be an endless sleep.

—Sir John Bland Sutton

453.   It is infamy to die, and not be missed.

—Carlos Wilcox

454.   Perhaps our fear of death is but embryonic fear of life.

—Dagobert D. Runes

455.   If some men died and others did not, death would indeed be a most mortifying evil.

—Jean de La Bruyère

456. Man's life is like unto a winter's day,
Some break their fast and so depart away,
Others stay for dinner, then depart full fed;
The longest age but sups and goes to bed.
—Author unknown

457. The child who enters life comes not with knowledge or intent.
So those who enter death must go as little children sent.
Nothing is known. But I believe that God is overhead;
And as life is to the living, so death is to the dead.
—Author unknown

458. There is nothing that Nature has made necessary which is more easy than death; we are longer a-coming into the world than going out of it; and there is not any minute of our lives wherein we may not reasonably expect it. Nay, it is but a moment's work, the parting of soul and body. What a shame is it then to stand in fear of anything so long that is over so soon!
—Seneca

Debate—Debates—Debating

459. Men are never so likely to settle a question rightly, as when they discuss it freely.
—Thomas Macaulay

460. The American tradition has always dictated that it is far better to debate an important matter without settling it than to settle it without debating it.

Debtor—Creditor——Debtors—Creditors

461. So long as a person who owes you is worried about it, you needn't be.

462. An accurate measure of a man is what he does for those who can't repay.

463. The proprietor of the grocery store had shown marked attention to one of his customers, almost bowing to the man as he left the store. Another customer, a newcomer to the town, had witnessed the proceedings and, thinking that the other man was a celebrity, remarked: "I noticed that you treated your last customer with some deference."

"Yes," replied the proprietor, "he's one of our early settlers."

"He doesn't appear over forty to me," said the customer.

"I don't know how old he is," answered the grocer, "but I do know he always settles his bill on the first of the month."

Decision—Decisions

464. Sound decisions are hammered out on the anvil of logic.

465. A decision delayed until it is too late is not a decision; it's an evasion.

466. It takes a mightly big man to share decision-making with others when he alone must shoulder responsibility for the results.

467. He is free who knows how to keep in his own hand the power to decide, at each step, the course of his life, and who lives in a society which does not block the exercise of that power.

—SALVADOR DE MADARIAGA

468. Do not rush headlong into a decision, or let yourself be rushed into one by others. No matter what you may decide, wait before you act. . . . Time gives you opportunity to weigh all factors and stamps your final action with the seal of maturity.

—BALTASAR GRACIÁN

469. Above all else in life we prize most the right of personal decision. Not only is this the inalienable right of free men, but it has proved to be the greatest strength of a free society. That is, free men, freely and fully committed to their personal responsibilities surpass the achievements of those whose obedience must be commanded.

—JOHN R. RHAMSTINE

470. The essence of civilization is the ability to make decisions and the willingness to live with the consequences. Democratic societies, above all others, have built and flourished on this basic truth. Whether we like it or not, the U. S. today is the primary showcase both for the blessings of free choice and for the sordid results when such freedom is abused.

—Better Living

471. While an open mind is priceless, it is priceless only when its owner has the courage to make a final decision which closes the mind for action after the process of viewing all sides of the question has been completed. Failure to make a decision after due consideration of all the facts will quickly brand a man as unfit for a position of responsibility. Not all of your decisions will be correct. None of us is perfect. But if you get into the habit of making decisions, experience will develop your judgment to a point where it is better to be right 51 per cent of the time and get something done, than it is to get nothing done because you fear to reach a decision.

—H. W. ANDREWS

Defeat—Defeats

472. Defeat never comes to any man until he admits it.

—JOSEPHUS DANIELS

473. SPORTSMANSHIP
Let others cheer the winning man,
There's one I hold worthwhile;
'Tis he who does the best he can,
And loses with a smile.
Beaten he is, but not to stay
Down with the rank and file;
That man will win some other day
Who loses with a smile.

—ANONYMOUS

Defeatism

474. If you think you are beaten, you are.
If you think you dare not, you don't.

If you'd like to win, but you think you can't,
  It's almost a cinch you won't.
If you think you'll lose, you've lost,
  For out of the world you find
Success begins with a fellow's will—
  It's all in the state of mind.
If you think you're outclassed, you are;
  You've got to think high to rise;
You've got to be sure of yourself before
  You can ever win a prize.
Full many a race is lost
  Ere ever a step is run;
And many a coward fails
  Ere ever his work's begun.
Think big and your deeds will grow;
  Think small and you'll fall behind;
Think that you can and you will—
  It's all in the state of mind.
Life's battles don't always go
  To the stronger or faster man
But soon or late the man who wins
  Is the fellow who thinks he can.

—Author unknown

Delusion—Delusions

475. The house of delusions is cheap to build but drafty to live in.
—A. E. Housman

476. When our vices quit us, we flatter ourselves with the belief that it is we who quit them.
—François de La Rochefoucauld

Demand and supply. See Supply and demand

Democracy

477. Puritanism, believing itself quick with the seed of religious liberty, laid, without knowing it, the egg of democracy.
—James Russell Lowell

478.   Democracy, if I understand it at all, is a society in which the unbeliever feels undisturbed and at home. If there were only half a dozen unbelievers in America, their well-being would be a test of our democracy, their tranquility would be a proof.

—E. B. WHITE

479.   It would be tragic if democarcy deteriorated into mass tyranny over the unconventional individual. We should then lose the diversity from which spring ideas; we should rob ourselves of the precious quality that distinguishes man from all other orders—his determination to think for himself; to be different.

—H. G. RICKOVER

480.   The essence . . . of democracy is that it is the one system devised to date premised on the manifest *fallibility* of man, the one system which asserts that all men and women (not just nobles, rich man, or Party members) are full members of the community entitled to a say in its destinies. Thus the leaders must look for public sanction and the people always retain the right to reject one set in favor of another. This may on occasion lead to demagoguery, "father images," and sheer incompetence, but the alternative is a frozen, self-validating, and inevitably dictatorial system. As Winston Churchill once observed in a moment of pessimism, "democracy is the worst system ever invented—except for all the rest."

—JOHN P. ROCHE

Desperation

481.   An Arab returned to his tent late one evening, very hungry. He lit a candle and searched until he found four dates. He took out his knife and cut one open; it was wormy, so he tossed it aside.

He took another one, cut it open, but it too was wormy.
He took a third date, cut it open and it was wormy.
Then he sighed, blew out the candle, and ate the last date.

BRUCE KILGORE

Difference—Differences

482.   You've got to love what's lovable and hate what's hateable. It takes brains to see the difference.

—ROBERT FROST

483.   The nature of men is always the same; it is their habits that separate them.

—Confucius

484.   There's only a small difference between men, but that small difference makes a big difference.

—Arnold Glasow

485.   It were not best that we should all think alike; it is difference of opinion that makes horse-races.

—Mark Twain

486.   Read every day something no one else is reading. Think something no one else is thinking, It is bad for the mind to be always a part of unanimity.

—Christopher Morley

487.   When a prisoner picked up for traffic violations argued with the judge that he was not drunk but had only been drinking, the judge assured him that would make a difference in the sentence. "I am not going to send you to jail for a month," the judge said, "but only for thirty days."

488.   Americans need to be warned about words and ideas which look much alike, but have different effects. For example, Americans often confuse size with importance, speed with progress, money with wealth, authority with wisdom, religion with theology, excitement with pleasure and enthusiasm with hollering.

—Carter Davidson

489.   A businessman from the States was traveling in the interior of a South American country. He flew into a fairly large town, and there found that he would have to take a local train to his destination, Naturally he bought a first-class ticket.

When the old, broken-down, wood-burning locomotive left the station, it was pulling only one coach. The American complained that there was no advantage in buying a first-class ticket since all passengers rode in the one coach.

The conductor assured him there was a difference and asked

him to wait and see. About halfway to its destination the train stopped. The conductor shouted something in Spanish, and all the other passengers got up and left the coach. Outside a trainman handed buckets to some and axes to the others.

Then the conductor explained to the American, "First-class passengers don't work. Second-class carry water and third-class chop wood."

Dignity

490.   A man's dignity is like his top-hat: the more he stands on it the less impressive it becomes.

—SIR RALPH WINDHAM

491.   It is well known that dignity will only bleed while you watch it. Avert your eyes and it instantly dries up.

—ARNOLD BENNETT

Discipline

492.   He that spareth his rod hateth his son.

—THE BIBLE

493.   God's law calls for discipline, both of ourselves and our children. It must be a discipline that will enable us to be masters of ourselves. It must be a discipline that will enable our children to meet life's challenge. . . . Discipline results in stamina, and stamina makes men and women of character.

Discouragement

494.   Don't let life discourage you; everyone who got where he is had to begin where he was.

—RICHARD L. EVANS

495.   If we want a thing badly enough, we can make it happen. If we let ourselves be discouraged, that is proof that our wanting was inadequate.

—DOROTHY L. SAYERS

Dishonesty

496. Discouragement is dissatisfaction with the past, distaste for the present, and distrust of the future. It is ingratitude for the blessings of yesterday, indifference to the opportunities of today, and insecurity of the strength of tomorrow, It is unawareness of the presence of beauty, unconcern for the needs of our fellow man, and disbelief in the promises of old. It is impatience with time, immaturity of thought, and impoliteness to God.

—Dr. William Arthur Ward

Dishonesty

497. The path of least resistance is what makes rivers and men crooked.

498. A department store manager wrapped a small empty package and placed it on a counter. It was quickly stolen. He wrapped a similar package 40 times that one day and 40 times it was stolen from the counter. The experiment was designed to give some idea of the amount of goods being taken daily by thieving customers.

—Norman Vincent Peale

Do-it-yourself

499. A self-made man is often a big argument against do-it-yourself.

Doubt—Doubts

500. The biggest cause of trouble in the world today is that the stupid people are so sure about things and the intelligent folks are so full of doubts.

501. Don't waste time in doubts and fears; spend yourself in the work before you, well assured that the right performance of this hour's duties will be the best preparation for the hours or ages that follow it.

—Ralph Waldo Emerson

Dream—Dreams—Dreaming

502. To dream is to think by moonlight, by the light of an inner moon.

503. Dream manfully and nobly, and thy dreams shall be prophets.
—EDWARD BULWER-LYTTON

504. Although there are various theories of dream interpretation, many psychoanalysts would agree to these basic points:

1. Our dreams reveal our innermost natures. They show us our secret selves, our hidden attitudes, wishes, impulses.

2. In our dreams we attempt to solve our most urgent problems. And this struggle goes on even when our waking minds don't even know that the problems exist.

3. Our dreams are difficult to understand, because we often don't want to face the truths which they expose—and also because our everyday intelligence cannot easily grasp the complex artistic symbolism of our dreams.

4. But we can understand our dreams—if we have the will, the patience, the intelligence and the courage to do so.
—WALTER WALKER

505. Dreams are an escape from yourself. They are a kind of magic carpet onto which one steps and flies away from his wounds, and his mediocrity. And they are more. As far as you can dream, so far you can one day go; for dreams are the lovely plans of the unknown reaching toward us to be fulfilled; they are the multicolored promise of that which can come to pass. What is a flower but the completed vision of a quiet seed dreaming in the dust? What are these terraced buildings all about us like strong hands lifted toward the skies in grave salute, but the dreams of men come true? What are the stars, and beyond, more stars too far for us to see—all the mystery and movement of the universe, but the reveries of God, expressed in form? When one no longer dreams of the beauty that could be, he has begun to die.

Drinking

506. It doesn't change the effect of alcohol to serve it in a cocktail room instead of a saloon.
—RUTH SMELTZER

507.   A rich oil man filled his swimming pool with martinis so that it would be impossible for him to drown. The deeper he went, the higher he got.

508.   Whenever we humans become too conceited about the intelligence of our species, we should think of this one fact. Spidermonkeys are much wiser than men. As Charles Darwin once pointed out, when a spidermonkey has once been made drunk on brandy, it will never touch the stuff again.

509.   All excess is ill, but drunkenness is of the worst. It spoils health, dismounts the mind, and unmans men. It reveals secrets, is quarrelsome, lascivious, impudent, dangerous, and mad. He that is drunk is not a man, because he is, for so long, void of reason that distinguishes a man from a beast.

—William Penn

Easter

510.   Easter, in the northern hemisphere, is in the spring. In fact, the name comes from an old Norse word of various spellings. Eastur or Ostara or some other variant meant the time when the sun came back—a pagan feast to celebrate the awakening of life after its winter dormancy. There are legends which tell of a Goddess of Spring, Eostre, who gave her name to the festival, but historians tend to discount old legends.

A pagan feast to celebrate the coming of spring might not have survived into modern times were it not for the most significant fact in human history—the birth and death of Jesus of Nazareth. The *Bible* tells us that He came out of the tomb where they had laid Him to assure His disciples that the Cross was not the end—that He was the Resurrection and that the promise of enduring life for all mankind would be fulfilled.

Easter changed from a pagan feast to welcome the annual springtime renewal of life on this earth to a Christian feast commemorating the Resurrection of Christ, and mankind's hope of a renewal of life beyond this earth. And over the centuries, as a Christian festival, Easter has spread all over the world.

Among the early Christians and even on into medieval times, Easter was an occasion to forgive. Authorities pardoned prisoners who were not dangerous to society. Feuding families, and individuals, agreed to end their animosities and to be civil to one another. It was a time when slaves were restored to human dignity through the gift of freedom.

In modern times Easter reflects the spirit of spring in clothing fashions. People like to wear something new and bright for Easter. In some communities there are Easter parades and in others more of a promenade by those who feel their Easter finery deserves attention.

Today our churches are filled on Easter Sunday, for deep down in their hearts most Christian people want to hear again the story of the Resurrection. They want to be told once more that this life is not all there is to being. They go to chucrh to be a part of the celebration of the true meaning of Easter.

Education

511. The supreme test of an educated person is his willingness to sacrifice for an abstract ideal.

—Francis P. Gaines

512. The education of our youth is this generation's debt to the future, and the future will judge how well we have discharged it.

513. The man who graduates today and stops learning tomorrow is uneducated the day after.

514. The richest man cannot *buy* an education for his son; he can only buy him the opportunity to *earn* one.

515. Give a man a fish, and he will eat for a day. Teach him how to fish and he will eat for the rest of his life.

—Old proverb

516. Education is a social process. . . . Education is growth. . . . Education is not preparation for life; education is life itself.

—John Dewey

517. No one can gain an education without some personal effort, no matter how many billions are spent to provide it.

518. Education has a two-fold purpose—to add to your capacity to earn a living and to your capacity to live with your earnings.

519. The main objective of education is not to show us how to earn our daily bread, but to make us appreciate more each mouthful.

520. The education of the young is always one generation out of date. We can only educate by the standards of our own generation, not by those of the next.

—Don Robinson

521. After schooling, education begins. . . . Education in its essence is the cultivation of the human mind. Education consists in the growth of understanding, insight and ultimately some wisdom.

—Mortimer J. Adler

522. Whatever educates us merely for its own use, without regard to us as living beings, whatever takes us for granted, degrades and impoverishes us. It does not matter that we are told it is for our own good.

—Daniel Long

523. The aim of education should be to teach us rather how to think than what to think,—rather to improve our minds, so as to enable us to think for ourselves, than to load the memory with the thoughts of other men.

—James Beattie

524. All great philosophers have understood that the education of youth is the primary function of society—the means by which humanity's inheritance is transmitted from one generation to another. . . . Each one of us is heir to all of the ideas and accomplishments of every human being who has ever lived.

—H. G. Rickover

525. There is no substitute for being educated. . . . My advice to the young might be summed up this way: You will never, during the rest of your life, possess the span of free time now available to you. . . . Use this time to *study*, to learn, to enrich your mind and spirit with ideas which are important and which you might otherwise never know how to absorb, master and use.

—LEO ROSTEN

526.   People today have come to regard a college degree in much the same way that their fathers regarded a high school diploma a generation ago. This is evidenced by the fact that the percentage of college age people going to college corresponds with the percentage of high school age children going to high school a generation ago. Whether parents have been to a college or not, they expect their children to go.

527.   The education received at school or college is but a beginning, and is valuable mainly inasmuch as it trains the mind and habituates it to continuous application and study. That which is put into us by others is always far less ours than that which we acquire by our own diligent and persevering effort. Our own active effort is the essential thing; and no faculties, no books, no teachers, no amount of lessons learned by rote will enable us to dispense with it.

—SAMUEL SMILES

528.   Excellence in education is not so much teaching a child what to think, but how to think, so that he goes on seeking, choosing and thinking, so developing the persistent habit of inquiry and reasoning, and if, years later, the knoweldge he has acquired in school has become irrelevant to his purpose, dated or forgotten, he still has the ability to acquire new knowledge, to understand events more clearly and to adapt himself to new circumstances. Quality education is not just providing information, it is developing wiser minds.

—E. J. OLIVER

Effort

529.   The only failure which lacks dignity is the failure to try.
—MALCOLM F. MACNEIL

530.   We get mostly what we go after—if we go after it hard enough. About the only thing that has ever come into our life without effort is trouble;

and much of that can be traced to a desire to take hold of the blossoms instead of the branches.

531.   We are like people on a moving sidewalk which is going the wrong way. If we stand still, our goal recedes. If we walk at an easy pace we barely keep from slipping back. Only through extra effort can we win real gains.

—HARRY K. WOLFE

532.   The Creator sells us good things at the price of labor, effort, drudgery and renouncement; a price in just proportion to the real value of the goods we are to get. We pay for our high ideals, sometimes, with great loneliness. We pay for life itself in effort to sustain it, in greater effort to train it into worthy channels, in unremitting effort to keep it there. We pay for our inevitable sorrows and losses and errors sometimes with anger and denunciation, sometimes with endurance and stoic quiet, or best, with tender and hopeful resignation; but whatever coin we give we know at least that nothing may be had for nothing.

Employe—Employers

533.   It is absolutely impossible for a boss to be as ignorant as his employes think he is.

534.   It's strange that so many smart people work for such ignorant bosses.

535.   Most employers these days are more interested in performance than conformance.

—HENRY FORD II

536.   When you cannot agree with a decision of your boss, explain your own thinking calmly and clearly, but work just as hard as if his decision were your own.

537.   If you work for a man, then in Heaven's name work for him. If he pays you wages that supply your bread and butter, work for him;

speak well of him; stand by him and stand by the institution he represents.

If put to a pinch, an ounce of loyalty is worth a pound of cleverness.

If you must vilify, condemn, and eternally disparage, why not resign your position? But as long as you are part of the institution, do not condemn it.

If you do, you are loosening the tendrils holding you to that institution, and with the first high wind that comes along you will be uprooted and blown away in the blizzard's track—and probably you will never know why.

—ELBERT HUBBARD

538. An employe is a human resource; and it must be determined, according to the American business system, what is expected of him. Also, in return, what he may reasonably expect as the fruits of his labor. If the employe looks upon his employer as no more than an instrument responsible for the production of goods or services, he is looking only at one side of the picture. Seen as a whole, business enterprise is a means of producing a certain percentage of our nation's needs for consumer goods and at the same time a source of employe livelihood.

—JOSEPH ARKIN

539. When the first Marshall Field was building his department store into one of Chicago's finest, he spent a good part of each working day on the sales floors observing everything.

One day a little girl, on a shopping trip with her mother, was telling another child whom she encountered in the aisle that her daddy ran one of the departments in the Field store. She talked about *his* store and *his* department as if he actually owned a part of it. Suddenly the little girl's mother recognized Mr. Field standing in the aisle listening to the child's patter. Fearing that he might not like what he heard, she started to apologize for her daughter.

Marshall Field checked her. "The little girl is right," he said. "I want her father to feel that it is *his* store and *his* department. If I could induce every employe to feel that way, I wouldn't have to be concerned about the success of this business."

Fortunate indeed is the employer whose workers feel that his business is their business. When they have that much interest in their work, he can be sure that it will be done cheerfully and done well.

Employment

540.   A man's mistake is to believe that he's working only for someone else.

541.   When questioned as to why she had written nothing in the space calling for "age" on her application for a position, the applicant replied: "I refuse to answer on the ground that it might eliminate me."

542.   A man's job is his best friend. It clothes and feeds his wife and children, pays the rent, and supplies the wherewithal to develop and become cultivated. The least a man can do in return is to love his job. A man's job is grateful. It is like a little garden that thrives on love. It will one day flower into fruit worthwhile for him and his to enjoy. If you ask any successful man the reason for his making good, he will tell you that first and foremost it is because he likes his work; indeed, he is wrapped up in it. He walks his work; he talks his work; he is entirely inseparable from his work, and that is the way every man worth his salt ought to be if he wants to make of his work what it should be, and make of himself what he wants to be.

—ARTHUR CAPPER

Enemy—Enemies

543.   The command is to love your enemies—you don't have to trust them.

544.   Have you fifty friends? It is not enough. Have you one enemy? It is too much.

—ITALIAN PROVERB

545.   Everybody has enemies. To have an enemy is quite another thing. One must be somebody in order to have an enemy. One must be a force before he can be resisted by another force.

—MADAME SWETCHWINE

546.   If we could read the secret history of our enemies, we should find in each man's life sorrow and suffering enough to disarm all hostility.

—HENRY WADSWORTH LONGFELLOW

Enthusiasm

547.   Enthusiasm without knowledge is like haste in the dark.

548.   None are so old as those who have outlived enthusiasm.
—HENRY DAVID THOREAU

549.   Enthusiasm is that temper of the mind in which the imagination has got the better of the judgment.
—WILLIAM WARBURTON

550.   A dash of enthusiasm is not a thing to be ashamed of in retrospect. If St. Paul had not been a very zealous Pharisee he would have been a colder Christian.
—ROBERT LOUIS STEVENSON

551.   When a man has the gift of enthusiasm which comes from living without reservation, nothing can stop him. It is to the men and women of the world who live in this manner that life gives its greatest prizes. Many men have learned that happiness is a by-product, and that it cannot be sought deliberately nor won consciously, but that it can come only as an incident in the greater job of giving to life and to our work everything we have. This gives life meaning and sense.
—HAL L. NUTT

552.   Enthusiasm is the greatest asset in the world. It beats money and power and influence. Single-handed the enthusiast convinces and dominates where the wealth accumulated by a small army of workers would scarcely raise any interest.

Enthusiasm tramples over prejudice and opposition, spurns inaction, storms the citadel of its object, and like an avalanche overwhelms and engulfs all obstacles. It is nothing more or less than faith in action.

Faith and initiative rightly combined remove mountainous barriers and achieve the unheard of and miraculous.

Set the germ of enthusiasm afloat in your plant, in your office, or on your farm; carry it in your attitude and manner; it spreads like contagion and influences every fiber of your industry before you realize it; it means increase in production and decrease in costs; it means joy, and pleasure, and satisfaction to your workers; it means life, real, virile; it means spontaneous bedrock results—the vital things that pay dividends.

—Henry Chester

Envy

553. When you make your mark in the world, watch out for guys with erasers.

554. How bitter a thing it is to look into happiness through another man's eyes!

—William Shakespeare

555. There is a time in every man's education when he arrives at the conviction that envy is ignorance.

—Ralph Waldo Emerson

556. To be rich in admiration and free from envy, to rejoice greatly in the good of others, to love, these are the gifts of fortune which money cannot buy, and without which—money can buy nothing.

—Robert Louis Stevenson

557. Do not begrudge someone else the possession of precious things. He is only their custodian and must worry about losing them, or seeing them overshadowed by new finds, while you may enjoy their beauty without sharing his anxieties.

—Baltasar Gracián

558. Other passions have objects to flatter them, and which seem to content and satisfy them for a while. There is power in ambition, pleasure in luxury, and pelf in covetousness; but envy can gain nothing but vexation.

—Michel de Montaigne

Equality

559. There are many in this old world of ours who hold that things break about even for all of us, I have observed, for example, that we all get the same amount of ice. The rich get it in the summertime and the poor get it in the winter.

—Bat Masterson

560.   Whether a man is tall or short, old or young, strong or weak, black or white, rich or poor, his place under the moral law is secure. Those who deny him his rights, who treat him unjustly, who deal with him cruelly and brutally, are offenders. Only those who are ignorant fail to act in harmony with the belief that all human beings are God's children.

—Thomas Dreier

561.   We in America have had too much experience of life to fool ourselves into pretending that all men are equal in ability, in character, in intelligence, in ambition. That was part of the claptrap of the French Revolution. We have grown to understand that all we can hope to assure to the individual through government is liberty, justice, intellectual welfare, equality of opportunity, and stimulation to service.

—Herbert Hoover

Eternity

562.   There are two eternities, a past and a future; of the past we know but little, of the future, nothing; between these two eternities lies a speck called time.

—E. P. Day

563.   As eternity is of greater importance than time, so ought men to be solicitous upon what grounds their expectations with regard to that durable state are built, and on what assurances their hopes or their fears stand.

—Samuel Clarke

564.   You reap what you sow—not something else, but that. An act of love makes the soul more loving. A deed of humbleness deepens humbleness. The thing reaped is the very thing sown, multiplied a hundredfold. You have sown a seed of life, you reap life everlasting.

—F. W. Robertson

Etiquette

565. God does nothing in vain. When He gives a power, it is for a purpose, it is that it may reach an end. Now what I argue is this: Since He has put in my soul a germ that can grow to eternity, He means that it shall grow to eternity.

It is our souls which are the everlastingness of God's purpose in this earth.

—WILLIAM MOUNTFORD

Etiquette

566. Manners are especially the need of the plain. The pretty can get away with anything.

—EVELYN WAUGH

567. Too much of the world is run on the theory that you don't need road manners if you drive a five-ton truck.

Evolution

568. It is man who claims kinship with the apes; no ape has yet acknowledged it.

569. While man's kinship to the ape may not yet be proved, his kinship with the ass is beyond question.

Examination—Examinations

570. An intelligence test sometimes shows a man how smart he'd have been not to have taken it.

571. There is an anecdote about Arturo Alessandri, one-time President of Chile. It is said that when he was attending law school, he took an oral examination with a very erratic professor. The professor said to the young man, "I don't want to waste much time. Therefore, I shall ask you only one question. If you answer it correctly you pass the course; if you don't I fail you. First, tell me your name."

"My name is Arturo Alessandri," said the young man, and since you have asked me one question and I have answered it correctly, I believe I have passed the course. Good day, Sir!"

And the story says that the professor, admitting the sharp mind of the young man and the indubitable legality of his passing, gave him a high grade.

—A. NOBL

Example—Examples

572. We can do more good by being good than in any other way.
—ROWLAND HILL

573. Few things are harder to put up with than the annoyance of a good example.

Experience

574. Few men are worthy of experience, the majority let it corrupt them.
—JOSEPH JOUBERT

575. Experience is a good teacher but a queer soul. She gives the test first, then explains the lesson.

576. Experience is very valuable. It keeps a man who makes the same mistake twice from admitting it the third time.
—BROOK BENTON

577. In time and as one comes to benefit from experience, one learns that things will turn out neither as well as one hoped nor as badly as one feared.
—JEROME S. BRUNER

578. It may serve as a comfort to us in all our calamities and afflictions that he that loses anything and gets wisdom by it is a gainer by the loss.
—SIR ROGER L'ESTRANGE

579.

WISDOM

When I have ceased to break my wings
  Against the faultiness of things,
And learned that compromises wait
  Behind each hardly opened gate,
When I can look Life in the eyes
  Grown calm and very coldly wise,
Life will have given me the Truth,
  And taken in exchange—my youth.

—Sara Teasdale

580. William Knudsen, who left the presidency of General Motors to become a Washington official during World War II, once gave some advice to a Senator who was trying to get war contracts. The Senator said that his clients did not have any experience in making airplanes but that they had plenty of money.

"Well," said Knudsen, "I have noticed that when a man with money meets a man with experience, the man with the experience gets the money and the man with the money gets the experience."

Fact—Facts

581. Get your facts first, then you can distort them as much as you please.

—Mark Twain

582. It is not the fact that's so important, but our treatment of it. The same mouth smiles or frowns depending on how we form our lips.

Failure—Failures

583. Learn how to fail intelligently.

—Charles F. Kettering

584. A has-been is proof that nothing recedes like success.

585. If you have tried your hand at something and failed, the next best thing is to try your head.

586. There is no greater failure than the man who devotes his life to the achievement of success.

587. The whole philosophy of failure can be summed up in a question of three words, *"What's the use?"*

588. If you set out to climb a mountain, however high you climb, you have failed if you cannot reach the top.

—WILLIAM GOLDING

589. Success comes to those who become success conscious. Failure comes to those who indifferently allow themselves to become failure conscious.

—NAPOLEON HILL

590. Every great improvement—has come after repeated failures. Virtually nothing comes out right the first time. Failures, repeated failures, are finger posts on the road to achievement.

—CHARLES F. KETTERING

591. It is a common mistake to think of failure as the enemy of success. Failure is a teacher—a harsh one, but the best. Pull your failures to pieces looking for the reason. Put your failure to work for you.

—THOMAS J. WATSON, SR.

592. We learn wisdom from failure much more than from success. We often discover what *will* do, by finding out what will not do; and probably he who never made a mistake never made a discovery.

—SAMUEL SMILES

593. Every failure is a step to success; every detection of what is false directs us toward what is true; every trial exhausts some tempting form of error. Not only so, but scarcely any attempt is entirely a failure, scarcely any theory, the result of steady thought, is altogether false; no tempting form of error is without some latent charm derived from truth.

—WILLIAM WHEWELL

Fair play

594. There are many wise failures. Often the failures know more than the successful people do. The answer seems to lie in the fact that the failures are receivers only. Into their minds they have poured facts and ideas. Like a sponge, they have soaked up knowledge and hoarded it selfishly. Successful people, fundamentally, are givers. Their minds act as channels through which ideas pass along to others—not as static storehouses. They do not merely read what others have thought and done—they have thoughts and ideas of their own and carry them into action. They live creatively.

Fair play

595. It is often surprising to find what heights may be reached by remaining on the level.

Faith

596. Faith is a flame in the heart—a fire in the soul.

597. Strike from mankind the principle of faith, and men would have no more history than a flock of sheep.

—EDWARD BULWER-LYTTON

598. What I admire in Columbus is not his having discovered a world, but his having gone to search for it on the faith of an opinion.

—A. ROBERT TURGOT

599. It is possible and right for the heart to believe many things which the mind cannot prove. . . . Faith certifies to us many of the most precious things of life and all of the things of eternal life.

600. Pity the human being who is not able to connect faith within himself with the infinite. He who has no faith has ego—ego swollen to the nth degree. And that never has a happy ending. He who has faith has also humility. He has an inward reservoir of courage, hope, confidence, calmness, an assuring trust that all will come out well—even though to the world it may appear to come out most badly.

—B. C. FORBES

601. Faith is one of the most precious treasures a man can possibly possess. It is a pity that so few understand what the *Bible* teaches about it. Faith is often confused with presumption, optimism, determination, superstition and imagination. Actually it is simply believing. . . . Obviously, faith honors God, while doubting His Word must insult and displease Him.

602. American history is replete with examples of men of business who dreamed dreams and saw visions with the result that the economy of the nation was advanced. Faith is not listed in the index of many textbooks on economics, but one cannot read the lives of the great entrepreneurs without realizing that faith was one element they all had in common. They all had "evidence of things not seen."

—I. E. HOWARD

False modesty. See Modesty, False

Fame

603. Fame is the fragrance of heroic deeds.

—HENRY WADSWORTH LONGFELLOW

604. Some people seem to achieve fame without deserving it; some seem deserving, but never achieve their fame; some deserve and achieve it; and then there are all the rest of us.

—BURTON HILLIS

605. Never get a reputation for a small perfection if you are trying for fame or a loftier area. The world can only judge by generals, and it sees that those who pay considerable attention to minutiae seldom have their minds occupied with great things.

—EDWARD BULWER-LYTTON

606. Soon after returning to the U. S. after her triumph in the capitals of Europe, Hildegarde and a friend went to visit The Versailles, which is now called The Roundtable, where she subsequently was to score her first big supper club success in New York. Not immediately recognized,

Family

Hildegarde was informed that she would have to wait for a table. "Tell them who you are," her friend whispered. "If I have to tell them who I am," Hildegarde replied quietly, "then I'm not."

Family

607. Your family is grown up when your kids stop asking you where they came from and refuse to tell you where they're going.

608. The ties of family and of country were never intended to circumscribe the soul. Man is connected at birth with a few beings, that the spirit of humanity may be called forth by their tenderness; and, whenever domestic or national attachments become exclusive, engrossing, clannish, so as to shut out the general claims of the human race, the highest end of Providence is frustrated, and home, instead of being the nursery, becomes the grave of the heart.

—WILLIAM ELLERY CHANNING, D. D.

Family life

609. Look for your misanthrope among the middle members of a big family; contrary to what people say, an only child has inestimable advantages and is the one to be interested in people in later life. The others get disillusioned in the nursery.

610. Family life is the source of the greatest happiness. This happiness is the simplest and least costly kind, and it cannot be purchased with money. But it can be increased if we do two things: if we recognize and uphold the essential values of family life and if we get and keep control of the process of social change so as to make it give us what is needed to make family life perform its essential function.

—ROBERT J. HAVIGHURST

Fanaticism

611. Fanaticism is the daughter of ignorance, and the mother of infidelity.

—JOHN BELLENDEN

612. This is fanaticism; when, by thinking too much of the other world, a man becomes unfit to live in this.

—CHRISTIAN NEVELL BOVEE

Farewell—Farewells

613. It is never any good dwelling on goodbyes. It is not the being together that it prolongs, it is the parting.

—ELIZABETH ASQUITH BIBESCO

614. The French do not use the word "adieu" in exactly the same sense that the English do. "Adieu" means really *"A Dieu"* ("To God I commend you"). It is used in Fench only when one departs on a long journey, involving an undertaking that presents danger coupled with the possibility of not returning. To use it as a synonym of "Good-bye" is an English corruption of the sense of the word.

Farm—Farms—Farming

615. Agriculture is an industry, indeed the largest industry we have. Its total investment exceeds $206 billion. It employs 7.1 million people— more than the combined employment in the steel, automotive, transportation and public utilities industries.

616. And he gave it for his opinion, that whoever could make two ears of corn, or two blades of grass, to grow upon a spot of ground where only one grew before, would deserve better of mankind, and do more essential service to his country, than the whole race of politicians put together.

—JONATHAN SWIFT.

Fate

617. A prudent man will think more important what fate has conceded to him than what it has denied.

—BALTASAR GRACIÁN

618.
  All are architects of Fate,
   Working in these walls of Time;
  Some with massive deeds and great,
   Some with ornaments of rhyme.
  Nothing useless is, or low;
   Each thing in its place is best;
  And what seems but idle show
   Strengthens and supports the rest.
  For the structure that we raise,
   Time is with materials filled;
  Our todays and yesterdays
   Are the blocks with which we build.
      —HENRY WADSWORTH LONGFELLOW

Fatherhood

619. The most important thing that any father can do for his children is to love their mother.

620. *Father's Day*—When a man who is proud of his family finds his family is proud of him.

621. Fathers should take note with some degree of wonder that fathers are accorded ONE special day a year while PICKLES get a whole week.

622.   **A Father's Ten Commandments**
  The National Father's Day Committee, organized to direct nationwide observance of Father's Day as a tribute to the fathers of America, several years ago formulated the following "ten commandments" for fathers, aimed at pinpointing Dad's responsibilities in the rearing of his children and thereby his potent obligations to America and the building of the future:
  1. Your sense of brotherhood instills in your child respect for his fellowman.
  2. Your fairness teaches him good sportsmanship in work and play.
  3. Your example instills in him an appreciation of the family spirit—the true backbone of society.

4. Your companionship creates a basis for mutual under-standing. Makes a pal of him.

5. Your teaching imparts a burning desire to love, honor, and obey his country's laws.

6. Your encouragement helps him to apply himself to difficult tasks.

7. Your leadership in community affairs teaches the importance of local participation in government.

8. Your self-reliance helps develop an independent spirit. Encourages do-it-yourself activities.

9. Your foresight in preparing for future security develops repsonsibility in him.

10. Your guidance prepares him for the duties and responsibilities of citizenship in a free society.

Fault-finding

623.　Some people find fault as if it were a buried treasure.
—F. O'WALSH

624.　Before flaring up at another's faults, one should take time to count ten—ten of his own.

Fear—Fears

625.　Fear is the darkroom where negatives are developed.

626.　Fear is an instrument of defeat, but it is also the side arm of caution.

627.　To be feared of a thing and yet to do it, is what makes the prettiest kind of a man.
—ROBERT LOUIS STEVENSON

628.　The function of fear is to warn us of danger, not to make us afraid to face it.

629. Hide your fears with courage to make up for those who bury their courage with fears.

630. Fear is nothing but faith in reverse gear! The foundation on which both faith and fear rests is belief in something.

—NAPOLEON HILL

631. Throughout the history of the world men's fears have robbed them of victories courage could have won. One such occasion occurred several centuries ago when the Tartars invaded Russia. The two armies were locked in combat along the banks of the Oka River. The Tartar force was larger, but for several days the Russians had held them at bay by preventing them from crossing the river.

The Russians were confident they could hold the invader as long as the river waters stood between them. But this was the fall of the year with a Russian winter in the offing. When a cold blast came sweeping out of the Urals, the Russian soldiers saw ice beginning to form on the river waters. To them this meant disaster, for the Tartars with their superior numbers could quickly cross on the solid ice once the river froze. That night the Russians panicked and under cover of darkness fled toward Moscow.

When morning came the Tartar sentries discovered the Russian flight. With the ice hardening on the river they could soon cross and take after the enemy. But fear began to haunt the Tartars. Were the Russians up to some trick? Did they vanish during the night with a plan to appear somewhere else and destroy them? Within a few hours the Tartars, too, were in full retreat.

The two armies were fleeing from each other, but in another sense they both fled from fear. No one can say that had courage prevailed the Tartars would have won, but certainly when fear prevailed they lost.

—*Nuggets*

Flattery

632. Flatterers are the worst kind of enemies.

—TACITUS

633. Flattery is the first step on the road to slander.

—DAGOBERT D. RUNES

634.   Most folks who slap us on the back expect us to cough up something.

635.   Flatterers are the cleverest of all mind readers—they tell us exactly what we think.

636.   More people are flattered into virtue than bullied out of vice.
—Robert Surtees

Forgetfulness

637.   It seems to be much easier to forget a favor than to forgive a wrong.

638.   There is nothing, nothing innocent or good, that dies, and is forgotten-forgotten! Oh, if the good deeds of human creatures could be traced to their source, how beautiful would even death appear; for how much charity, mercy, and purified affection, would be seen to have their growth in dusty graves!
—Charles Dickens

Forgiveness

639.   If it is divine to forgive, it is manly to forget.
—Dagobert D. Runes

640.   Always forgive your enemies ... nothing annoys them so much.

641.   The truly great man is as apt to forgive as his power is able to revenge.
—Sir Philip Sidney

642.   Forgiveness does not leave the hatchet handle sticking out of the ground.

643. Forgiveness is a funny thing—it warms the heart and cools the sting.

—Dr. William Arthur Ward

644. Women are always ready to forgive and forget, but they never forget what they forgive.

645. We should forgive our enemies but not forget them—after all, they may not have forgiven us.

646. It is very easy to forgive others their mistakes; it takes more grit and gumption to forgive them for having witnessed your own.

—Jessamyn West

647. There is no better evidence of a large and generous nature than memory to forgive and forget every injury, imagined and otherwise and thereby be superior to the petty feelings of resentment, pride, and unforgiveness, which work mischief alike to the one who holds them and to the one who has done the injury.

—Rodman R. Clayson

648. Forgiveness does not have an analogy in bookkeeping. It is not a question of "balancing the books," and Jesus' answer to Peter about forgiving seventy-times-seven is a clear indication that forgiveness is not a legal transaction. When we try to reduce it to that level we miss the spiritual nature of it.

—Erroll T. Elliott

Freedom

649. Freedom requires discipline to save it from anarchy.

650. Freedom, our heritage from the past, should be our legacy to the future.

651. Freedom means that people should be able to express themselves freely but not outrageously.

652. The basic test of freedom is perhaps less in what we are free to do than in what we are free not to do.

—Eric Hoffer

653. If ever our American freedoms are lost, it will not be because the enemy was so strong, but because we, ourselves, were so lazy that we preferred to play at piety rather than to work at responsibility.

—Robert A. Cook

654. Freedom is an indivisible word. If we want to enjoy it, and fight for it, we must be prepared to extend it to everyone, whether they are rich or poor, whether they agree with us or not, no matter what their race or the color of their skin.

—Wendell Willkie

655. A climate of freedom is in itself conducive to greatness. Greatness is nurtured by the right to think and argue and reason, and to act as reason dictates. The free market place produces not only the best goods but also the best minds. Great minds reach for freedom just as plants seek the sun for growth and flowering.

—Dell Murphy

656. The winning of freedom is not to be compared to the winning of a game—with the victory recorded forever in history. Freedom has its life in the hearts, the actions, the spirit of men and so it must be daily earned and refreshed—else like a flower cut from its life-giving roots, it will wither and die.

—Dwight D. Eisenhower

657. The moment one makes a free choice, he limits his own freedom by that choice. . . . For instance, being a free moral agent, man is free to choose the path of goodness or of evil. When once he has made the choice, restrictions are immediately set up by that choice. If he chooses to follow the path of goodness, he is not free then to do evil.

658. In no society and at no time in the history of human civilization has freedom been successfully destroyed. Freedom, like the phoenix, rises from the flames of falling tyranny. The kings, emperors, dictators and "isms" all have their day; but freedom, though capable neither of creation nor destruction by the hand of man, was, is and shall always be a desire, basic to his character. And those who try to destroy freedom are bound to destroy themselves in the process.

—CHANG CHUN-HA

659. Freedom can never mean license because the world we live in just does not function that way. Individuals do not live isolated lives; they live with their fellowmen. If we are to live as civilized human beings, we must respect the rights and needs of others. No one is free to hurt someone else.

The hunger for freedom that lies in the hearts of all men will never work automatically. Individuals have to make it work and to do that means the recognition of responsibility and the exercise of restraint. Only when people are willing to live up to their responsibilities can they expect to live in freedom.

Freedom of speech. See Speech, Freedom of

Friendliness

660. The only really friendless people in the world are those who, rich in means, but poor in spirit, are too well off to need benefits, and too selfish to confer them.

—CHRISTIAN NEVELL BOVEE

661. When you are friendly you are automatically inviting, and unconsciously developing, potential business. . . . The odds are always with the friendly representative, all other things being equal; and in many instances friendliness can compensate when all other things are not precisely equal.

—HENRY W. HAYES

Friendship—Friendships

662. If you have her for a friend, you don't need any enemies.
—June Allyson

663. He alone has lost the art to live who cannot win new friends.
—S. Weir Mitchell

664. Friendship stands or falls on sincerity; a false friend is no friend.
—Arnold H. Glasow

665. Friendship is largely a matter of putting up with each other's peculiarities.

666. In the adversity of our best friends we often find something that does not displease us.
—François de La Rochefoucauld

667. Be on such terms with your friend as if you knew that he might one day become your enemy.
—Decimus Laberius

668. A true friend doesn't sympathize with your weakness; instead he helps summon your strength.

669. Let friendship creep gently to a height; if it rush to it, it may soon run itself out of breath.
—Thomas Fuller

670. The finest kind of freindship is between people who expect a great deal of each other but never ask it.
—Sylvia Bremer

671. Friendship is a living thing that lasts only as long as it is nourished with kindness and understanding.

672. The friendships which last are those wherein each friend respects the other's dignity to the point of not really wanting anything from him.

—CYRIL CONNELLY

673. Whatever the number of a man's friends, there will still be times in his life when he has one too few; but if he has only one enemy, he is lucky indeed if he has not one too many.

—EDWARD BULWER-LYTTON

674. Friendship is like an image in a mirror. The nearer we approach, the clearer and more perfect in outline is the image, and just in the proportion that we recede from it, does it become dim and finally fade.

—AUGUSTUS THOMAS

675. The comfort of having a friend may be taken away, but not that of having had one. . . . Let us therefore make the best of our friends while we have them; for how long we shall keep them is uncertain. . . . He that has lost a friend has more cause of joy that he once had him, than of grief that he is taken away.

—SENECA

676. Rivers are like lives. The more contributions they gain from friendships, the bigger they grow, Friendly, quiet little streams that join them in their long, troublesome journey to the sea, make them strong and mighty. The helpful contributions of love and kindness we gain from friends make our journey of life better and richer.

677.
    If you have a friend worth loving,
      Love him. Yes, and let him know
    That you love him, ere life's evening
      Tinge his brow with sunset glow;
    Why should good words ne'er be said
      Of a friend till he is dead?

—AUTHOR UNKNOWN

Frustration—Frustrations

678.   We have to have frustrations. You just have to learn how to live with them. Sometimes you win, and sometimes you lose; but don't allow yourself to be made a fool of by either success or failure. It's religion to be able to rise above both success and failure.

—ROBERT FROST

679.   The world is full of people who believe that their talents have been frutsrated by an unkind fate; they are convinced that they could write, paint, or perhaps excel in music if their lives were only differently ordered. But they lack the resolution to do that necessary reordering.

They are not liars, these people, but they are probably deceiving themselves. The talent that is not backed up with sufficient resolution to ensure its expression is only doubtfully existent.

—ALICE CURTAYNE

Fund-raising

680.   A clergyman, famous for begging abilities, was speaking to a group of Sunday school children. When comparing himself—the pastor of a church—to a shepherd, and his congregation to the sheep, he put the following question to the children: "What does the shepherd do for the sheep?"

To the amusement of those present, a little fellow in the front row answered, "Shears them!"

Future, The

681.   The future belongs to those who live intensely in the present.

682.   The future belongs to those who see and trust the best things in the worst times.

—REV. HAROLD BLAKE WALKER

683.   Everyone should take an interest in the future—that's where he will spend the rest of his life.

684. Everyone's future is, in reality, an urn full of unknown treasures from which all may draw unguessed prizes.

—LORD DUNSANY

685. The world is full of people whose notion of a satisfactory future is, in fact, a return to the idealized past.

—ROBERTSON DAVIES

Garden—Gardener—Gardening

686. When a woman wants her husband to make a garden, the first thing he'll usually dig up is a good excuse.

687. If he spades up a few worms for himself, he is a fisherman; if he spades up half the yard for his wife, she's a gardener.

688. *Soil Bank.* A real gardener does not cultivate flowers; he cultivates soil. He is a creature who digs himself into the earth and leaves the sight of what is *on* it to us gaping good-for-nothings. He lives buried in the ground and builds his monument in a heap of compost. If he came into the Garden of Eden he would sniff excitedly and say, "Good Lord, what humus!"

—KAREL CAPEK

689. It doesn't matter as to the size of your garden. It may be only a window-box in a single room, but, if growing from that soil is something of you—your patience, your interests, your love, and perhaps a touch of your faith in God, in the goodness of mankind, and a cheerful hopefulness— your heritage should be that of a healthy, happy human being.

—GEORGE M. ADAMS

Generosity

690. Generosity is giving what you could use yourself.

—MARIANNE MOORE

691.   He who allows his day to pass by without practicing generosity and enjoying life's pleasures is like a blacksmith's bellows—he breathes but does not live.

—Sanskrit proverb

Genius

692.   Genius may conceive, but patient labor must consummate.

—Horace Mann

693.   The test of genius is not originality; the test of genius is universality.

—Dr. Preston Bradley

694.   A genius is not a man who was made in some other image. He is just a man driven to constructive action by a great enthusiasm. Enthusiasm feeds on challenge.

—Dr. Wilder Penfield

695.   Not everyone has the gift of genius, but everyone can work at whatever task he has at hand. Not everyone can reach the heights of accomplishment achieved by those rare individuals who stand out so far above other men. But anyone who is willing to work patiently and intelligently can contribute enough to the world to earn a comfortable living and sometimes even renown. No one can be sure that he is a genius, but everyone knows whether he is using the brains and skills he has to the best of his ability—and that is the only thing that really counts.

Gift—Gifts

696.   Don't worry so much about what you give your wife for Christmas. If she likes you, she will like anything.

697.   In choosing presents people should remember that the whole point of a present is that it is an extra.

—E. V. Lucas

Giving

698.   Books make gifts of a very special kind. They don't break, they don't wilt, they don't age. They are like the cake in the fairy tale, which can be eaten but still doesn't diminish.

699.

It ain't the gift a feller gits;
    It ain't the shape ner size
That sets the heart to beatin;
    An' puts sunshine in yer eyes.
It ain't the value of the thing,
    Ner how it's wrapped ner tied;
It's something else aside from this
    That makes you glad inside.
It's knowin' that it represents
    A love both deep an' true
That someone carries in his heart
    An' wants to slip to you
It's knowin' that someone loves you
    An' tells you in this way—
Just sorta actin' out th' things
    They really long to say.
So, 'taint th' gift a feller gits,
    Ner how it's wrapped ner tied,
It's knowin' that there's folks like you
    That makes you glad inside.

—AUTHOR UNKNOWN

Giving

700.   One must be poor to know the luxury of giving.

GEORGE ELIOT

701.   Real charity doesn't care if it's deductible or not.

702.   It is better to give others a piece of our heart than a piece of our mind.

703.   It's not how much you give that counts; it's how much you have left!

—BISHOP FULTON J. SHEEN

704. You may give without loving—but you can't love without giving.

705. *Church Sign:* Since you can't take it with you why not leave it here?

706. That which is given with pride and ostentation is rather an ambition than a bounty.

—SENECA

707. It's a matter of giving more to this world than you take from it, so when you die, you don't owe it anything.

—GORDON PARKS

708. I can testify that it is nearly always easier to make $1,000,000 honestly than to dispose of it wisely.

—JULIUS ROSENWALD

709. Real and lasting generosity requires that an individual do more than make up his mind to give. He must also make up his heart.

—DR. WILLIAM ARTHUR WARD

710. "What! Giving again?" I ask in dismay,
"And must I keep giving and giving away?"
"Oh, no," said the angel looking me through,
"Just keep giving till the Master stops giving to you."

—from the Diary of a humble
English blacksmith

711. Give with a heart glowing with generous sentiments; give as the fountain gives out its waters from its own swelling depths; give as the air gives its vital breezes, unrestrained and free; give as the sun gives out its light, from the infinite abysses of its own nature.

712. To give alms is nothing unless you give thoughts also. It is written, not "blessed is he that feedeth the poor," but "blessed is he that considereth the poor." A little thought and a little kindness are often worth more than a great deal of money.

—JOHN RUSKIN

713.   The art and skill of conferring benefits is, of all human duties, the most absolutely necessary to the well-being. He that does good to another man does good also to himself; not only in the consequence, but in the very act of doing it; for the conscience of well-doing is an ample reward.

—SENECA

714.   Most of us know people in dire need to whom we would like to be good neighbors, but who are too proud to accept our help. William Thackeray had such a neighbor, an elderly widow who fell ill without the means for medical care. But he had a writer's imagination. He secured a pillbox from his druggist, filled it with gold coins and wrote on the box: "One to be taken when required." He wrapped it up and left it at her door.

—ROBERT W. YOUNGS

715.   Anyone who has to go out and try to collect money for a Community Fund or some other worthy cause might find this advice of Benjamin Franklin helpful. He said, "First, call upon those who you know will give something; next apply to those you are uncertain whether they will give or not; and finally to those you are sure will give nothing, for in some of these you may be mistaken."

716.

We are helped by helping others,
    If we give we also get;
Seeing others as our brothers
    Is life's safest, surest bet;
If we give what folks are needing
    It will pay us in the end;
And we just can't help succeeding
    In this game of life, my friend.

—ANON.

717.   The rich philanthropist is not always among the happiest men in the world. In fact the life of such a man is not necessarily one to be envied. He is besieged by the unworthy as well as the worthy. He is flattered, cajoled, and unmercifully exploited by his artful friends. Since no purse is deep enough to satisfy all demands, some appeals must be refused. Those who fail to share in his generosity resent his discrimination and dislike him more than if he gave to no one at all.

718.　The real joy of giving is reserved for the man of modest means. This man sees where his money goes when he lends a few dollars to a needy neighbor, sends an occasional check to a married daughter, or at Christmas presents clean, new currency to his aging parents. Even the occasional half-dollar he gives in response to a hard-luck story on the city street gives him a glow of satisfaction. Because his giving is emotional, he gets emotional satisfactions from it. The rich man would like to indulge his emotions, too, but he does not dare. One can afford to be sentimental with ten dollars, but not with ten million.

719.　The story is told of the mother of Marshall Field who gave to the University of Chicago the handsome sum of one million dollars. When the Board of Directors of Northwestern University, also located in the city of Chicago, heard of this gift, they commissioned one of their members to make a query concerning why a smiliar gift was not made to the latter school. A tactful approach was made to a member of Mrs. Field's family and when the Board of Directors of Northwestern University was told why they were not recipients of such a gift, they heard the important words, "Northwestern didn't ask me."

—HAL L. NUTT

720.　A witty person once said: "There are three kinds of givers in the world—the flint, the sponge, and the honeycomb."

To get anything out of a flint, you must hammer it, and then you get only flint and sparks.

To get anything out of a sponge, you must squeeze, and the more you squeeze the sponge, the more you will get.

But the honeycomb overflows with its own sweetness.

Some people are stingy and hard; they give nothing away if they can help it.

Others are good-natured; they yield to pressure, and the more they are pressed, the more readily and abundantly they give.

A few delight in giving without being asked at all, and of these, the Bible says: "The Lord loveth a cheerful giver."

Goal—Goals

721.   The course of a river is almost always disapproved of by its source.

—JEAN COCTEAU

722.   If you have no idea where you want to go, it makes little difference how fast you travel.

723.   If a man does not know what port he is steering for, no wind is favorable to him.

724.   Many are stubborn in pursuit of the path they have chosen, few in pursuit of the goal.

—FRIEDRICH WILHELM NIETZSCHE

725.   Most of us serve our ideals by fits and starts. The person who makes a success of living is the one who sees his goal steadily and aims for it unswervingly.

—CECIL B. DE MILLE

God—Man

726.   The best way to know God is to love many things.

—VINCENT VAN GOGH

727.   Most men forget God all day, and ask Him to remember them at night.

728.   The person who often looks up to God rarely looks down on any man.

—DR. WILLIAM ARTHUR WARD

729.   The true tragedy of the world is that God calls and men refuse to answer.

730.   If, like Jacob, you trust God in little things, He may answer you by great things.

—J. R. MacDuff

731.   Man is a peculiar, puzzling paradox, groping for God and hoping to hide from Him at the selfsame time.

—Dr. William Arthur Ward

732.   Never should we so abandon ourselves to God as when He seems to abandon us. Let us enjoy light and consolation when it is His pleasure to give them to us; but let us not attach ourselves to His gifts, but to Him; and when He plunges us into the night of pure faith, let us still press on through the agonizing darkness.

733.   As the flowers follow the sun, and silently hold up their petals to be tinted and enlarged by its shining, so must we, if we would know the joy of God, hold our souls, wills, hearts, and minds, still before Him, whose voice commands, whose love warns, whose truth makes fair our whole being. God speaks for the most part in such silence only. If the soul be full of tumult and jangling voices, His voice is little likely to be heard.

—Alexander Maclaren

Golden Rule, The

734.   Do not do unto others as you would that they should do unto you. Their tastes may not be the same.

—George Bernard Shaw

735.   I learned over an over again that there is scarcely anything more difficult than to love one another.

—Ranier Maria Rilke

Golf

736.   Forget your opponents; always play against par.

—Sam Snead, Golf champion

737.   A golf ball should be hit every time—but not too often.

738.   A policy of absolute honesty can be the making of a man's character and the ruination of his golf game.

739.   In Africa some of the native tribes have the custom of beating the ground with clubs and uttering spine-chilling cries. Anothropologists call this a form of primitive self-expression. Here in America we call it golf.

740.   Father O'Malley met one of his parishioners on the street one day and after exchanging greetings the lady asked him, "Father, is it a sin for my husband to play golf on Sunday?"

With a twinkle in his eye, Father O'Malley answered without hesitation, "The kind of golf he plays is a sin any day he plays it."

—LEO J. SHEEHAN

741.   To the average masochist, golf is not only a game that humbles but one that frustrates, tortures and ruins. Unlike team sports—such as baseball, football and basketball—in which mistakes can be covered up through the interplay of teammates, golf exposes the individual for what he is: a failure, a dedicated failure. Unlike tennis, in which the individual has hundreds of strokes in which to bargain with perfection, golf allows no margin for error. A man gets around eighteen holes in the absolute minimum of strokes or he loses to a man who can. Unlike almost all other sports, in which a man can take savage pleasure in facing an opponent, golf demands that he somehow defeat his own most human failings.

—WILLIAM BARRY FURLONG

742.   Golf is the simplest looking game in the world when you decide to take it up and the toughest after you have been at it ten or twelve years. It is probably the only known game a man can play as long as a quarter of a century and then discover that it was too deep for him in the first place.

Golf is a physical and mental exertion made attractive by the fact that you have to dress for it in a $200,000 club house. It is what letter-carrying, ditch-digging and carpet-beating would be if those three tasks had to be performed on the same afternoon in colored socks, jersey and pants by gouty-looking gentlemen who require a different implement for every mood.

The game is played on carefully selected grass with little white balls and as many clubs as a player can afford. These little balls cost from fifty cents up and it is possible to support a family of ten people (all adults) for five months on the money represented by balls lost by players in a single afternoon.

A golf course is eighteen holes, seventeen of which are unnecessary and just put around the course to make the game harder. A "hole" is a tin cup in the center of a "green." A green is a small patch of grass costing $1.98 per blade and is usually located between a lake and a couple of fruit trees, or a lot of unfinished excavations called sand traps. The idea is to get the ball from a given point into each of the eighteen holes in the fewest number of strokes and with the greatest number of words. A favorite expression among players is, "I think you are in a trap, I hope."

The ball must not be thrown, pushed or carried. It must be propelled by a lot of curious devices designed especially to provoke the player. Each device has a specific purpose and in time the players get to know which to use. However, those who do are the exception.

After each hole has been played the golfer counts his "strokes." Then he subtracts six and says: "Made that one in five. That's one over par. Shall we play for fifty cents on the next hole, too?" After the final or eighteenth hole, the player adds up his score and stops when he reaches eighty-seven. Then he takes a swim, sings "Sweet Adeline" with a group of other liars and calls it the end of a perfect day.

—Author unknown

Goodness

743.   Goodness consists not in the outward things we do, but in the inward thing we are. To be good is the great thing.

—Edwin Chapin

744.   A good man doubles the length of his existence; to have lived so as to look back with pleasure on our past existence is to live twice.

—Martial

745.   A good deed is never lost; he who sows courtesy reaps friendship, and he who plants kindness gathers love; pleasure bestowed upon a grateful mind was never sterile, but generally gratitude begets reward.

746. An act of goodness is of itself an act of happiness. No reward coming after the event can compare with the sweet reward that went with it.

—Maurice Maeterlinck

747. The work an unknown good man has done is like a vein of water flowing hidden underground, secretly making the ground green.

—Thomas Carlyle

Gossip

748. A report may be true, yet should not be repeated if it helps nobody and hurts somebody.

749. There would not be so many open mouths if there were not so many open ears.

—Bishop Hall

750. Gossip: a woman who can quickly change an earful into a mouthful.

751. The nicest thing about an egotist: he never goes around talking about other people.

752. The difference between gossip and news depends on whether you hear it or tell it.

753. When a woman wants to let another woman know what she thinks of her she confides in a mutual friend.

754. Live your life so that you won't be afraid to be the first woman to leave a women's bridge party.

755. With men, it isn't gossip—it's just repeating rumors they heard but don't believe.

756.   Gossips have been catalogued in three different types:
1: Vest-button type—always popping off.
2: Vacuum-cleaner type—always pick up dirt.
3: Liniment type—always rubbing it in.

Government—Governments

757.   Whatever the faults of our government—we primarily are to blame because our government is ourselves.

—EUGENE P. BERTIN

758.   Experience teaches us to be most on our guard to protect liberty when the government's purposes are beneficent.

—JUSTICE LOUIS D. BRANDEIS

759.   A constantly swelling government is a sure sign of the moral sickness of the people under it. Governments swell when and because the people shrink.

—CLARENCE MANION

760.   No matter how sincerely and hard the government tries it can't solve all human problems. Most of these problems must be solved by individual thinking and hard work.

761.   Government is only a necessary evil, like other go-carts and crutches. Our need of it shows exactly how far we are still children. All governing overmuch kills the self-help and energy of the governed.

—WENDELL PHILLIPS

762.   The tendency of government is to grow in power. Old governments do not simply wither away, but invariably and inevitably die by violence at the hand of superior forces that may be either externally or internally initiated; a government is dead when it can no longer defend itself.

—PAUL L. POIROT

763. The legitimate object of government is to do for a community of people whatever they need to have done, but cannot do at all, or cannot do so well themselves, in their separate and individual capacities. In all that the people can individually do as well for themselves, government ought not to interfere.

—ABRAHAM LINCOLN

764. Government exists to defend the weak and the poor and the injured party; the rich and the strong can better take care of themselves. . . . We want a state of things in which crime will not pay; a state of things which allows every man the largest liberty compatible with the liberty of every other man.

—RALPH WALDO EMERSON

765. Let a man's sphere of governing be ever so limited, he learns to appreciate some of the difficulties of government in general. He finds how hard a thing it is to make men of one mind, and to get real business of any kind carried forward, where there is great freedom of discussion and of action. Also he becomes cognizant of some of those matters concerned with government, which only experience can teach.

—SIR ARTHUR HELPS

766. Good government starts with you as much as with anyone. Bad politicians are elected by good people who don't vote. The punishment of wise men who refuse to take part in government is to live under government of unwise men. Government depends upon men rather than men depending on government. Either you run government, or government runs you.

—EUGENE P. BERTIN

767. To be governed is to be watched over, inspected, spied on, directed, legislated at, regulated, docketed, indoctrinated, preached at, controlled, assessed, weighed, censored, ordered about. . . . To be governed means to be, at each operation, at each transaction, at each movement, noted, registered, controlled, taxed, stamped, measured, valued, assessed, patented, licensed, authorized, endorsed, admonished, hampered, reformed, rebuked, arrested.

—PIERRE JOSEPH PROUDHON

Grandparent-Grandchild

768.   The nice thing about grandchildren is that you aren't too busy supporting them to have time to enjoy them.

769.   We cannot educate our grandmother, we say; but there are grandmothers whom we can educate. The children of today are the grand-mothers of the future; we can educate them.

—ALICE WELLINGTON ROLLINS

770. **What is a Grandmother?**

A grandmother is a combination of work-worn hands, after a lifetime of toil, a loving heart, and endless stories of the days when her family was young.

Grandmothers wear old age with dignity and composure. You don't notice what grandmothers wear, you only see the love and tenderness in her face as she fondles her youngest grandchild.

Grandmothers have spent a whole lifetime, cooking meals that statisticians would be unable to record, keeping house, helping neighbors, drying the tears of the past generation as well as the present, and pray that they may be allowed to go on doing it for a few more years.

Grandmothers have run the whole gamut of human emotions, joy, defeat, success, failure, heartache, sorrow and perhaps tragedy, and have come through with the wisdom and tranquility endowed to those whose tears have been replaced by the calm acceptance and quiet outlook given only to those who have weathered life's battles.

The nicest possible place to hear a story is in grandmother's lap. Giants and ogres hold no terrors when held in the warmth and love of a grandmother with one's head pillowed on her breast.

Grandmothers can always be counted on to produce sweets, cookies and candies that seem to taste nicer from her than from anyone else.

Grandmothers just don't believe that their grandchildren have any faults, and can be relied upon to champion the underdog, lost causes, and when a chap is in trouble for not washing behind the ears, she will console him by telling him that his Dad was almost *nine* before he overcame that problem.

Grandmothers can soothe an unruly weeping young boy or girl just by rocking them on her lap and crooning in a soft voice that manages to sound just right in spite of being old.

Grandmothers give the impression of being all wisdom and

love whether it is in giving help or advice to a neighbor or making a hurt finger better with a kiss.

God has a special place for them in heaven and when grandmother does eventually go there she will be smiling down, and on her lap will be one of God's littlest angels—the one that reminds her of YOU.

—Elizabeth Faye

Gratitude

771. Be grateful for what you have, not regretful for what you haven't.

772. He enjoys much who is thankful for little. A grateful mind is a great mind.

—T. Secker

773. The gratitude of most men is but a secret desire of receiving greater benefits.

—François de La Rochefoucauld

774. There is nothing grateful but the earth; it will continue to repay tenfold the pains and labor bestowed upon it.

—Lord Ravensworth

775. Our thanks should be as fervent for mercies received, as our petitions for mercies sought.

—Charles Simmons

776. Express gratitude generously and sincerely; receive gratitude humbly and graciously; expect gratitude rarely if ever.

—Dr. William Arthur Ward

777. Gratitude is a feeling we have for what we enjoy or possess. The more we experience it, the more good we attract to us. We cannot be grateful and at the same time disturbed by some imperfection; nor can we claim poverty while we express appreciation for our abundance. When we are giving attention to what is right, we are not anxious over what is wrong. This is good, for we invite whatever we center our attention upon. And so it is that much is gained by praise, which brings forth increase.

Greatness

778. The reward of great men is that, long after they have died, one is not quite sure that they are dead.

—JULES RENARD

779. None think the great unhappy but the great.

—EDWARD YOUNG

780. Great hopes make great men.

—THOMAS FULLER

781. One out of ten men are born to labor for the tenth. Resolve to be the tenth.

—WALTER BESANT

782. That man is great who can use the brains of others to carry on his work.

—DON PIATT

783. Great men are those who find that what they ought to do and want to do are the same thing.

784. There are no great men; only great challenges that ordinary men are forced by circumstances to meet.

785. No matter how great a man is, the size of his funeral usually depends on the weather.

786. Greatness of soul is shown as well by what is attempted, as by what is achieved.

—CHRISTIAN NEVELL BOVEE

787. If any man seeks for greatness, let him forget greatness and ask for truth, and he will find both.

—HORACE MANN

788. One should never feel any discomfiture at being called great as long as he is not called upon to prove it.

—CHARLES G. DAWES

789. Greatness is not found in possessions, power, position or prestige. It is discovered in goodness, humility, service and character.

—DR. WILLIAM ARTHUR WARD

790. Every man has the germ of greatness in his soul. If he does not wear a great man's crown, he still can possess the same high ideals. A humble streetcleaner may have more noble qualities than a king.

—BALTASAR GRACIÁN

791. The tests of life form the background for true greatness. They will help us or be against us, as we allow them. Trouble, they say, may demolish a man's business but it can build up his character. A blow to the outward man is very often the greatest blessing to the inner man.

792. He is great who feeds the minds of others. He is great who inspires others to think for themselves. He is great who pulls you out of your mental ruts, lifts you out of the mire of the commonplace, whom you alternately love and hate, but whom you cannot forget.

793. The broad-minded give due credit to others and do not mind sharing with them the honor of achievement. . . .The big-hearted act nobly out of compassion, the big-minded out of understanding. To hold out a hand to the vanquished without gloating shows both kindliness and statesmanship.

—BALTASAR GRACIÁN

794. Beverley Baxter, M. P., once said of Churchill: "If this astonishing man had been born in Spain, he would have been a bullfighter. If he had lived in France, he would have either declared a new republic or restored the monarchy. If he had been in the United States he would have been President. . . . I have never in my life seen such a man, such competence, such genius.

Habit—Habits

795.   Habit, unlike instinct, must be acquired by practice. We are not born with habits as animals and birds are born with instincts. We are given the opportunity of choosing what habits we will form, good or bad.

Handwriting

796.   If you can read the handwriting on the wall, it was not written by the average adult.

797.   Bad handwriting has sometimes been considered a sign of cleverness, even of intellectual genius. Many great men have, in fact, been atrocious writers. Shakespeare would not pass a simple clerk's examination for readable handwriting today; nor would Napoleon, one of whose intimate letters to the Empress Josephine, when captured by his enemies, led the German generals to believe they had seized his rough plan of campaign!
—David Gunston

Happiness

798.   No one can be said to be happy until he is dead.
—Solon

799.   He who has no wish to be happier is the happiest of men.
—W. R. Alger

800.   Happiness adds and multiplies as we divide it with others.

801.   Happiness makes up in height for what it lacks in length.
—Robert Frost

802. All the Constitution guarantees is the pursuit of happiness; you have to catch up with it yourself.

803. Happiness held is the seed; happiness shared is the flower.

804. To be truly happy is a question of how we begin, and not how we end, of what we want and not what we have.

—ROBERT LOUIS STEVENSON

805. If there is a dearth of happiness in this world, it is because more people are trying to share it than produce it.

806. Happiness is the only good. The place to be happy is here. The time to be happy is now. The way to be happy is to help make others so.

—ROBERT G. INGERSOLL

807. Happiness is a butterfly, which, when pursued, is always just beyond your grasp, but which, if you sit down quietly, may alight upon you.

—NATHANIEL HAWTHORNE

808. If we want our share of happiness, we must accept our share of misery; and we suffer more than our share of misery only when we try to claim more than our share of happiness.

809. The art of living does not consist in preserving and clinging to a particular mood of happiness, but in allowing happiness to change in form without being disappointed by the change. For happiness, like a child, must be allowed to grow up.

810. If there were in the world today any large number of people who desired their own happiness more than they desired the unhappiness of others, we could have a paradise in a few years.

—BERTRAND RUSSELL

811.   Happiness may be described as a state of contentment, which is a result of doing that which we consider right, and becoming what the heart most desires. It consists of appreciation for opportunities, surroundings, family, and friends.

812.   Those who do not take an interest in the bigger things hurt themselves as well as everybody else.

No one, I am convinced, can be happy who lives only for himself. The joy of living comes from immersion in something that we know to be bigger, better, more enduring, and worthier than we are. The pitiful people are those who in their living elect to be spectators rather than participants; the tragic ones are those sightseers who turn their backs deliberately on the procession.

The only true happiness comes from squandering ourselves for a purpose.

—JOHN MASON BROWN

Haste

813.   Speed is good when wisdom clears the way.

—EDWARD R. MURROW

814.   Whoever is in a hurry, shows that the thing he is about is too big for him.

—LORD CHESTERFIELD

Hatred

815.   I hate nobody; I am in charity with the world.

—JONATHAN SWIFT

816.   Hatred is the vice of narrow souls; they feed it with all their littleness, and make it the pretext of base tyrannies.

—HONORÉ DE BALZAC

817.   Hate I consider is an internal sin. And hate is closely associated with fear. I think fear breeds defeatism, and that is a disease that we cannot afford in this country if we're going to maintain our position in the family of freedom-loving people.

—GENERAL DAVID M. SHOUP

Hell

818.   Hell is truth seen too late.

—ALEXANDER ADAM

819.   While the wish of many individuals is to arrive at heaven, we daily behold them on the way to hell.

—WILLIAM SCOTT DOWNEY

820.   Hell is simply the displeasure of God mingled with your condemnation of yourself. Brimstone fires are nothing in comparison with the flames of remorse and self-reproach.

—GEORGE H. HEPWORTH

821.   Good men have their hell in this world, that they may know there is a heaven after death to reward the virtuous; and wicked men escape torments in this world, because they shall find there is a judgment to come, wherein the wicked shall have punishment according to the number of their offenses.

—LUCIUS LACTANTIUS

Helpfulness

822.   To live is not to live for one's self alone; let us help one another.

—MENANDER

823.   A man also succeeds when he helps another reach the heights which he could not attain himself.

824.   God has not made it possible for each of us to be a great painter or leader or businessman or great anything. But God has given each of us the opportunity to live successfully. We all can develop humility and tolerance. And what life ever was described as a failure that has been spent in doing for others?

—MILTON CANIFF

825.   A distinguished executive addressed a class of seniors. "Before I leave," he said, "I'm anxious to know what your objectives in life are. You in the front row," he said, pointing his finger, "what's yours?"

The young man jumped up. "I'm not sure, specifically," he said, "but I'm going to try to get somewhere."

How many others feel that way?" the executive asked.

There was only one dissenting voice—a young girl's.

"What is your objective?" and the executive smiled at the dissenter.

"Well," the girl said timidly, "I guess I'm more interested in helping someone than I am just in getting somewhere."

"Young lady," the executive said, "you can't live according to that philosophy without getting somewhere."

—LOWELL W. RAYMOND

Hero-Heroism

826.   The occasion doesn't make the hero; it only discovers him.

827.   A writer once interviewed a man who had performed an outstanding act of physical courage in saving the lives of several children. The writer asked him if he actually realized the danger he was in, and, if he did, how did he put down the fear that he surely must have felt.

The hero thought for a moment and then explained, "No, I don't think it occurred to me that I was in any danger. I only realized that the *children* were in danger, and something had to be done about it right now. But after they were safe, I must admit that I suddenly felt very weak in the knees. I am afraid that I am just not a brave man at heart."

Hesitancy

828.   He who hesitates is sometimes saved.

—JAMES THURBER

Hindsight

829. He who sees a need and waits to be asked for help is as unkind as if he had refused it.

—ALIGHIERI DANTE

Hindsight

830. Everybody had 20/20 hindsight.

History

831. History makes haste to record great deeds, but often neglects good ones.

—HOSEA BALLOU

832. History is in constant flux, filled with false starts, dead ends, ambiguities, contradictions, but also with progression from one stage to another in time.

—DR. LELAND HINE

833. In our history books lives the soul of the past, the achievements and makers of the past, who, when understood, can provide guidance for the future. Looking backward and evaluating what has happened is an important part of looking forward and planning for the future.

—HAROLD H. EIBLING

834. History is not merely "the doubtful story of successive events;" the facts of history are the facts of life. The distant past was once the pulsating, living present and the inscrutable, or even at times frightening future. There is no basis for our society or church, save its past. History is the source of our very identity. It tells us about the "success or failure of men and societies in the great, turbulent, confused experiment of living," about how we arrived at today's pleasures and sorrows—the efforts, struggles, and sufferings that wrung our civilization, culture, or church out of the fabric of the past.

—B. B. BEACH

Holiness

835.   The essence of true holiness consists in conformity to the nature and will of God.

—RICHARD LUCAS, D.D.

836.   Holiness is in religion what taste is in the philosophy of mind; it is a state of the soul, and not an emotion of the heart; it is not a distinct and specific virtue itself, but it makes everything which it affects and touches, virtuous; it is not itself an independent grace, but it gives the hue, and throws the odor of graciousness on everything accomplished by the soul.

—JOHN PARKHURST

Home—Homes

837.   A house is made of walls and beams; a home is built with love and dreams.

—DR. WILLIAM ARTHUR WARD

838.   What the world needs most today is happy homes. Not rich homes. Not frustrated homes. Not empty homes.

—ELSIE LANDON BUCK

839.   The Church can preach, the schools can teach, but the home must convert sermons and lessons into a way of life.

—ISADORE GARSEK

840.   Even animals love their home. A zoo keeper once said that the best way to recapture an escaped animal is simply to leave its cage door open and wait for it to return.

841.   Home and heaven are not so far separated as we sometimes think. Nay, they are not separated at all, for they are both in the same great building. Home is the lower story, and is located down here on the ground floor; heaven is above stairs, in the second and third stories; and, as one after another the family is called to come up higher, that which seemed

135

to be such a strange place begins to wear a familiar aspect; and, when at last not one is left below, the home is transferred to heaven, and heaven is home.

—ALEXANDER DICKSON

842. A home which is merely soporific is no better than a hospital. For home is a place to work and to play as well as to rest, a place for activity —but activity minus agitation. The most peaceful household in town may well be the busiest and the liveliest, simply because the energies and enthusiasms of its members are uninhibited by frustrations, distractions and discord. A household that is truly tranquil takes goings and comings, noise and quiet, youngsters and oldsters, guests and the lack of them, all in competent stride. There are rarely any crises because the household is geared to cope with the emergencies that spark crises before they have time to blow up.

Honesty

843. As a man can never be truly honest unless he be religious, so on the other hand, whatever show of religion a man may make, he cannot be truly religious in God's judgment unless he is honest in his conversation toward his neighbor.

—RICHARD MANT, D.D.

844. Honesty is the cornerstone of character. The honest man or woman seeks not merely to avoid criminal or illegal acts, but to be scrupulously fair, upright, fearless in both action and expression. Honesty pays dividends both in dollars and in peace of mind.

B. C. FORBES

Hope

845. Everything that is done in the world is done by hope.

—MARTIN LUTHER

846. Hope is itself a species of happiness, and perhaps the chief happiness which this world affords.

—DR. SAMUEL JOHNSON

847. Hope is the belief that something we desire will happen . . . Hope is the belief that the good news we desire will come about. But hope is likely to be a delusion if we merely wait for desire to be fulfilled. If we would turn hope into confident expectation, we must help make good news happen.

—Margaret Jenkins

Hopelessness

848. He only is hopeless who has ceased to hope.

—Dr. William Arthur Ward

849. When you say a situation or a person is hopeless, you are slamming the door in the face of God.

Host-Guest—Hosts-Guests

850. A host and hostess are judged by the company that leaves.

851. Some guests can't arrive too early and others can't come too late.

852. It is not the quantity of the meat, but the cheerfulness of the guests, which makes the feast.

—Edward Clarendon

853. Give no more to every guest
Than he's able to digest.
Give him always of the prime
And give him little at a time.
Give to all, but just enough,
Let them neither starve nor stuff.
And that each may have his due,
Let your neighbor carve for you.

—Sir Walter Scott

Human relations

854. No small part of the cruelty, oppression, miscalculation, and general mismanagement of human relations is due to the fact that in our dealings with others we do not see them as persons at all, but only as specimens or representatives of some type or other. . . . We react to the sample instead of to the real person.

—ROBERT J. MACIVER

Humility

855. Sense shines with a double luster when it is set in humility. An able and yet humble man is a jewel worth a kingdom.

—WILLIAM PENN

856. The greatest ornament of an illustrious life is modesty and humility, which go a great way in the character even of the most exalted princes.

—NAPOLEON BONAPARTE

Humor

857. Humor is emotional chaos remembered in tranquility.

—JAMES THURBER

858. If Adam came on earth again the only thing he would recognize would be the old jokes.

—LORD THOMAS ROBERT DEWAR

859. Repetition is a mighty power in the domain of humor. If frequently used, nearly any precisely worded and unchanging formula will eventually compel laughter if it be gravely and earnestly repeated, at intervals, five or six times.

—MARK TWAIN

Humor, Sense of

860.   A man without mirth is like a wagon without springs. He is jolted disagreeably by every pebble in the road.

—Henry Ward Beecher

861.   A keen sense of humor helps us overlook the unbecoming, understand the unconventional, tolerate the unpleasant, overcome the unexpected, and outlast the unbearable.

—Dr. William A. Ward

Husband—Wife

862.   A good husband is a gentleman to his wife.

863.   A man is boss in his home when he doesn't hesitate to wipe his hands on a guest towel.

864.   The best time for a man to assert his authority and let his wife know who's boss is the first time he gets up the courage.

Hypocrisy

865.   Better the world should know you as a sinner, than God know you as a hypocrite.

—Danish proverb

866.   The natural man has a difficult time getting along in this world. Half the people think he is a scoundrel because he is not a hypocrite.

—E. W. Howe

Idea—Ideas

867.   If you can't think up a new idea, try finding a way to make better use of an old idea.

868.   When we change our ideas we change our friends, because our friends are only the embodiment of our ideas.

—GEORGE MOORE

869.   Just how good a red-hot idea is usually depends on how much heat it retains when somebody throws cold water on it.

870.   Giving birth to an idea isn't enough; you have to nurse it, develop it, and test it before you can put it to work.

871.   A new idea is delicate. It can be killed by a sneer or a yawn; it can be stabbed to death by a quip and worried to death by a frown on the right man's brow.

—CHARLES BROWER

872.   There was a time when people thought the ability to create ideas was like the ability to wiggle your ears. Either you were born with it or you weren't. We know better now. Experiment after experiment indicates that everyone has the ability to originate ideas. But the same experiments underscore the fact that most of us don't utilize this ability to the fullest possible degree.

873.   What's greater than an idea? An idea is new—newer than a new car ... An idea is a reflection of an individual's personality. It displays thinking, background, a point of view. It points to the future. Ideas rarely come from committees. An idea can be a split-second inspiration or it can evolve from lengthy consideration. It can be good or it can be bad. Ideas can be big or little. My big idea may be insignificant to you. Yours may be the same to me. Our world is shaped of ideas. And ideas continue to alter this world. Because of yesterday's ideas we live better today. And the ideas we conceive today will be the realities of tomorrow.

Ideal—Ideals

874.   Ideals may be beyond our reach, but never beyond our hopes.

875.　Always keep your ideals high enough that you have to keep stretching to reach them.

876.　Life is a race between our conduct and our ideals and our conduct never quite catches up.

877.　It is well to keep one's ideals high, but not so high that they can't be reached once in a while.

Idleness

878.　Idleness is leisure gone to seed.

—ELI J. SCHLEIFER

879.　To do great work a man must be very idle as well as very industrious.

—SAMUEL BUTLER

880.　When an idler sees a completed job, he is sure he could have done it better.

881.　Time is the only thing that can never be retrieved. One may lose and regain a friend; one may lose and regain money; opportunity that is once spurned may come again; but the hours that are lost in idleness can never be brought back to be used in gainful pursuits.

Illusion—Illusions

882.　Illusions are created to soften the sharp edge of reality.

883.　Don't part with your illusions. When they are gone you may still exist, but you have ceased to live.

—MARK TWAIN

Imagination

884. Reporting facts is the refuge of those who have no imagination.
—Luc de Clapiers Vauvenargues

885. Imagination can be creative or destructive, depending upon whether you control it or let it run wild.

886. Imagination is more important than knowledge, for knowledge is limited whereas imagination embraces the entire world.

887. Imagination is the beginning of creation. You imagine what you desire; you will what you imagine; and at last you create what you will.
—George Bernard Shaw

888. The first of our senses which we should take care never to let rust through disuse is that sixth sense, the imagination. I mean the wide open eye which leads us always to see truth more vividly, to apprehend more broadly, to concern ourselves more deeply, to be, all our life long, sensitive and awake to the powers and responsibilities given to us as human beings.
—Christopher Fry

Imitation—Imitations

889. A good imitation is the most perfect originality.
—Voltaire

890. A successful imitation is never anything more.

891. Don't be a carbon copy of someone else—make your own impression.

892. Wine produced in California under the name of champagne bears a label which says: *Beware of French imitations.*

893. One of the most tragic mistakes man makes is to strive to be what some other person is. To emulate another man's virtues is wisdom. To try to fit ourselves into his shoes, however, is folly.

—Alvin H. Goeser

Immortality

894. We do not believe in immortality because we have proved it, but we forever try to prove it because we believe it.

—James Martineau

895. To believe in immortality is one thing, but it is first needful to believe in life. Denunciatory preachers seem not to suspect that they may be taken gravely and in evil part; that young men may come to think of Time as of a moment, and with the pride of Satan wave back the inadequate gift. Yet here is a true peril; this it is that sets them to pace the graveyard alleys and to read, with strange extremes of pity and derision, the memorials of the dead.

—Robert Louis Stevenson

Impossible, The

896. Nothing is impossible to the man who doesn't have to do it himself.

897. When somebody says something can't be done, it only means he can't do it.

898. Nothing is impossible to the man who can will, and then do; this is the only law of success.

—Honore Mirabeau

899. Because your own strength is unequal to the task, do not assume that it is beyond the powers of man; but if anything is within the powers and province of man, believe that it is within your own compass also.

—Marcus Aurelius

Inaction

900. It is the greatest of all mistakes to do nothing because you can only do little.

—SYDNEY SMITH

901. If you insist on standing still, stand aside; others may be going somewhere.

Income tax

902. When submitting a Federal income tax return, a good rule to follow is that it is better to give than deceive.

Indecision

903. Habit is the enormous flywheel of society, its most precious conservation agent. There is no more miserable human being than one in whom nothing is habitual but indecision. Full half of the time of such a man goes to the deciding, or the regretting, of matters which ought to be so ingrained in him as practically not to exist for his consciousness at all.

—WILLIAM JAMES

Indispensability

904. Make yourself necessary to somebody.

—RALPH WALDO EMERSON

905. History is the cemetery of men who were sure they were indispensable.

906. Make yourself indispensable and you will move up. Act as though you are indispensable and you will move out.

Individualism

907. A society in which each is willing to surrender only that for which he can see a personal equivalent is not a society at all; it is a group already in process of dissolution, and no one need concern himself to stay its inevitable end; it would be a hard choice between it and a totalitarian society. No Utopia, nothing but Bedlam, will automatically emerge from a regime of unbridled individualism, be it ever so rugged.

—LEARNED HAND

Indolence

908. By nature's laws, immutable and just, enjoyment stops where indolence begins.

—ROBERT POLLOK

909. In making life too easy for someone we love, we may do them more harm than good. Struggle seems to be a part of nature's plan. We do not strengthen our muscles by sitting around and letting them grow flabby. Nor do we sharpen our mind by idle daydreaming. The Scriptural admonition that man must earn his bread by the sweat of his brow is less a punishment than an opportunity. It is through use that we develop our physical and mental powers to their fullest flower.

Industry—Industriousness

910. In the ordinary business of life industry can do anything which genius can do, and very many things which it cannot.

—HENRY WARD BEECHER

911. If you have great talents, industry will improve them; if moderate abilties, industry will supply the deficiencies. Nothing is denied to well-directed labors; nothing is ever to be attained without it.

—JOSHUA REYNOLDS

Inflation

912. While people seem to think that money still talks, actually it's more of a sneer.

Initiative

913. Inflation, once started, is like going over a waterfall; the only stopping place is on the rocks at the bottom.

—Lord Liverdale

Initiative

914. Doing the opposite of what you are asked to do doesn't necessarily mean that you are showing initiative.

915. America, in the eyes of the world, typifies above all else the quality of initiative. "Where there is no vision, the people perish," says the Sacred Book. Ideas are the most valuable commodity in the world. And ideas are born of initiative, the children of men and women of initiative. Advancement is applied initative. Don't imitate. Initiate.

Inspiration

916. Inspiration without perspiration is usually sterile.

917. You have lived well if something of your influence survives to inspire others to live well.

—Ralph Lee Goodman

Instalment purchase—Instalment purchases

918. The modern line of least resistance is the dotted one at the bottom of the instalment contract.

919. When tempted to buy something on easy payments, it is well to remember that the collector will be even more persistent than the salesman.

Insurance

920. "Hindsight is better than foresight," mused the old-timer, looking at an accident insurance policy that had expired because of his age.

"Here is something I paid for through more than fifty years when I didn't really need it."

Insurance, Life

921. Life insurance has its highest value at the moment it is needed most.

922. Life insurance is a matter of taking intelligent advantage of natural laws.

923. It's a mistaken kindness to provide for oneself or for others so well today that no provision can be made for tomorrow.

924. Life insurance is the golden net stretched under the tightrope of existence.

925. Life insurance is like a parachute. If you ever need it and haven't got it, you will never need it again.

Integrity

926. Honesty is the best policy—don't let the premiums lapse.

927. Let unswerving integrity ever be your watchword.
—BERNARD BARUCH

928. It is a fine thing to be honest, but it is also very important to be right.
—WINSTON CHURCHILL

929. Society is built on trust, and trust upon confidence in one another's integrity.
—ROBERT SOUTH

Intolerance

930. Aaron Burr was a more brilliant man than George Washington. If he had been loyal to truth, he would have been an abler man; but that which made George Washington the chief hero in our great republic was the sagacity, not of intellectual genius, but of the moral element in him.

—A. E. DUNNING

Intolerance

931. If the bell of intolerance tolls for one, it tolls for all.

—HENRY SEIDEL CANBY

932. A man with a single-track mind has no way to sidetrack a prejudice—so he produces intolerance.

Invention—Inventions

933. Napoleon could have ridden in an automobile. Shakespeare could have made "talkies" of his best plays. Caesar could have telephoned the news of his victories to Rome. Cleopatra could have had a steam yacht. Socrates could have recorded his dialogues on phonograph records. The principles on which all modern inventions are based, the materials out of which they are made, and the forces which operate them, *have always existed.* The world had to wait for a few men to discover and utilize them. In the years before us, amazing inventions and improvements will be made in every line of work. Opportunities for fame and wealth await men of intelligence, imagination, and ingenuity who can perceive new or better ways to serve mankind, and put them into operation.

Investment—Investments

934. Never invest your money in anything that eats or needs repainting.

—BILLY ROSE

Involvement, Total

935. A chicken and a pig were traveling together. They reached a town, hungered by a long march, where they spied a sign outside a restaurant, which read: "Ham and Eggs, $1."

"Seems fair enough to me," said the chicken. "Let's try it."

"Not me!" exclaimed the pig. "For you it's a contribution, but for me it's total involvement."

Jealousy

936. Success is often hard to take—especially when it's the other fellow's.

937. At men of deeds are jealous slanders thrown,
As stones are cast at fruitful trees alone.
—From the Hindustani

938. Jealousy makes us smaller in the hearts of our friends, weaker in the eyes of our adversaries, and defenseless in the hands of our enemies.
—Dr. William Arthur Ward

Judge—Judges

939. A judge has no constituents.
—George Sutherland, 47 Cong. Rec. 2801 (1911) (Said when Senator).

940. JUDGE'S PRAYER

O God of all truth, knowledge and judgment, without whom nothing is true or wise, or just, look down with mercy upon Thy servants whom Thou sufferest to sit in earthly seats of judgment, to administer Thy justice to Thy people. Enlighten their ignorance and inspire them with Thy judgments. Grant them grace, truly and impartially to administer Thy Justice and to maintain Thy truth in the glory of Thy name. And of Thy infinite mercy so direct and dispose of my heart that I may this day fulfill all my duty in Thy fear, and fall into no error of judgment. Give me grace to hear patiently, to consider diligently, to understand rightly, and to decide justly. Grant me due sense of humility, that I be not mislead by my wilfulness, vanity or egotism. Of myself I humbly acknowledge my own unfitness and unworthiness in Thy sight, and without Thy gracious guidance I can do nothing right. Have mercy upon me, a poor weak, frail sinner, groping in the dark; and give me grace so to judge others now, that I may not myself be judged when Thou comest to judge the world with Thy truth. Grant my prayer, I beseech Thee, for the love of Thy son, our Saviour, Jesus Christ. Amen.

—EDWARD G. RYAN, CHIEF JUSTICE OF WISCONSIN SUPREME COURT. PRAYER WAS FOUND AMONG HIS PAPERS AFTER HIS DEATH.

Kindness

941. Persistent kindness conquers the ill-disposed.

—CICERO

942. Kindness has converted more sinners than either zeal, eloquence, or learning.

—F. W. FABER

943. Kindness is very indigestible. It disagrees with very proud stomachs.

—WILLIAM THACKERAY

944. After years of living with the coldest realities I still believe that one reaps what one sows and that to sow kindness is the best of all investments.

—JOSEPH W. MARTIN, JR.

Know-it-all

945. The fellow who thinks he knows it all is especially annoying to those of us who do.

Knowledge

946. Knowledge is folly unless grace guide it.

—GEORGE HERBERT

150

947. We know too much for one man to know much.
—J. ROBERT OPPENHEIMER

948. Seeking to know is only too often learning to doubt.
—ANTOINETTE DESHOULIERES

949. Knowledge of itself has little value unless confirmed by personal conviction.
—CAMERON McLEAN

950. Knowledge is one thing that does not become secondhand when it is used.

951. The great enemy of all people is he who restricts the free and full flow of knowledge.
—SIR. ROBERT WATSON-WATT

952. The object of knowledge should be to mature wisdom and improve character.
—SAMUEL SMILES

953. No knowledge we can ever acquire is so important as a knowledge of what to say and how to say it; except, perhaps, a knowledge of what not to say and when not to say it.

954. What a man knows should find its expression in what he does; the value of superior knowledge is chiefly that it leads to a performing manhood.
—CHRISTIAN NEVELL BOVEE

955. Let me always remember that it is not the amount of religious knowledge which I have, but the amount which I use, that determines my religious position and character.
—ALEXANDER MACLAREN

956. There are more men of knowledge in the service of men of power than men of power in the service of men of knowledge. Knowledge seldom lends social power to the man of knowledge.

—C. Wright Mills

957. To serve a truly useful purpose in the world, a man must not only be able to acquire knowledge, but he must be able to interpret and apply it. For, the men who have contributed to the progress of the world used knowledge, not as a showpiece, but as a tool.

958. Some people confuse "knowledge" with "intelligence." Very often the ones with the greatest "book learning" have a remarkably poor understanding of life in general. Wisdom comes from doing battle with life's problems, not from simply reading about them.

959. There is oftentimes a great deal of knowledge where there is but little wisdom to improve that knowledge. It is not the *most knowing* Christian but the *most wise* Christian that sees, avoids, and escapes Satan's snares. Knowledge without wisdom is like mettle in a blind horse, which is often an occasion of the rider's fall.

—Thomas Brooks

960. There are some who desire knowledge merely for its own sake; and that is shameful curiosity. And there are others who desire to know, in order that they may themselves be known; and that is vanity, disgraceful too. Others again desire knowledge in order to acquire money or preferment by it; that too is a discreditable quest. But there are also some who desire knowledge, that they may build up the souls of others with it; and that is charity. Others, again, desire it that they may themselves be built up thereby; and that is prudence. Of all these types, only the last two put knowledge to the right use.

—St. Bernard

Language

961. The English characterize unintelligible speech by saying "That's Greek to me"; the Russians and Rumanians by "That's Chinese

to me"; the French by "That's Hebrew to me"; the Germans by "That's Spanish to me," and the Poles by "I'm listening to a Turkish sermon."
—NOAH JONATHAN JACOBS

Laughter

962. The man who can make others laugh secures more votes for a measure than the man who forces them to think.
—MALCOLM DE CHAZAL

963. If you want to make people weep, you must weep yourself. If you want to make people laugh, your face must remain serious.
—GIOVANNI CASANOVA

964. No one is born happy, but all of us are born with the ability to create happiness. A laugh expresses the joy of living, and the person who laughs is a delight to be with. But more important—he is enjoying his own life.
—EUGENE P. BERTIN

Law—Laws

965. We have every right to disagree with a law, but no right to disobey it.
—ATTRIBUTED TO JOHN F. KENNEDY

966. The law does not generate justice, the law is nothing but a declaration and application of what is already just.
—P. J. PROUDHON

967. The essence of jurisprudence is that, however inexact may be the decisions of a court, a court is a far superior method of reaching a decision than a battlefield.
—ERNEST CUNEO

968. The life of the law has not been logic: it has been experience. The felt necessities of the time, the prevalent moral and political theories. . . .

In order to know what it is, we must know what it has been, and what it tends to become. . . . The substance of the law at any given time pretty nearly corresponds, so far as it goes, with what is then understood to be convenient. . . . The law is always approaching, and never reaching, consistency.

—OLIVER WENDELL HOLMES

969. Law is a most conservative profession. The object of law is not to plan a better society. Politics does the planning, while law carries it out and suits it to existing changes in the way of life. Hence changes in law, in both contents and its working, are gradual. Remnants of old laws can be found in every legal system. To understand the existing law, the judge and the lawyer must sometimes sink deep into the past. There is an old saying among lawyers that laws never die; even abolished laws still rule from their graves.

—ELIEZER MALCHI

970. Law is an instrument of justice. Justice is rendering to every man what is due him. What is due to a man depends upon his nature, and by virtue of his nature man is a rational, free, spiritual being, whose happiness is an end in itself, and whose dignity therefore must always be respected. Law is a means to an end, and the end is the common good of man and society. If we do not respect the true nature of man and society, we will not respect the law which serves that end. Disrespect for ends is a deeper crisis than disrespect for means. If the ends are correct, the genius of a people will find the right means. If the ends are wrong, the situation is hopeless. In other words, law is designed to respect something, and if we do not respect that which the law is designed to respect, we will not respect the law itself.

—HAROLD R. McKINNON

Laziness

971. Lazy people are always eager to be doing something.

—FRENCH PROVERB

972. What is often called indolence, is in fact the unconscious consciousness of incapacity.

—H. C. ROBINSON

973. Three faults . . . found together . . . infect every activity: laziness, vanity, cowardice. If one is too lazy to think, too vain to do a thing badly, too cowardly to admit it, one will never attain wisdom. Yet it is only the thinking which begins when habit-thinking-leaves off . . . that is worth pursuing. A comfortable person can seldom follow up an original idea any further than a . . . pigeon can fly.

—Cyril Connelly

974. A farmer went into a big country store one day and heard a dog barking in the rear of the store. He said to the store keeper, "What in the world is the matter with that dog?" The store keeper said, "He is sitting on a cocklebur." The farmer said, "Why doesn't he get off of it?" The store keeper replied, "It takes less energy for him to bark and howl than to get off the cocklebur."

—J. I. Cossey

Leadership

975. The climax of leadership is to know when to do what.

—John R. Scotford

976. True leadership is the art of changing a group from what it is into what it ought to be.

—Virginia Allan

977. One of the tests of leadership is the ability to recognize a problem before it becomes an emergency.

978. In the simplest terms, a leader is one who knows where he wants to go, gets up, and goes.

—John Erskine

979. The leader must know, must know that he knows, and must be able to make it abundantly clear to those about him that he knows.

—Clarence B. Randall

980. Two qualities make the difference between leaders and men of average performance. They are curiosity and discontent. I have never known an outstanding man who lacked either. And I have never known a man of small achievement who had both.

—CHARLES H. BROWER

981. Being a leader is like being a parent. You work like a slave and nobody notices. You are taken for granted when you sacrifice, but are resented when you discipline. You give and give until you have nothing left to give. And then you give some more.

—JOHN WHITE

982. Leadership is complicated. It is intellectual; it is emotional; and it is physical. It is inherited, and it is learned. It is the summation of the total man which must square with the myriad desires of the group.

—EMERY STOOPS

983. Leaders do not rest on their laurels for long if they expect to remain leaders. Initiative is a necessary quality for anyone who aspires to rise above the crowd clustered at the foot of the ladder of success; it is characteristic of all true leaders.

—BOYD LINDOP

984. The new leader is clearly distinguished from the old-style boss. A boss creates fear, a leader confidence. A boss fixes blame, a leader corrects mistakes. A boss knows it all, a leader asks questions. A boss makes work drudgery, a leader makes it interesting. A boss is interested in himself, a leader in the group.

985. Leadership is a relationship which exists between one individual and the other members of a group. . . . Effective leaders display a multitude of common qualities, and characteristics—human understanding, professional competence, and a strong, independent character. A moment's reflection reveals effective leadership as a totality. Everything the leader does contributes to his success. As a teacher, administrator, trainer or counselor, his every action is part of the total relationship which must exist between him and his contemporaries.

986.   SOME MUST FOLLOW

Someone must play the minor parts,
Someone must hold the spear,
And someone, when the music starts,
Must follow in the rear.

Not everyone can be the star,
That shines with great white light,
But some must twinkle from afar
To harmonize the night.

—RUBY INGRAHAM

987.   Leadership carries responsibilities and obligations. It is easy to be ambitious for leadership, but it is difficult to bear the burdens which *real* leadership entails. A real leader must be creative, must encourage creativity when it would be easier to hew to the status quo. A real leader must see his own assets and liabilities realistically, even when it hurts. He must dare to be unpopular when circumstances require, though, like all men, he feels a deep, emotional need for approval. . . . He must learn that the rewards of his work are often delayed over long periods of time without recognition or satisfaction. He must be able to withstand stress, emotional and otherwise. And he must have that magic capacity which has been described this way: "Leadership, at its highest peak, consists of getting people to work for you when they are under no obligation to do so."

—BEN S. GILMER

Learning

988.   Those who cannot learn must be entertained.

—FELIX MORLEY

989.   One is on the way to being useless when he stops learning.

—RUTH SMELTZER

990.   The man who is too old to learn was probably always too old to learn.

—HENRY S. HASKINS

991. Seeing much, suffering much and studying much are the three pillars of learning.

—BENJAMIN DISRAELI

992. Your unused learning is an unused taper:
A book, tight shut, is but a block of paper.

—FFOM THE CHINESE

993. Learning is a link that connects the individual with the totality of his surroundings—nature and art, men and animals, the atom, the earth, the cosmos. As long as we don't know about them, they don't exist for us.

994. Suddenly it occurs to you that the process of learning is the process of discovering really to be true what at the beginning they told you was true, but you didn't quite capture it then.

—ARCHIBALD MacLEISH

995. Formal education is only the beginning of learning for all learning does not come from books and lectures. Much of it comes from experience in doing things, working with people, from grappling with problems, from the exercise of judgment, and from mistakes.

Leisure

996. If it weren't for having more leisure time these days, many men would never finish the work they take home from the office.

—FRANKLIN P. JONES

997. Leisure time is no longer a problem. Thanks to modern methods of transportation, one uses it all up going to and from work.

998. Leisure is like an empty bottle. It depends on what you put into it. . . . More leisure does not automatically mean more culture, more happiness. It may mean more crime, more boredom, more time-killing activities.

—KRASTYU KRASTEFF

999. In Greek the term for leisure is *skole*, and in Latin *scola*—from which we derive our word *school*. Leisure thus conceived is an aspect of the educational or learning process. The spirit of leisure is the spirit of learning, of self-cultivation. Leisure provides the climate for the growth of man's whole being—for contemplation of man's ultimate concerns, for activities which enrich the mind, strengthen the body, and restore the soul. Like education, leisure takes discipline, training, cultivation of habits and tastes, discriminating judgments. It is not something one drifts into.

—Robert Lee

Letter-writing

1000. Letter-writing is the only device for combining solitude and good company.

—Lord Byron

Liberty

1001. The real destroyer of the liberties of any people is he who spreads among them bounties, donations and largess.

—Plutarch

1002. Liberty is no heirloom. It requires the daily bread of self-denial, the salt of law, and above all, the backbone of acknowledging responsibility for our deeds.

—Bishop Fulton J. Sheen

1003. Liberty lies in the hearts of men and women; when it dies there, no constitution, no law, no court can save it; no constitution, no law, no court can even do much to help it. While it lies there it needs no constitution, no law, no court to save it.

—Learned Hand

Lie—Lies

1004. White lies are but the ushers to black ones.

—Frederick Marryat

Life

1005. The art of living is the art of knowing how to believe lies.
—CESARE PAVESE

Life

1006. Life and religion are one, or neither is any thing.
—GEORGE MACDONALD

1007. The difficulties of life are intended to make us better, not bitter.

1008. No life is so hard that you can't make it easier by the way you take it.
—ELLEN GLASGOW

1009. Prepare to live by all means, but for Heaven's sake do not forget to live.
—ARNOLD BENNETT

1010. All life is an experiment. The more experiments you make, the better.
—RALPH WALDO EMERSON

1011. One's real life is so often the life that one does not lead.
—OSCAR WILDE

1012. Life is the garment we continually alter but which never seems to fit.

1013. The ladder of life is full of splinters, but you never realize it until you begin to slide down.

1014. One cannot control the length of his life, but he can have something to say about its width and depth.

1015. Creative man lives many lives; some men are so dull they do not live even once.

—Dagobert D. Runes

1016. Dost thou love life, then do not squander time, for that is the stuff life is made of.

—Benjamin Franklin

1017. The time of life is short;
To spend that shortness basely were too long.

—William Shakespeare

1018. The longer you live the more you will realize that forgiveness, consideration and kindness are three of the great secrets of life.

1019. Life is a language in which certain truths are conveyed to us; if we could learn them in some other way, we should not live.

—Arthur Schopenhauer

1020. Very few of the great philosophers have made a greater contribution to the science of happiness than the hardworking old Negro woman who had a thoroughly likable but unusually lazy husband. When asked why she put up with him, she replied, "Well, I'll tell you. It's this way. I makes the living and he makes the living worthwhile."

1021. Be not afraid of life. Believe that life *is* worth living, and your belief will help create the fact.

—William James

1022. The reason many people don't live within their incomes is that they don't consider that living.

1023. I have lived long enough to be battered by the realities of life and not too long to be downed by them.

—John Mason Brown

1024. The secret of a happy and successful life is to be content with the abilities God gave and discontented with the use you make of them.

—BURTON HILLIS

1025. Life was meant to be lived, and curiosity must be kept alive. One must never, for whatever reason, turn his back on life.

—ELEANOR ROOSEVELT

1026. Life's a pretty precious and wonderful thing. You can't sit down and let it lap around you. You have to plunge into it; you have to dive through it!

—KYLE CRICHTON

1027. We act as though comfort and luxury were the chief requirements of life, when all that we need to make us really happy is something to be enthusiastic about.

—CHARLES KINGSLEY

1028. The person fears death most who fears life most, and the one who lives with the realization that he has but one life to enjoy is the person who, in his waning years, is as happily satisfied as ever.

—JOHN M. DORSEY

1029. Our life is like some vast lake that is slowly filling with the stream of our years. As the waters creep surely upward, the landmarks of the past are, one by one, submerged. But there shall always be memory to lift its head until the lake is overflowing.

—ALEXANDRE BISSON

1030. Life without love is a bird without song. Life without trust is a night without day. Life without faith is a tree without root. Life without hope is a year without Spring. Life without friends is a sun without shade. Life without work is a bloom without fruit.

—DR. WILLIAM ARTHUR WARD

1031. There is no life so humble that, if it be true and genuinely human and obedient to God, it may not hope to shed some of His light. There is no life so meager that the greatest and wisest of us can afford to despise it. We cannot know at what moment it may flash forth with the life of God.

—PHILLIPS BROOKS

1032. It is not enough for a man to say that he lives. The question is, what does he live for? From what source does he derive his inspiration? Does he spend his days in the cellar of his being or the dome? The wise man is he who identifies himself with his community and seeks to make it better. The person who thinks that the object of living is nothing but work must regard the workhouse or the prison as a stepping stone to the ideal. He should not have been born a man but a bee or an ant. We exist merely in a state of coma unless we be of service to mankind.

—JAMES J. DAVIS

1033. Have you ever thought how solemn a thing it is to live? If you are grateful for your life, set a value on it: find out how much it is worth, and if it falls below what you would have it, begin to increase its value. Take as your motto, "For God and Humanity," and live up to it. Be consistent and conscientious; live for a purpose; have faith in God and man; be full of hope and love, and resolve to make as much out of life as you can.

—IDA SCOTT TAYLOR

1034. To start out in the world knowing that someone loves you— to achieve and know that there is someone to rejoice with you—to face difficulties and know that someone is cheering and applauding your perseverance and courage—to work long hours and know that someone appreciates your sacrifices—to feel confident and strong and know that someone taught you to be so—to be confronted with a problem of lack, sickness, fear or temptation, and know that someone is ready to sympathize and help— that, indeed, is to be truly blessed in your journey up the road of life to your ideal!

Life insurance. See Insurance, Life

Listening

1035. Most "good listeners" are usually thinking about something else.

1036. You can learn without listening and you can learn to listen. Listening is like reading. You learn what the other fellow said and ponder what he meant. A good listener is both tender-hearted and tough-minded. The tender-hearted listener gets the feel of the situation, is sensitive to the needs of others, builds emotional kinship. The tough-minded listener knows how to tell a fact from an opinion, is neither a slave to unrelated facts nor at the mercy of sweeping generalizations. He is becoming an educated man.

—EDGAR DALE

1037. Listening is not something that comes naturally; it is an acquired art. For most of us, listening, whether in a social conversation or around the table at a conference, is just a pause we feel obliged to grant a speaker until we again have a chance to air our own opinions. This is not real listening, in any sense of the word. Listening is not a passive activity during which we let our own thoughts intrude upon what someone else is saying. To actively listen to another person requires willpower, concentration, and great mental effort.

—J. C. PENNEY

1038. Good listening is actually the foundation of good sportsmanship, good manners and intelligent citizenship . . . Experts doing research in listening estimate that we spend 70 per cent of our time communicating with others by reading, writing, speaking and listening. Most of us spend only about one-tenth of that time communicating in writing but nearly one-third of the time in talking. Listening, up to now the orphan of education and the forgotten art of the twentieth century, occupies the greatest single part (42 per cent) of our communicating time.

—JEAN R. KOMAIKO

Little things

1039. Paying attention to simple little things that most men neglect makes a few men rich.

—HENRY FORD

1040. He enjoys much who is thankful for little; a grateful mind is both a great and a happy mind.

—WILLIAM SECKER

1041. Life is made up, not of great sacrifices or duties, but of little things, in which smiles and kindness, and small obligations given habitually, are what preserve the heat and secure comfort.

—HUMPHREY DAVY

1042. Experience proves that most time is wasted, not in hours, but in minutes. A bucket with a small hole in the bottom gets just as empty as a bucket that is deliberately kicked over.

—PAUL J. MEYER

1043. Your little candle may not light the room but it can light the candle next to it, which in turn can do the same, until all the candles are lighted and darkness is gone.

—RUTH SMELTZER

1044. I should never have made my success in life if I had not bestowed upon the last thing I have ever undertaken the same attention and care that I have bestowed upon the greatest.

—CHARLES DICKENS

1045. The difference between men consists, in great measure, in the intelligence of their observation. It is the close observation of little things which is the secret of success in business, in art, in science, and in every pursuit of life.

—SAMUEL SMILES

1046.
The nail secures the shoe,
The shoe the horse,
The horse the man,
The man the castle,
The castle the land.

—FROM THE GERMAN

Livelihood

1047. If you think the world owes you a living, hustle out and collect it.

1048. The world owes you a living only when it is in debt to you. The first part of the transaction is yours. You have to contribute something the world wants and needs, before you can honestly say the world owes you anything in return.

Loneliness

1049. Much of a man's life can be lonely unless he is willing to accept work as a companion.

1050. Loneliness is a negation of the self, while solitude is the prerequisite of self-discovery. Loneliness is the symptom of atrophy, while solitude is a necessity for growth. We should never shrink from being alone at times, for when we are alone, and only then, do we reflect upon existence and receive life. Loneliness is a defeat, but solitude is a triumph, for it opens the gate toward a mature character and social responsibility.

—Samuel Terrien

Love

1051. To love is to stop comparing.

1052. To love at all is to be vulnerable.

—Clive S. Lewis

1053. He who cannot love must learn to flatter.

—Johann Wolfgang von Goethe

1054. Those who love deeply never grow old; they may die of old age, but they die young.

1055.   First love is only a little foolishness and a lot of curiosity.
—GEORGE BERNARD SHAW

1056.   Greater love has no man than in teaching his wife to drive or play golf.

1057.   It has been wisely said that we cannot really love anybody at whom we never laugh.
—AGNES REPPLIER

1058.   It is a mistake to speak of a bad choice in love, since as soon as a choice exists, it can only be bad.
—MARCEL PROUST

1059.   Love is the same old game it was in prehistoric times, except for one thing: Diamonds have now replaced clubs.

1060.   Love develops slowly, for it is a capacity requiring growth. It cannot spring full blown at first sight, as infatuation can.
—F. ALEXANDER MAGOUN

1061.   Love cannot endure indifference. It needs to be wanted. Like a lamp, it needs to be fed out of the oil of another's heart, or its flame burns low.
—HENRY WARD BEECHER

1062.   Many people behave, when bereaved or disappointed in love, not in the least as they would if they had never read about the similar experiences of heroes and heroines. In fact much of their melancholy is pure "literary grief" and could be blown away by a little ruthless self-examination.
—ELIZABETH CROSS

1063.   Love is the deep and superlative reciprocal relationship which evolves when two or more people can feel and understand together sufficiently to remain separate in their independence, yet happy in their unity, because their individual needs continue to be fulfilled in better ways than would have been possible without each other.

—F. ALEXANDER MAGOUN

1064. Love fulfills our need to be sympathetically understood by someone to whom we can pour out our troubles, by whom we can be comforted, with whom we can go on to find gladness. It is a relationship forever renewed . . . an emotional closeness which prevents a person from feeling alone inside. Loved ones are always there to some degree, even after death.

—F. ALEXANDER MAGOUN

Loyalty—Loyalties

1065. I admire men who stand up for their country in defeat, even though I am on the other side.

—WINSTON CHURCHILL

1066. If vitality gives a man's perspectives color, if community bonds give them breadth, if awareness of the land makes them realistic, a deep sense of loyalty gives them personal meaning and integrity.

—HARRY HUNTT RANSOM

Luck

1067. Luck is good when it isn't bad.

1068. Luck may win a few deals, but in the long run it is the better player who scores the highest. Chance may throw a fortune into anyone's lap, but what is termed luck usually is the fruit of shrewdness and persistency.

—BALTASAR GRACIÁN

1069. The difference between bad luck and good luck is the difference in our attitude toward circumstances and events. The human mind sometimes converts the greatest blessings into the most sordid evils. But the spiritual-minded person takes whatever comes and at once seeks the blessing contained therein. By looking, we always locate what we seek.

—ADELAIDE HENSLEY

Man—Men

1070.   Man is an enigma. He wants to live a long time, yet is constantly threatening himself with annihilation. He desires the enjoyment of good health, yet regularly ignores the basic rules for it. He longs for immortality, yet often lives a life not fit to live forever. He loves liberty, yet steadily makes himself a slave to false masters. He has the possibility of being a saint, yet so often chooses to be a sinner. He is the only creature that can stoop below itself, becoming a "rat," a "skunk," a "cur," a "snake-in-the-grass," yet he can ascend through God's grace to angelic heights.

—GILBERT L. GUFFIN

1071.   THE MEASURE OF A MAN

Not—"How did he die?"
But—"How did he live?"
    Not—What did he gain?"
But—"What did he give?"
    These are the units
To measure the worth
    Of a man, as a man,
    Regardless of birth.

Not—"What was his station?"
But—"Had he a heart?"
    And—"How did he play
His God-fearing part?"
    Was he ever ready
With words o' cheer,
    To bring back a smile,
To banish a tear?

Not—"What was his church?"
Nor—"What was his creed?"
    But—"Had he befriended
Those really in need?"
    Not—"What did the sketch

In the newspaper say?"
But—"How many were sorry
When he passed away?"

—Author unknown

Mankind

1072.   Man seeks to acquire a rank among his fellow men, whom he detests, but without whom he cannot live.

—Immanuel Kant

1073.   The real problem is in the hearts and minds of men. It is not a problem of physics but of ethics. It is easier to denature plutonium than to denature the evil spirit of man.

—Albert Einstein

Man-Woman—Men-Women

1074.   Nothing so excites a man's curiosity as the silence of a woman.

1075.   Being a woman is a terribly difficult task, since it consists principally in dealing with men.

—Joseph Conrad

1076.   Women have the same desires as men, but do not have the same right to express them.

—Jean Jacques Rousseau

1077.   In some cases, when a woman makes a fool of a man, it's an improvement.

1078.   Men are attracted to two types of women—those who wear well and those who wear little.

1079.   It's only the men who consider the 50-mile hike as training in physical fitness. Women merely call it shopping.

1080. Man once subscribed to the theory of male superiority—then woman cancelled his subscription.

—SHANNON FIFE

1081. Ever since Eve gave Adam the apple there has been a misunderstanding between the sexes about gifts.

1082. There is not a war in the world, no, nor an injustice, but you women are answerable for it; not in that you have provoked, but in that you have not hindered. Men, by their nature, are prone to fight; they will fight for any cause, or for none, It is for you to choose their cause for them, and to forbid them when there is no cause. There is no suffering, no injustice, no misery in the earth, but that the guilt of it lies lastly with you.

—JOHN RUSKIN

Manners

1083. To the Frenchman manners are of great importance—and always have been, as the following extract from a 16th-century *Livre de Civilité* (Book of Etiquette) shows:

"When I am a guest at table," asks the young man, "must I eat little or much?"

"Eat as much as you possibly can," says the old man without hesitation, "for if you are invited by a friend, he will be flattered thereby, and if by an enemy he will be annoyed."

What more could you want?

Marriage

1084. Marriage simplifies your life but complicates your days.

1085. Marriage is terrifying, but so is a cold and forlorn old age.

—ROBERT LOUIS STEVENSON

1086. A successful marriage requires falling in love many times with the same person.

—MIGNON McLAUGHLIN

1087. So live that when a man says he's married to you, he'll be bragging.

1088. Independence is the price a woman is ready to pay for the happiness of being married.

—Paul Tournier

1089. Love is the star men look up to as they walk along, and marriage is the orbit they fall into.

—Charles Kennedy

1090. Entirely too many women get excited over nothing and then marry him.

1091. An old farmer, asked why he had never married, explained, "Well, I'd rather go through life wanting something I didn't have than having something I didn't want."

1092. Many a marriage could have been saved if the couple had remembered this: that their hearts belong to each other, but their souls belong to God!

—Louis H. Evans

1093. Advice to mothers who worry because their sons don't want to get married: they may show no interest now, but just wait until the wrong girl comes along.

1094. Marriage is an adventure in cooperation. The more we share the richer we will be; and the less we share the poorer we will be.

—Harold B. Walker

1095. The greatest charm of marriage, in fact that which renders it irresistible to those who have once tasted it, is the duologue, the permanent conversation between two people who talk over everything and everyone till death breaks the record.

1096. "Dad," the boy said after running home from school, "I've got my first part in a play. I play a man who's been married for 25 years."

"That's a good start, son," his father replied. "Just keep at it and one of these days you may get a speaking part."

1097. The golden rule of married life is, "bear and forbear." Marriage, like government, is a series of compromises. One must give and take, refrain and restrain, endure and be patient.

—SAMUEL SMILES

1098. Apparently our forefathers didn't take too bright a view of marriage, for with them the word *wed* once meant "to wager" and later on "to marry." In their spelling you would *weddian* your money on a racehorse. Or you could *weddian* a woman, "for fairer, for fouler" as they put it in their quaint marriage ceremony.

Again, "to put in *wed*" was "to put in pawn." To "take out of *wed*" was to redeem. On the other hand, a *wedman* was a married man, and a *wed-break* was an adulterer. In later history the word *wed* lost its gambling significance.

1099. A prominent judge attended the church wedding of the daughter of one old friend to another old friend's son. After the minister pronounced them man and wife, the happy couple came down the aisle smiling gaily at relatives and friends. As they passed the judge's pew, he felt a strong urge to step out and tell them to make this a lifelong partnership. He wanted to tell them never to let anything drive them into the divorce courts where far too many marriages are being terminated today. He didn't do it. The very thought of divorce seemed to him a desecration at so beautiful a wedding.

Later in his study at home, the judge thought of the contrast between the happiness of a wedding day and the harshness of so many days in court. He pondered the excuses given by those who are determined "to put asunder what God hath joined together." From his courtroom experience, he set down ten commandments for marriage. Perhaps they might help married couples retain the happiness of their wedding day.

1. Avoid the first quarrel.
2. Don't argue, nag or find fault.
3. Let there be no boss rule in the house.
4. "Ours" and not "Mine" should be the possessive pronoun.

Married life

     5. Confine your intimacies to yourselves; don't share them with your social friends.

     6. Don't live with your in-laws. No matter how humble, have a home of your own.

     7. A little love and affection, as you used to display during your courtship days, will prevent many petty quarrels.

     8. Husbands must keep in mind that running the household is a tough, tedious and tiresome job. Be considerate and overlook the wife's nerves.

     9. Keep respect for each other. When respect goes love vanishes.

     10. Protect the home with love insurance by having as many children as you can afford.

Married life

1100.   A married couple usually work out a budget together and then break it separately.

1101.   Women who insist on wearing the pants frequently discover it is the other woman who is wearing the chinchilla.

1102.   The secret of a married man's success is to live as a bachelor: A quiet life with one's books, music and friends.

                                    —GEORGE SANDERS

Martyrdom

1103.   The tyrant dies and his rule is over; the martyr dies and his rule begins.

                                  —SOREN KIERKEGAARD

Maturity

1104.   The awareness of the ambiguity of one's highest achievements (as well as one's deepest failures) is a definite symptom of maturity.

                                  —PAUL TILLICH

1105. To bear defeat with dignity, to accept criticism with poise, to receive honors with humility—these are the marks of maturity and graciousness.

—DR. WILLIAM ARTHUR WARD

1106. Maturity is the ability to deal with people of widely differing opinion, temperament, and taste without allowing these differences to interfere with the effectiveness of work or the warmth of human acceptance.

—DON ROBINSON

Mediocrity

1107. To be content with mediocrity is a tragedy.

—RUTH SMELTZER

1108. Persevering mediocrity is much more respectable, and unspeakably more useful than talented inconstancy.

—DR. JAMES HAMILTON

Meditation

1109. Meditation is to the sermon what the harrow is to the seed— it covers those truths which else might have been picked up or washed away.

—REV. CHARLES THOMAS

1110. Without meditation we do but talk one after another like parrots, and take up things by mere hearsay, and repeat them by rote, without affection and life, or discerning the worth and excellency of what we speak. It is meditation that maketh truth always ready and present to us.

—THOMAS MANTON, D.D.

Meekness

1111. If you are right, take the humble side—you'll help the other fellow. If you are wrong, take the humble side—and you'll help yourself.

Memorial Day

1112. Memorial Day is a good time to remember our wonderful heritage, and some of the blessings we so take for granted. We often treat with indifference the sound foundations of our nation's life that were laid by consecrated and industrious hands. We should be grateful for our Constitution, which has safeguarded our liberty and protected its destruction by malicious minds or by blinded political prejudice. Every day is not too often to remember those men and women of vision and valor who bought our liberty, and particularly should they be remembered on Memorial Day.

—SIR ORACLE

1113. There is some dispute as to who originated the idea of decorating the graves. Some historians believe the idea began with three Civil War veterans who met at Crab Orchard Christian Church near Carbondale, Illinois, in April 1866. Others credit the idea to Captain Asgill Connor, who is believed to have organized the first decoration of graves in Carbondale the same year. Still another version credits the idea to the wife of Gen. John A. Logan, commander-in-chief of the Grand Army of the Repulic. Gen. Logan issued an order that May 30 be set aside as Memorial Day "for the purpose of strewing with flowers the graves of comrades who died in defense of their country." The general's orders also suggested that the occasion would be marked annually.

Memory—Memories

1114. Happy memories, like a lighted candle, light the dark places of later life.

—RUTH SMELTZER

1115. Memory is the vapor trail left by rocketing years; an inscription written on the waters of time to perish as a wave breaking on the shore.

—DOUGLAS MEADOR

1116. Someone once said that in our early years we should build the foundations for happiness, so that in our later years we can begin to enjoy what we have built. The older we grow the more important memories of the past become. It is the character of these memories which gives us a feeling of achievement from a life lived well, or a sense of remorse for wasted years. Every day we are deciding our happiness by how we live. Wisdom suggests that we live right every day, so that any shadows of the past will fade and every promise for tomorrow will become even brighter than before.

Mercy—Mercifulness

1117. As freely as the firmament embraces the world, or the sun pours forth impartially his beams, so mercy must encircle both friend and foe.

—JOHANN SCHILLER

1118. None of us is so close to perfection that he can be a spiritual policeman over the lives of everybody else. And since every one of us stands constantly in need of mercy more than justice, it behooves all of us to center more on being merciful than on being judge.

Mind, Change of

1119. Don't ever slam a door; you might want to go back.

—DON HEROLD

1120. It is by presence of mind in untried emergencies that the native metal of man is tested.

—JAMES RUSSELL LOWELL

Minority—Minorities

1121. If 10 million people do a wrong thing it is still wrong. Don't be afraid to stand with the minority.

Minority groups

1122. What a minority group wants is not the right to have geniuses among them, but the right to have fools and scoundrels without being condemned as a group. Every group has its wrongdoers. But when wrongdoers are identified with a group, their number is magnified in the minds of other people. Minorities would gladly give up the reflected glory of their great men if only the world didn't burden them with the ignominy of their scoundrels. Both great men and scoundrels belong to mankind as a whole, and mankind as a whole shares the sorrow as well as the honor.

—AGNES ELIZABETH BENEDICT

Misfortune—Misfortunes

1123. The greatest misfortune of all is not to be able to bear misfortune.

1124. Let us be of good cheer, however, remembering that the misfortunes hardest to bear are those which never come.

—JAMES RUSSELL LOWELL

1125. Life is thickly sown with thorns, and I know no other remedy than to pass quickly through them. The longer we dwell on our misfortunes, the greater is their power to harm us.

—VOLTAIRE

Mistake—Mistakes

1126. More erroneous conclusions are due to lack of information than to errors of judgment.

—LOUIS D. BRANDEIS

1127. It may take two to make a bargain, but it takes only one to make a mistake.

1128. The man who does things makes many mistakes but he never makes the biggest mistake of all—doing nothing.

—BENJAMIN FRANKLIN

1129. In order to profit from your mistakes, you have to get out and make some.

1130. A blunder at the right moment is better than cleverness at the wrong time.

1131. The only time to worry over past mistakes is when they don't teach you anything.

1132. One thing worse than making a mistake is to dicover that you are so unimportant nobody noticed it.

1133. If only one could have two lives: the first in which to make one's mistakes; which seem as if they have to be made; and the second in which to profit by them .

—D. H. LAWRENCE

1134. We learn wisdom from failure much more than from success. We often discover what will do by finding out what will not do; and probably he who never made a mistake never made a discovery.

—SAMUEL SMILES

1135.   Ten mistakes to avoid:
            Remorse over yesterday's failure.
            Anxiety over today's problem.
            Worry over tomorrow's uncertainty.
            Waste of the moment's opportunity.
            Procrastination with one's present duty.
            Resentment of another's success.
            Criticism of a neighbor's imperfection.
            Impatience with youth's immaturity.
            Skepticism of our nation's future.
            Unbelief in God's providence.

—DR. WILLIAM ARTHUR WARD

Moderation

1136. In everything the middle course is best: all things in excess bring trouble to men.

—PLAUTUS

Modern age

1137. There is a limit to enjoyment, though the sources of wealth be boundless; and the choicest pleasures of life lie within the ring of moderation.

—Martin Farquhar Tupper

1138. Moderation may be a virtue, but it is an extremely minor one. The person who is always careful never to overstate will not say anything that is really memorable, while the person whose main interest lies in never making mistakes will end by making no important accomplishments. The safe road turns out finally to be dull, because it does not go anywhere.

—Dr. D. Elton Trueblood

Modern age

1139. The trouble with our age is all signposts and no destination.

—Louis Kronenbergr

1140. This is the age of the half-read page
And a quick hash and a mad dash;
The bright night with the nerves tight
The plane hop and the brief stop
The lamp tan in a short span
The big shot in a soft spot
The brain strain and the heart pain
The cat naps 'til the spring snaps
This is our culture!

Modesty

1141. A farmer went with his son into a wheat field to see if it was ready to harvest, "See, father," exclaimed the boy, "how straight these stems hold up their heads! They must be the best ones. Those that hang their head down I am sure cannot be good for much." The farmer plucked a stalk of each kind and said, "See here, foolish child! This stalk that stood so straight is light headed and almost good for nothing; while this that hung its head so modestly is full of the most beautiful grain."

—Dwight L. Moody

Money

1142.   Money doesn't make you happy, but it quiets the nerves.
—SEAN O'CASEY

1143.   Money talks, but dollar for dollar its voice keeps getting weaker and weaker.

1144.   The art of living easily as to money is to pitch your scale of living one degree below your means.
—HENRY TAYLOR

1145.   Money is the measure of appreciation. Compliments are pleasant, but it is the cash that counts.
—ELBERT HUBBARD

1146.   It annoys me when people boast that they know nothing about money as if it were a virtue instead of a symptom of bad citizenship.

1147.   Money is human happiness in the abstract: he, then, who is no longer capable of enjoying human happiness in the concrete devotes himself utterly to money.
—ARTHUR SCHOPENHAUER

1148.   Money, once you start to consider it carefully, is a hydra-headed monster. You need it to sustain life, to run an efficient society, and keep meaningful accounts. But ill-managed it can wreck homes, bring down governments, and reduce whole populations to destitution.

1149.   Money is that which, if you don't have any, worries you. It can be tight or loose, hot or cold, easy or uneasy, saved or squandered. When money loses its value, that's inflation. When it stays put, that is a miracle. When it evaporates, that is a calamity.

1150.   Dollar bills are lasting longer these days for three reasons, according to banking institutions: 1) Wider use of credit cards does away with the need of folding money; 2) Increased use of checking accounts; 3) Stronger paper for folding money.

Yes, they're longer lasting but faster spending.

Monument—Monuments

1151.   The only monuments most of us can expect to leave will be the loving memories of those who were glad they knew us.

1152.   We shall lose the advantage of a man's dying if we are to have a statue of him forthwith. It is very offensive to my imagination to see the dying stiffen into statues at this rate. We should wait till their bones begin to crumble—and then avoid too near a likeness to the living.

—HENRY DAVID THOREAU

1153.
What monument shall you erect
To foil Oblivion's lethal scheme,
When Death his customs shall collect,
And terminate this fleeting dream?
Build not of stone, for stone is cold,
And heartless, thru Time's deathless reign;
No tenderness, doth mortar hold
Where mem'ries spring to life again.
Build not of tyranny nor greed,
Nor blood-drenched garments of the slain;
Build not of mother's tears that plead
The safety of their sons in vain.
Build not of precious stones and gold,
For such as these beget but strife;
No lasting grandeurs these can hold
Will worthily reflect your life.
But build of honesty and grit,
With consciousness of virtue's might,
With force of wisdom, grace of wit,
Determination for the right.
And build of courage, worthy deeds,
With selfless service to your kind;
Yes, build of thoughts for others' needs,
Adorned with cheerfulness of mind.

Thus thru the ages shall survive
This monument you've builded then,
Your inmost self kept still alive
Within the living souls of men.

—HENRY C. CHURCHMAN

Mother—Mothers—Motherhood

1154. A man never sees all that his mother has been to him till it's too late to let her know that he sees it.

—WILLIAM DEAN HOWELLS

1155. Motherhood will always remain the best profession for women. Besides it's the only one entirely free from male competition.

1156. This automation you hear so much about is something that gets all the work done while you just sit there. When we were younger, this process was called Mother.

1157. God alone knows the fears that weigh upon the hearts and minds of mothers in this sometimes terrifying modern world. Every mother prays that the politicians and statesmen will find a way to let every mother's son grow up and live in peace. But every American mother knows that when the security of her country is threatened by those who would destroy freedom everywhere, her sons and daughters will meet their responsibilities with courage.

1158. Motherhood . . . is not a matter of bearing children. The bearing of children is a biological event. Motherhood is a matter of living a life in the midst of a family and thus of having a very great deal of influence on the character of that family—on its tastes, its quality, its approach to itself, its expectations, and its ability to cope with the world around it. In some societies other than ours, mothers, grandmothers and great- grandmothers are assigned specific roles in the community and each is respected for the role she plays. Often they are the arbiters of community attitudes. They control the community through their authority in the family and its kinship relations, which determine who is who and what is what.

—HAROLD TAYLOR

1159. WHAT IS A MOTHER

A mother is a woman who can bake a cake with six other hands helping her, and still have it turn out fine.

Mother's shoulders sometimes smell of sour milk, and if you are very observant, you will note safety-pin holes in her clothes, even her Sunday best.

Mothers frequently have runs in their hose. Likely as not junior didn't park his trike off the sidewalk.

A mother is different. She likes chicken wings and backs, things the kids and Daddy always spurn. She never takes the last chop on the plate, and she always saves the candy from her tray at the club to bring home to the children.

A mother may not have ulcers, but she has versatile tears. They show anger, weariness, hurt or happiness. Once, when Daddy forgot an anniversary, Mother cried. One Saturday night he brought home chocolates when it wasn't her birthday or anything, and she cried then, too.

Sometimes it's hard to know just what kind of tears a mother is weeping.

A mother is someone who can repair the kitchen sink—after Daddy has spent time, tools and expended not a few cuss words.

A mother is a person who can change diapers all day, feed the baby at two a.m. and still share Daddy's delight when baby's first words are "da da."

A mother is put together of wondrous things—soft hands to caress a tired head, firm fingers to guide a growing child along the right path, and a warm breast to shield her little one against the world.

When a mother dies, she must face Him with her record of accomplishments. If she's been tops in taking care of her children, she'll get the most sought-after position in heaven, that of rocking baby angles on soft white clouds, and wiping their celestial tears with the corner of her apron.

—WANDA BEAL

Mother's Day

1160. The only mothers it is safe to forget on Mother's Day are the good ones.

—MIGNON McLAUGHLIN

1161. Foreign comment: You Americans are strange people. You devote one day out of the year to your mothers and an entire week to pickles.

1162. While there are only two countries in the world—the United States and her northern neighbor, Canada—that set aside a day each year in which to honor mothers, the custom itself reaches far back in history.

The Chinese, centuries before the coming of Christ, held motherhood in awe and reverence. About the only good thing that can be said about the merciless Huns and the vicious Tartars is their esteem for their mothers.

The Romans held an annual feast in honor of Hilaria, the mother goddess. Historians record the holding of flower festivals in honor of Chicomehutal, the mother goddess of Mexico's Nahuan Indians, more than a thousand years ago.

During the seventeenth century, when boys and girls were apprenticed to factory owners, well-to-do families, and farmers in England, there was the day of "Going a-Mothering," on which the young people were allowed to visit their mothers, carrying small gifts furnished by their employers.

Credit for America's first Mother's Day usually goes to Miss Anna M. Jarvis, a Sunday school teacher, who in 1908 planned and conducted a memorial service in honor of her mother in the Andrews Methodist Church in Grafton, West Virginia.

The idea proved so popular locally that Miss Jarvis began a personal campaign for the widespread recognition of the contributions that motherhood has made to the nation. So successful were her efforts that, in 1914, President Woodrow Wilson signed a Congressional resolution setting aside the second Sunday of May as Mother's Day. That resolution also calls for the display of the American flag in honor of the nation's mothers.

As the carnation was the favorite flower of Miss Jarvis' mother, it has been adopted as the official Mother's Day flower—red or pink for the living mother, and white in memory of the mother who has passed away.

—Helen Mull

Motive—Motives

1163. Do not fear your motives being misunderstood or not understood at all. Fear far more for them to be understood in their entirety.

—Franz Marchault

1164. The motive for a deed usually changes during its performance: At least, after the deed has been done, it seems quite different.

—FRIEDRICH HEBBEL

Music

1165. I love music, but I do not try to play myself. I love music too much to spoil it.

—ANNA PAVLOVA

1166. Music is a thing of the soul, an instrument of God. It lightens labor and speeds play, it soothes the sad, refreshes the weary, breaks human barriers, stirs patriotic impulses and dignifies the activities of mankind. It is the ultimate form of culture.

—EUGENE P. BERTIN

1167. Music is a gift of God which gives deep enrichment to life through the wordless language of its melodies and harmonies. Music is a bridge between the seen and unseen worlds; it stands at the juncture of mind and matter and is related to both and yet different from either. Music links the inner life of man with the world outside himself. Through the language of tonal forms and colors the creative musician expresses realities of thought and experience that cannot easily be put into words.

—R. HAROLD TERRY

1168. Music speaks with emotion that words alone do not arouse. This emotional content may stir us to noble action, or quietly establish a sense of peace that sets us free from the disturbances of outer conditions. Being free from language barriers, its function affects most people, and its influence remains far-reaching. Although a baby does not understand the words to the lullaby that puts him to sleep, his body responds to the tender love that is expressed in the lilt of his mother's song. He relaxes, sleeps in peace, and awakes refreshed and contented. Music continues with us throughout life to give us comfort, to inspire, and to refresh us. When we listen, it brings us into rhythmic action and causes us to move with greater ease and lightness of heart.

Name—Names

1169. She called her husband Theory—because he so seldom worked.

1170. Researchers finally discovered how Eleva, Wisconsin, got its name changed from New Chicago. Late in 1899, workmen got part of the word "elevator" painted on the side of a new grain elevator when cold weather forced them to give up. The painted letters spelled "ELEVA." Residents decided they liked that better than New Chicago and changed the name officially.

Nation—Nations

1171. In the life of a nation ideas are not the only things of value. Sentiment is also of great value; and the way to foster sentiment in people, and to develop it in the young, is to have a well-recorded past and to be familiar with it. . . . A people that studies its own past and rejoices in the nation's proud memories is likely to be a patriotic people, the bulwark of law and the courageous champion of right in the hour of need.

—JOSEPH ANDERSON

Nature

1172. Nature does not bestow virtue; to be good is an art.

—SENECA

1173. It's just plain bad planning on nature's part, having the days shortest when there is most to do.

1174. If I were to name the three most precious resources of life, I should say books, friends, and nature; and the greatest of these, at least the most constant and always at hand, is nature.

—JOHN BURROUGHS

Neglect

1175. Whenever you feel neglected, remember Whistler's father.

Newness

1176. There's nothing new, except what has been forgotten.

1177. The mind likes a strange idea as little as the body likes a strange protein and resists it with similar energy. If we watch ourselves honestly, we shall often find that we have begun to argue against a new idea even before it has been completely stated.

—ARTHUR KOESTLER

New Year, The

1178. This is the year you expected so much of last year.

—E. W. HOWE

1179. The trouble comes when the New Year's resolutions collide with the old year's habits.

1180. Our friends can wish us a happy new year but only we can make their wishes come true.

1181. If the calendar did not provide a New Year's Day, we would have to devise one. We need an annual breaking point—a time to stop and take stock of ourselves—a time to renew our determination—a time to recheck our goals—and a time to make a fresh start.

1182. The new year brings opportunity, for there is always much to be done. And perhaps the greatest opportunity will be that of making a fresh start. We can put the mistakes of the old year, its frustrations, its disappointments, and muffed chances out of our mind. We can remember only what we learned from our experience—and the wisdom, if you please—that the old year gave us.

1183. FOR THE NEW YEAR

This I would like to be: Braver and bolder,
Just a bit wiser because I am older,

Just a bit kinder to those I may meet,
Just a bit manlier taking defeat.

This I would like to be: Just a bit finer,
More of a smiler and less of a whiner,
Just a bit quicker to stretch out my hand
Helping another who's struggling to stand.

This I would like to be: Just a bit truer,
Less of the wisher and more of the doer,
Broader and bigger, more willing to give,
Living, and helping my neighbor to live.

This for the New Year my wish and my plea:
Lord, make a regular man out of me.

1184.   WHAT IS THE NEW YEAR?

One poet says:
    "It is a door,
By which we reach new fields
Of service for our God and fellow man:
    A door by which we can explore
    Wide spheres of usefulness
    Our world to bless;
And reap the sheaves God's Word of witness yields.

    "It is a task
Set by the Master of our souls,
A little part of our life's work below:
    And so we ask
The holy wisdom, which alone controls
Our labor, teaching what and where to sow.
That the year, and its end,
May show God's glory and man's profit blend.

    "It is a book
With many pages and as yet all white,
On which to write
The history of thought, and deed, and word
    In this new group of days,
    We pray thee, Lord,
    As thou shalt look
Upon the book, when written o'er, may all be to thy praise,"
                                        —WILLIAM OLNEY

Nonconformity

1185. Many a person might have become outstanding but for the fear of being different.

1186. Majorities, of course, start with minorities, but you have to have a crocodile's hide to last that long. That is why the nonconformist, the agitators and left-wingers become so fanatical and dangerous. The others hold them back too long, patronize them too much and concede too little.

—Robert Moses

1187. Strangely, the expounders of many of the great new ideas of history were frequently considered on the lunatic fringe for some or all of their lives.

If one stands up and is counted, from time to time one may get knocked down. But remember this: a man flattened by an opponent can get up again. A man flattened by conformity stays down for good.

—Thomas J. Watson

Obstacle—Obstacles

1188. While no one can afford to quit because the road gets rough, anyone can afford to take a second look to see if there is a smoother road to the same destination.

1189. Our strength often increases in proportion to the obstacles which are imposed upon it; it is thus that we enter upon the most perilous plans after having had the shame of failing in more simple ones.

—René Rapin

Old age

1190. To deprive elderly people of their bogies is as brutal as snatching from babies their stuffed bears.

—Logan Pearsall Smith

1191.   Age involves loss of power to act, but not so much loss of wisdom to judge. Old men, therefore, though less fitted for executive stations, are still the best of counsellors.

—CHRISTIAN NEVELL BOVEE

1192.   He who would pass the declining years of his life with honor and comfort, should, when young, consider that he may one day become old, and remember, when he is old, that he has once been young.

—JOSEPH ADDISON

1193.   A man's not old when his hair turns grey,
And a man's not old when his teeth decay;
But he's on his way to that final sleep,
When his mind makes appointments his body can't keep.

—ANONYMOUS

1194.   Age is a quality of mind—
If you have left your dreams behind,
    If hope is cold,
If you no longer look ahead,
If your ambition's fires are dead
    Then you are old.
But if from life you take the best,
And if in life you keep the jest,
    If love you hold,
No matter how the years go by,
No matter how the birthdays fly—
    You are not old!

—ANONYMOUS

Openmindedness

1195.   The fellow who says that he has an "open mind" on a subject, sometimes means he never cared enough to be informed about it.

Opinion—Opinions

1196.   There is a limit to the legitimate interference of collective opinion with individual independence.

—JOHN STUART MILL

Opportunism

1197. It is refreshing to find a man who has really opinions of his own, even where they are opposed to our own. . . . What we call our opinions, are in general, in matters of importance, only the prejudices of our class, party or sect.

—Christian Nevell Bovee

Opportunism

1198. The pessimist spends all his time worrying about how he can keep the wolf from the door.

The optimist refuses to see the wolf until he seizes the seat of his pants.

The opportunist invites the wolf in and appears the next day in a fur coat.

Opportunity—Opportunities

1199. The sure way to miss success is to miss the opportunity.

—Victor Chasles

1200. The gates of opportunity and advancement swing on these four hinges: initiative, industry, insight and integrity.

—Dr. William Arthur Ward

1201. Every successful business in the world is in existence because its founder recognized in a problem or need an opportunity to be of service to others. Every problem or need in your life is in reality an opportunity to call forth inner resources of wisdom, love, strength, and ability.

—J. Sig Paulson

1202. To suggest that peeling potatoes offers an opportunity for anything more than getting the job over with would likely provoke a laugh. Yet one sailorman in the British merchant navy found an opportunity for himself when he faced a huge mound of potatoes to be peeled for the ship's mess. Being a man who would do any job to the best of his ability, he peeled those potatoes with a little more care than the average housewife or the sullen soldier doing KP. All the eyes and blemishes were carefully scraped away. Ship's cooks began to boast about the clean smoothness of the spuds he peeled, until his reputation spread throughout the shipping lanes.

Today the ex-sailorman is a small businessman in London. He supplies select potatoes, peeled to perfection, to the best restaurants in the city.

Perhaps his name will not go down in history. He may never enjoy more than a small but profitable little business. But of the millions who peel potatoes all over the world, Gerald Pereth was one who saw his opportunity for achievement in doing a lowly job better than anyone else was doing it.

—NUGGETS

Opposition

1203. Men often oppose a thing merely because they have had no agency in planning it, or because it may have been planned by those whom they dislike.

—ALEXANDER HAMILTON

Oppression

1204. I learned that assistance given to the weak makes the one who gives it strong; and that oppression of the unfortunate makes one weak.

—BOOKER T. WASHINGTON

Optimism

1205. Keep your face to the sunshine and you cannot see the shadow.

—HELEN KELLER

1206. Be an optimist, and shadows will fall behind you, cheerfulness will walk beside you, opportunity will rise in front of you, and doors will open for you.

—DR. WILLIAM ARTHUR WARD

1207.   If earth were just a crystal ball
              With naked eye we'd pierce it thru
              To find the sun is always up—
              The down is just our point of view!
                                    —MILDRED HOSKINSON

Optimism—Pessimism

1208. Sometimes a pessimist is the man who backed an optimist.

1209. The optimist has a reason for every success, the pessimist an excuse for every failure. The optimist sees a green near every sand trap; the pessimist sees a sand trap near every green. The optimist goes out and rings the bell; the pessimist gives up and wrings his hands.
                                    —DR. WILLIAM ARTHUR WARD

1210. The rains that nourish the optimist's flowers make the pessimist's weeds grow; and the drouth that does what the pessimist predicted for the flowers does what the optimist hoped for the weeds.

1211. A pessimist is one who counts each second as being just one second nearer to his grave. On the contrary, an optimist is one who looks forward to the possibilitiy of utilizing every remaining second of his life to being of service to others.
                                    —ARTHUR A. OSBURN

1212. The pessimist finds fault; the optimist discovers a remedy. The pessimist seeks sympathy; the optimist spreads cheer. The pessimist criticizes circumstances; the optimist changes conditions. The pessimist complains about the apple seeds; the optimist plants them. The pessimist disparages; the optimist encourages. The pessimist imagines impending peril; the optimist sees signs of prosperity. The pessimist creates loneliness; the optimist finds friends. The pessimist nibbles at the negative; the optimist is nourished by the positive. The pessimist builds barriers; the optimist removes roadblocks. The pessimist invents trouble; the optimist enriches his environment.
                                    —DR. WILLIAM ARTHUR WARD

Ostentation

1213. What is your name? Whatever it is, it isn't "Mister," believe us. For Pete's sake introduce yourself as "John Jones," "Henry Smith," or just plain "Poindexter Leffingwell." It's very poor taste to tell people that you are "*Mister* Brown." "Mister" means "Master"—and to use it in referring to yourself is ostentatious and egotistical.

1214. Do not stand out too prominently above the crowd. The tower, which glitters in the sun, is easily struck by lightning. The ace in the deck gets dog-eared first; the too popular song becomes tiresome. Keep your brilliancy in check, so it may not become offensive to others; instead, take satisfaction in its mere possession.

—Baltasar Gracian

Outer space

1215. The reason life is probably extinct on other planets is that their scientists are a little more advanced than ours.

Parent—Child

1216. When their children fail to charm others, few parents can stay neutral.

—Mignon McLaughlin

1217. Too many parents tie up their dogs and let their 16-year-old's run loose.

1218. A mother's patience is like a tube of tooth paste—never quite all gone.

1219. The fundamental defect of fathers is that they want their children to be a credit to them.

—Bertrand Russell

1220. Usually parents who are lucky in the kind of children they have, have children who are lucky in the kind of parents they have.

1221. You will get better results if you ask a child to do something rather than command him to.

—RUTH SMELTZER

1222. No boy appreciates how much his parents did for him until he has children of his own.

1223. Today's parents surrender the logical dictatorship of the adult for the irresponsible dictatorship of the juvenile, and then dare call it "democracy."

—FRANZ MARCHAULT

1224. Every mind was made for growth, for knowledge; and its nature is sinned against when it is doomed to ignorance.

—WILLIAM ELLERY CHANNING

1225. Probably one of the toughest problems faced by a lot of children nowadays is learning good manners without seeing any.

1226. All parents think their children are gifted, and all children think their parents are retarded.

1227. The voice of parents is the voice of gods, for to their children they are heaven's lieutenants.

—WILLIAM SHAKESPEARE

1228. Some boys don't follow in their father's footsteps because the old man didn't make any tracks.

1229. One of the difficulties with parents these days is that they expect their children to behave as well as they never did.

1230.   We have been so anxious to give our children what we didn't have that we have neglected to give them what we did have.

1231.   When parents cannot control children in the home, it is difficult for the government to control them on the streets.

1232.   The male parent in suburbia can spend little time in the home. But the value of a father to a child is not the time spent with him or her, but the kind of image a father leaves in the child's mind. Unless he represents understanding, security and love, a man can spend all day at home and be not only a nuisance but a detriment.

1233.   Discipline is vital to success and happiness, for both the child and the adult. We all recognize that self-disciplined people go far in the world. Well, where does self-discipline come from? It is taught in the home. The child who learns early in life to accept the authority of his parents can more readily control his own emotions, overcome laziness and direct his energies to a constructive end.

—ISABELLE P. BUCKLEY

1234.   "Listening" to a youngster is an art which every parent should develop. It is more than simply hearing what he has to say. He may be unable to put his feelings into words. We may have to receive his message by observing the way he behaves. Irritation, temper, or tears may be an indication of weariness or illness or of an emotional disturbance which is unrelated to the incident of the moment. He does not understand this. He expects *us* to understand, and expects *us* to *help*! So we must listen, not just with our ears, but the heart and mind as well. Then communication may become complete, and bring about a real partnership.

1235.   Let every man so live that his mother can always be proud of his character, whatever his material success or failure may be. Let him so live that she will never be embarrassed by anything he does, nor hurt by something he failed to do when he should have. Let him fix firmly in his mind and heart the precious truths and values that he learned from her teaching and example. Let every man so live that he cannot fail to make a life that will be a credit to her memory.

Parting

1236. Every parting gives a foretaste of death; every coming together again a foretaste of the resurrection. This is why even people who were indifferent to each other rejoice so much if they come together again after twenty or thirty years' separation.

—ARTHUR SCHOPENHAUER

Past, The

1237. We cannot say "the past is past" without surrendering the future.

—WINSTON CHURCHILL

1238. Always forget the past. No man ever backed into prosperity.

1239. When thinking longingly of the past, we can never be sure where memory leaves off and imagination begins.

1240. The true past departs not; no truth or goodness realized by man ever dies, or can die; but all is still here, and, recognized or not, lives and works through endless change.

—THOMAS CARLYLE

Past—Present—Future

1241. The future is written in the past for those who have the skill to read it.

1242. Take your hats off to the past, but take your coats off to the future.

—CLARE BOOTHE LUCE

1243. Every man's life lies within the present, for the past is spent and done with, and the future is uncertain.

—MARCUS ANTONINUS

1244. One of man's greatest enemies is the illusion that there will be more time in tomorrow than there is in today.

1245. We live in the present, we hope for the future, we learn eternal truths from the past.

1246. It's a fast age. The impossibility of yesterday becomes a luxury today and a necessity tomorrow.

1247. Those who are ashamed of the past and afraid of the future don't find the present so hot either.

1248. The ultimate in wisdom is to live in the present, plan for the future and profit from the past.

1249. A really contented man has his yesterdays all filed away, his present in order, and his tomorrow subject to instant revision.
—CHARLES M. DWELLEY

1250. Today's troubles can be overcome. It is tomorrow's anxiety that worries us to death.
—R. BRYANT MITCHELL

1251. Tomorrow does not exist. It is only today that is a reality. If we dream of having success and happiness, we must do today that which makes such success and happiness.
—TOM D. EILERS

1252. For some the Present is difficult, others dread the unknown Future; but the worst foe of the soul is the Past, because the Past has in it the power to become a dreadful Present.
—REV. CLARENCE EDWARD MACARTNEY

1253. It is not the cares of today, but the cares of tomorrow that weigh a man down. For the needs of today we have corresponding strength given. For the morrow we are told to trust. It is not ours yet.
—GEORGE MACDONALD

1254.　As today is the fruit of yesterday, it is also the seed of tomorrow. If today is not to our liking, we know mistakes were made which must now be corrected. If tomorrow is to be an improvement, we must use today to make it so.

1255.　It is common to overlook what is near by keeping the eye fixed on something remote. In the same manner present opportunities are neglected, and attainable good is slighted by minds busied in extensive ranges and intent upon future advantages.

—Dr. Samuel Johnson

1256.　It has been said that the lessons of the past are always ignored by the inhabitants of the present, and this may be so. But the past plays its part in our lives whether we wish it to or not, and the inescapable truth remains that yesterday was once today—a moment yet unformed, unspoiled, promising the best or the worst only as man himself saw fit to create it.

1257.　An observing philosopher once said that he could watch a person walking and tell whether his thoughts were on the future, the present, or the past. He added that young men are inclined to look upward; their thoughts are on the future. Middle-aged men are more likely to look straight ahead; their thoughts are on the present. Old men look downward; their thoughts are on the past.

1258.　There are two days in the week upon which and about which I never worry—two carefree days kept sacredly free from worry and apprehension. One of these days is yesterday. Yesterday with its cares and frets and all its pains and aches, all its faults, its mistakes and blunders have passed forever beyond recall. It was mine; it is God's .And the other day that I do not worry about is tomorrow. Tomorrow with all its possible adversities, its burdens, its perils, its large promise and poor performance, its failures and mistakes, is as far beyond my mastery as its dead sister, yesterday. Tomorrow is God's day; it will be mine.

　　　　There is left for myself, then, but one day in the week— today.

—Robert J. Burdette

Patience

1259. Patience is out of place in the quicksand.

—DAGOBERT D. RUNES

1260. Patience is power; with time and patience the mulberry leaf becomes silk.

—CHINESE PROVERB

1261. How poor are they who have not patience! What wound did ever heal but by degrees?

—WILLIAM SHAKESPEARE

1262. Never think that God's delays are God's denials. Hold on; hold fast; hold out. Patience is genius.

—G. L. L. BUFFON

1263. It takes time to succeed because success is merely the natural reward for taking time to do anything well.

—JOSEPH ROSS

1264. This would be a fine world if all men showed as much patience *all* the time as they do while they're waiting for a fish to bite.

—VAUGHN MONROE

1265. The word "patient" comes from the Latin "*patior*," which means "to suffer." A patient person may be defined as one who "exercises quiet endurance or forbearance under distress, pain, injury, insult, or suspense."

Patriotism

1266. Patriotism is the sum of three cardinal virtues: Faith, hope and charity—faith in the principles of our government; hope in the future of our country; and charity toward all and malice toward none.

1267. No citizen of this nation is worthy of the name unless he bears unswerving loyalty to the system under which he lives, the system that gives him more benefits than any other system yet devised by man. Loyalty leaves room to change the system when need be, but only under the ground rules by which we Americans live.

—John A. Hannah

1268.　　　A NATION'S BUILDERS

Not gold, but only men can make
　A people great and strong—
Men who, for truth and honor's sake,
　Stand fast and suffer long.
Brave men, who work while others sleep,
　Who dare while others fly—
They build a nation's pillars deep
　And lift them to the sky.

—Ralph Waldo Emerson

Peace

1269. If a conference lasts a long time, it must end in peace; no one can keep on defying his enemies all day.

—Alfred Duggan

1270. Peace will not be preserved by pious sentiments expressed in terms of platitudes or by official grimaces and diplomatic correctitude.

—Winston Churchill

1271. The important thing to remember is that peace comes from within your own heart and mind, not from some outside source, and when you refuse to be disturbed by things about you, life will flood your being with dynamic energy.

1272. Too many of us think of peace in terms of being idle—sitting beside the road and watching the world go by. Nothing could be further from the truth. Peace is not something we earn for the future. It is a gift we accept now. This means that the virtue of peace lies in what we are thinking and doing at the present moment. Peace is an active quality, compounded of interest, attention, desire, joy, and achievement. It is the satisfaction of knowledge gained and applied; the acceptance of the laws of life and living by them; and the willingness to live and let live.

Perfection

1273. It is one of the strongest and saddest lessons of history that the worst crimes, the most terrible acts of cruelty and tyranny, are often committed not for greed or lust or sheer deviltry, but as a part of a dedicated, unselfish effort to realize some perfectionist ideal.

—WILLIAM H. CHAMBERLAIN

1274. There is no joy which surpasses that which springs from consciousness of work well done, whether it be driving an engine or managing a railroad, sweeping the floor of a bank or filling its presidential chair, selling a bill of goods or directing a vast sales force, operating a machine at the bench or running a great factory. The stenographer who types a perfect letter, the mechanic who turns out a perfect tool, the chauffeur who takes pride in keeping his car in perfect condition, is just as much an artist as the painter or the sculptor whose productions attract thousands to art galleries.

—B. C. FORBES

1275. In the world in which we live no one should ever expect to find perfection in anything. If we want to get a reasonable degree of enjoyment out of life, we must learn to take things as they are. This does not mean that we have to be completely satisfied. It only means that if improvement is practical it is our job to achieve it.

We cannot expect to find things perfect, nor can we expect to make them perfect. We can only hope to make them better. That is the challenge. Misery is the lot of those who resent the challenge. Happiness is possible for those who meet the challenge, who take things as they are in the hope that through their efforts improvement can be made.

—NUGGETS

Performance

1276. It isn't the hope, or the wish or the dream; it isn't the vision, the thought or the scheme; it isn't the aim and it isn't the plan—it's just what you do that determines the man.

—ROBERT GUILLIAM

Perseverance

1277. In your strife for success, do not expect an unbroken string of triumphs. Even the ablest general cannot win all his battles. . . . Likewise, when judging others, do not judge them by one trial. A horse may lose one heat and still win the race. Grant lost his first battle, yet won the war. That is what counted.

—Baltasar Gracián

Perseverance

1278. No one ever would have crossed the ocean if he could have gotten off the ship in the storm.

—Charles F. Kettering

1279. A good beginning is a great advantage, but is no guarantee of a winning race.

1280. Perseverance is a prime quality in every pursuit. . . . Men fail much oftener from want of perseverance than from want of talent.

—William Cobbett

1281. Perseverance and tact are the two great qualities most valuable for all men who would mount, but especially for those who have to step out of the crowd.

—Benjamin Disraeli

1282. Some men give up their designs when they have almost reached the goal; while others, on the contrary, obtain a victory by exerting, at the last moment, more vigorous efforts than before.

—Polybius

1283. All the creativeness in the world adds up to little if another quality is lacking, perseverance. Good ideas, spewed forth in abundance, and responsible to the most critical problems, are of no value until they are carried out. And the execution of even great ideas can call for perseverance on a heroic scale.

1284. Do you know the story about two frogs that fell into a bucket of cream?

They tried over and over to get out by climbing up the side of the bucket. But each time they would slip back into the cream.

Finally one frog said: "We'll never get any place doing this. I give up!" So down he went and drowned.

The other frog, seeing the consequences of giving up, decided to keep trying. Even if he didn't succeed, it would be better to go down fighting.

So time and time again he tried to climb with his front legs while he kicked with his back legs. Suddenly he hit something solid.

He turned to see what it was. Lo and behold, he found that all his kicking had churned up a lump of butter! So hopping on top of it, he leaped out of the pail to safety.

Plan—Plans—Planning

1285. Men don't plan to fail—they just fail to plan.

1286. Planning is essential for success but it is results that pay off.
—Harry F. Banks

1287. Any plan that depends upon luck to succeed isn't a plan; it's a gamble.

Pleasure

1288. There are few pleasures in the world so reasonable and so cheap as the pleasure of giving pleasure.

1289. If having a good time were all there is to life, monkeys have mankind outdistanced completely—both in amusing others and in being amused.

Poet—Poets—Poetry

1290. For poetry there exists neither large countries nor small. Its domain is in the heart of all men. Poetry is necessary to the world we live in, harassed as it is by fear and anxiety.
—Giorgos Seferiades

Point of view

1291. The poet's art is not only the most ancient of the literary arts. It is also the profoundest and the most demanding in the rigid discipline it imposes on the author. At the same time the poet's art seems to be disarmingly simple. This is why there are so many aspiring poets. For every one person who feels a deep compulsion to write a novel or a play there are a hundred who attempt poems. Of these, many ought not to try—not at least until they have done some hard work in mastering the elements of poetry and until they have saturated themselves with the sound and vision of great poetry.

—Paul Bechtel

Point of view

1292. It is said that every rose has a thorn but there is another side if we but have the wisdom to see it—every thorn has a rose.

1293. One man's justice is another's injustice; one man's beauty is another's ugliness; one man's wisdom another's folly; as one beholds the same objects from a higher point of view.

—Ralph Waldo Emerson

1294. A canny Maine farmer was approached by a stranger one day and asked how much he thought his prize Jersey cow was worth.

The farmer thought a moment, looked the stranger over, and said: "Are you the tax assessor or has she been killed by a train?"

1295. A familiar adage advises us to look at life through rose-colored glasses. This is often good advice, yet it is wise to look at the dazzling brightness of the sun through dark glasses of moderation and control. Many are dazzled by vistas of selfishness. They need the glasses of obligation to share and to sacrifice. Many are dazzled by life's glamor and glitter, seeing it as a brightly colored fantasy. They need the dark glasses of realism, remembering that life is real and life is earnest.

Politician—Politicians

1296. Statesmen see themselves as handmaidens of history; politicians see the state as a handmaiden of themselves.

—Dagobert D. Runes

1297. It's a smart politician who can keep the note of envy out of his voice while accusing his opponent of fooling the public.

1298. If a politician tries to buy votes with private money, he's a dirty crook; if he tries to buy them with the people's own money, he's a liberal.

1299. I have never seen difficulties that prevented leading politicians of great maturity and strong personalities from getting together when they felt it made sense.

—DAG HAMMARSKJÖLD

1300. Politics is a gamble and appeals to gamblers. Politicians often have built-in personality defenses as well as remunerative law practices to fall back on. But failure is a test of character. It is a strong man and often a happy one who, stooped in defeat, stands erect again to rebuild his pulverized political career or a local political machine.

—FLORA RHETA SCHREIBER & MELVIN HERMAN

Politics

1301. Yesterday's political promises are today's taxes.

1302. Politics is not a game. It is an earnest business.

—WINSTON CHURCHILL

1303. In politics, people are friends or enemies. In business, they are customers or former customers.

1304. What is politics but persuading the public to vote for this and support that and endure these for the promise of those?

—GILBERT HIGHET

1305. He who is firmly seated in authority soon learns to think security, and not progress, the highest lesson of statecraft.

—JAMES RUSSELL LOWELL

1306. A political leader must keep looking over his shoulder all the time to see if the boys are still there. If they aren't still there, he's no longer a political leader.

—BERNARD BARUCH

1307. The difference between North American politics and Latin American politics is that our politicians start running for office *before* the election.

1308. Anybody can succeed in politics. All you need do is get votes from the have-nots and campaign funds from the rich by promising to protect each group from the other.

1309. A candidate for public office needs five hats: One to wear, one to throw in the ring, one to pass around for donations, one to talk through, and one to pull rabbits out of.

1310. Politics is the most challenging profession in this challenging world of ours. It is more exciting than any sport. It is more difficult than any job. It is more rewarding than any prize. No other field of endeavor requires more of a man, for a politician must profess to know at least something about everything.

—JIM WESBERRY, JR.

1311. Politics is not and never can be a science. The human race is not that logical or inert or controllable. Politics is an art, one that has been called the art of the possible. The best possible preparation for the practice of this art, in my opinion, is a good, sound liberal education given relevance to world affairs by taking the world for its province as it ought to do anyway.

—A. WHITNEY GRISWOLD

1312. A businessman with money is respected. A politician with money is suspected. In business, reciprocity is necessary, prudent and wise. In politics it's called "a deal." . . . The businessman offers a bribe, "that's business." A politician accepts a bribe, "that's a crime." . . . It's smart for a "working man" to get more than he's worth, for working less than he's able. But the politician is expected to "sacrifice," to accept less than he's worth, but be always "on duty."

—PAUL HARVEY

1313. Two candidates for mayor of a small town were appearing before a town meeting to give their reasons for seeking election. Finally, the claims of each took on a belligerent flavor when one pointed his finger at his opponent accusingly and challenged: "You tell these good people about the powerful interest that controls you!" With that the other candidate jumped up, shook his first in his accuser's face and bellowed: "You keep my wife out of this!"

1314. Three ambitious politicians were walking along a beach, planning a strategic move to defeat a powerful rival, when they came upon several boys looking for crabs. As each crab was caught it was put into a wicker basket. One of the men warned: "You boys should cover the basket, otherwise the crabs will climb out and run away." Replied a freckled-faced lad: "Oh, no, sir! If one crab tries to climb up, the others will pull him down."

1315. If politics means anything, it means an all-embracing interest in the total affairs of the community. It means the interconnection of everything and an attempt to get a perspective of the whole. It is that comprehensive function which gives to politicians their greatest satisfaction and which—even more than the prospects of power—keeps them enthralled by their work. To identify the problems of contemporary society, to locate the men and women who are working for a solution, to evolve policies from ideas, to organize mass movements, to campaign for these policies to convince the people to accept them, to carry through the program by consent, lubricating the process by wise compromises without losing sight of the objective as he goes along—these are the tasks of the politician.

—ANTHONY WEDGWOOD BENN

Popularity

1316. Woe unto you when all men speak well of you!

—*The Bible*

1317. Popularity is a crime from the moment it is sought; it is only a virtue where men have it whether they will or no.

—MARQUIS OF HALIFAX

1318. I cannot see why people are ashamed to acknowledge their passion for popularity. The love of popularity is the love of being loved.

—WILLIAM SHENSTONE

Possession—Possessions

1319. The value of a possession is in the use that is made of it.

—CHRISTIAN NEVELL BOVEE

1320.   POSSESSIONS

My neighbor has a mansion high
Filled with the things which wealth can buy.
I have a roof that's quaint and low,
But it keeps out the rain and snow.

My neighbor has a hot-house where
Are gathered costly orchids rare.
I have a few old-fashioned flowers
That bless and brighten all my hours.

My neighbor has fine cars which come
To bear him from and to his home.
I have two feet, but they can go
In paths a car will never know.

My neighbor has so much, I fear
That life for him is sometimes drear.
I have but little, yet my days
Are full of happiness always.

—EDWIN CARLILE LITSEY

Poverty

1321. Less coin, less care; to know how to dispense with wealth is to possess it.

—C. REYNARD

1322. I've never been poor, only broke. Being poor is a frame of mind. Being broke is only a temporary situation.

—MIKE TODD

1323. It's a great advantage to have no money. Poverty compels you to use whatever talent you've got. I've never believed in hiding lights under bushels.

—SIR MALCOLM SARGENT

1324. There is not such a mighty difference as some men imagine between the poor and the rich; in pomp, show, and opinion, there is a great deal, but little as to the pleasures and satisfactions of life. They enjoy the same earth and air and heavens; hunger and thirst make the poor man's meat and drink as pleasant and relishing as all the varieties which cover the rich man's table; and the labor of a poor man is more healthful, and many times more pleasant, too, than the ease and softness of the rich.

—BISHOP SHERLOCK

Power

1325. Many people who covet positions of authority have no desire for the accompanying responsibilities.

1326. Not the exercise of power, but the love of power, makes a man corrupt and tarnishes all that he touches.

1327. The men who create power make an indispensable contribution to the nation's greatness. But the men who question power make a contribution just as indispensable—for they determine whether we use power or power uses us.

1328. No one is fit to be trusted with power. . . . No one. . . . Any man who has lived at all knows the follies and wickedness he's capable of. If he does not know it, he is not fit to govern others. And if he does know it, he knows also that neither he nor any man ought to be allowed to decide a single human fate.

—C. P. SNOW

1329.   If fortune has favored you with a high position, use it for the common good. Power, if molded into a whip, is dangerous to those who are at its mercy and equally so to the one who wields it; but if divorced from self-aggrandizement, power can produce a horn of plenty from which flow blessings in an unending stream.

—BALTASAR GRACIÁN

Praise

1330.   Praise makes good men better and bad men worse.

—THOMAS FULLER

1331.   Tell part of a person's praise in his presence and all of it in his absence.

—*The Talmud*

1332.   Be grateful for both praise and criticism; praise gives you confidence and criticism keeps you from overconfidence.

1333.   The trouble with most of us is that we would rather be ruined by praise than saved by criticism.

—NORMAN VINCENT PEALE

1334.   Praise is warming and desirable, what the human race lives on like bread. But praise is an earned thing. It has to be deserved like an honorary degree or a hug from a child. A compliment is manna, a free gift.

—PHYLLIS McGINLEY

Prayer—Prayers

1335.   Only man, among living things, says prayers. Or needs to.

—PETER BOWMAN

1336.   He who cannot pray when the sun is shining will not know how to pray when the clouds come.

1337. Too many people pray like little boys who knock at doors then run away.

1338. If he prayed who was without sin, how much more it becometh a sinner to pray!

—St. Cyprian

1339. Prayer can keep us out of trouble a lot easier than it can get us out of trouble.

1340. What more people need is the faith of the little old lady who declined a last minute invitation to a garden party because she had already prayed for rain.

1341. How many people who pray for God's help for others are willing to be one of the means by which He answers their prayers?

1342. There is nothing the Supreme Court can do to keep a child who has learned to pray at home from quietly saying a prayer in school.

1343. Prayer is a state of being alone in God's presence. Prayer is being so alone that God is the only witness to your existence. Thus we hear God speak to us.

1344. Whatever we are directed to pray for, we are also exhorted to work for; we are not permitted to mock Jehovah, asking that of Him which we deem not worth our pains to acquire.

—E. L. Magoon

1345. When George Washington took the oath as first President of the United States, on April 30, 1789, he spontaneously added this four-word prayer of his own: "*So help me God*," an invocation still used in official oaths by those taking public office, in courts of justice and in other legal proceedings.

1346. It is not the arithmetic of our prayers, how many they are; nor the rhetoric of our prayers, how eloquent they may be; not the geometry of our prayers, how long they may be; nor the logic of our prayers, how argumentative they may be; nor the method of our prayers, how orderly they may be; it is the fervency of spirit which availeth much!

Preaching

1347. It requires as much reflection and wisdom to know what is not to be put into a sermon as what is.

—Rev. Richard Cecil

1348. A preacher who preaches so children can understand him, usually finds his whole audience attentive.

—Ruth Smeltzer

1349. A minister, without boldness, is like a smooth file, a knife without an edge, a sentinel that is afraid to let off his gun. If men will be bold in sin, ministers must be bold to reprove.

—Rev. W. Gurnall

1350. The object of preaching is, constantly to remind mankind of what mankind are constantly forgetting; not to supply the defects of human intelligence, but to fortify the feebleness of human resolutions; to recall mankind from the by-paths where they turn, into that broad path of salvation which all know, but few tread.

—Sydney Smith

Precedent—Precedents

1351. Following a precedent is an easy substitute for thinking.

—Ruth Smeltzer

1352. Do not be guided by precedent alone. . . . To its idolizers nothing is right unless it has happened before. If science were guided by precedence, it would cease to function.

—Baltasar Gracián

Prejudice—Prejudices

1353. Prejudice: an opinion that belongs to someone we dislike.

1354. It is easy to mistake our prejudice for patriotism, our rationalization for reason, our littleness for logic, our theories for truth, and our fervor for fact.

—Dr. WILLIAM ARTHUR WARD

Pride

1355. Pride is a kind of pleasure produced by a man thinking too well of himself.

—BENEDICT SPINOZA

1356. They are proud in humility; proud in that they are not proud.

—ROBERT BURTON

1357. Pride is the spring of malice and desire of revenge, and of rash anger and contention.

—ROBERT LEIGHTON

1358. Pride is an established conviction of one's own paramount worth in some particular respect; while vanity is the desire of rousing such a conviction in others. Pride works from within; it is the direct appreciation of oneself. Vanity is the desire to arrive at this appreciation indirectly, from without.

—ARTHUR SCHOPENHAUER

Principle—Principles

1359. It is often easier to fight for principles than to live up to them.

—ADLAI E. STEVENSON

1360. Whenever he says it's not the money but the principle of the thing he cares for, just offer him the money and see how quickly the principle vanishes.

—RUTH SMELTZER

1361.   The value of an individual as well as the value of an organization depends upon the willingness to stand up when a need arises. An individual must determine the basic precepts that are to guide his activities and these must not be compromised. Without a set of principles an individual or an organization is without value.

Problem—Problems

1362.   There is no such thing as a "perfect" solution to any human problem.

—Dr. William J. Reilly

1363.   The biggest problem in the world could have been solved when it was small.

—Witter Bynner

1364.   Most of life's problems are really like those cloverleaf exchanges we find on our highways: It may not seem like it at first, but there is a way out.

1365.   It is unwise to try to be conclusive at any cost at any time. Anyway, you cannot settle problems; you can only try to create conditions that enable problems to evolve toward solution.

—Jean Monnet

1366.   It often happens that I wake at night and begin to think about a serious problem and decide I must tell the Pope about it. Then I wake up completely and remember that I am the Pope.

—Pope John XXIII

1367.   Two small boys were playing with a wagon one day. They were each trying to ride at the same time, but there was little evident enjoyment. Finally one of the youngsters turned to the other and said, "You know, one of us could have a lot more fun if you would get off."

1368. The solutions to our problems are not going to be found in any new and brilliant idea. They are going to be found in making the old, proven ideas work—an honest day's work, respect for the given word, living within income, and the willingness to make necessary sacrifices to attain a worthwhile goal.

Procrastination

1369. The wise man does at once what the fool does finally.
—Baltasar Gracián

1370. Tomorrow is one of the greatest labor-saving inventions of all time.

1371. Procrastination is the fertilizer that makes difficulties grow.

1372.   "JUST A MINUTE"

Whene'er he faced a task and knew
    He should begin it,
He could not start to put it through
    For "just a minute."
And, though the case demanded speed
He could not move just then; but he'd
Be ready for it, yes, indeed!
    In "just a minute."

His purposes were out of rhyme
    By "just a minute."
The whole world seemed ahead of time
    By "just a minute."
He could not learn to overhaul
His many duties, large and small,
But had to beg them, one and all,
    To "wait a minute."

In manhood he was still delayed
    By "just a minute."
He might have won, had Fortune stayed
    For "just a minute."

> But at the end of life he railed
> At "cruel Fate," and wept and wailed
> Because he knew that he had failed
> By "just a minute."
>
> NIXON WATERMAN

Progress

1373. Panic of error is the death of progress.
—ALFRED NORTH WHITEHEAD

1374. Progress comes from the intelligent use of experience.
—ELBERT HUBBARD

1375. All human progress, like baseball, involves a certain amount of risk. You can't steal second while keeping one foot on first.

1376. The most successful man is the man who holds onto the old just as long as it is good, and grabs the new just as soon as it is better.
—ROBERT P. VANDERPOEL

1377. Progress is inevitable only when we have the will and determination to make it so.

1378. The world owes all its onward impulses to men ill at ease. The happy man inevitably confines himself within ancient limits.

1379. Progress is not a broad road with people marching, but a piecemeal affair, a push here, an idea there, a dedicated man working quietly yonder, lights burning into the night in some laboratory, a few steps toward the dawn.

1380. The history of much of the progress made in the world is a history of insult and injury to those who have advocated change based upon new discoveries or new ideas. Without discounting the brilliance of their minds, we must marvel at the patience of those who slowly convince others that they must accept and use a new idea.

1381.   This is a story that is reported to have happened in the life of Thomas Edison. He and a friend were watching a big new earth mover in operation. The friend said sadly, "That machine will put a lot of men out of work." Edison turned to him and said, "Many more men could be put to work if they would move that earth with teaspoons."

—Wayne A. Johnston

1382.   Scientific advances cannot be refused. You may not always like them. But it is useless to turn out the electric light or bring back the trotting horse. The scientist cannot undiscover any dangerous or trouble-some fact. He can only go on seeking the truth. Meanwhile, society, for itself, must learn to control its desitmy by a corresponding spiritual achieve-ment in moral and political fields.

—Dr. Wilder Penfield

Promise—Promises

1383.   Better to refuse any request with firmness and courtesy than to make a promise you can't keep.

1384.   In religion, not to do as thou sayest is to unsay thy religion in thy deeds, and to undo thyself by doing.

—R. Venning

1385.   You cannot live on other people's promises, but if you promise others enough, you can live on your own.

—Mark Caine

1386.   PROMISES

The sunset is the promise of the sunrise.
The darkness is the promise of the dawn.
The winter is the promise of the springtime.
The hilltop of the road that rambles on.

The longing is the promise of fulfillment.
The dream the promise of its coming true.
The planting is the promise of the harvest,
The old the promise of the certain new.

The reaching is the promise of the grasping.
The need is promise of its own supply.
The plodding is the promise of arrival,
And patience finds its answer by and by.

Promises made in words may break and fail us.
Promises written down may not endure.
But promises recorded in the silence
That dwells in life's reality are sure.

—CLARENCE EDWIN FLYNN

Promotion—Promotions

1387. Someone has said the greater part of promotion is motion.

—RUTH SMELTZER

1388. The best way for a man to get out of a lowly position is to be conspicuously effective in it.

—D. JOHN HALL

1389. You never get promoted when no one else knows your current job. The best basis for being advanced is to organize yourself out of every job you're put into. Most people are advanced because they're pushed up by the people underneath them rather than pulled by the top.

—DONALD DAVID

1390. A man being promoted to a new job must be made aware that he is not receiving a deed to his new job but a contract on which he must deliver. The point that must be driven home is that the primary accountability for his making a success at the job is his own—not the accountability of the men who gave him the promotion.

Public opinion

1391. Public opinion is all-important in a democracy. If aroused it will correct any serious defect in our society. In most cases there will be voluntary compliance with the will of the people. Where this is not forthcoming, public consensus may bring about legislative action. What sparks this rectifying process is nearly always a lone critic who sets out to convince his fellow citizens that something is amiss and must be remedied. We must not let organized might, abetted by public apathy, crush this lone critic, this gadfly on the body politic.

—H. G. RICKOVER

Public speaking

1392. While a great speech can never move mountains, it can move people to the mountains and stir them to begin their necessary tasks.

—RICHARD H. HUNT

1393. The relationship of the toastmaster to speaker should be the same as that of the fan to the fan dancer. It should call attention to the subject without making any particular effort to cover it.

1394. All public speakers fall into geometrical patterns: those who have no depth try to make up for it in length, and those without breadth make up for it by going around in circles.

1395. Enthusiasm is the most convincing orator; it is like the infallible law of nature. The simplest man, fired with enthusiasm, is more persuasive than the most eloquent man without it.

—FRANKLIN FIELD

1396. Disturbed by conversation during the anthem, the pastor adopted a drastic device to break up the thoughtless practice. Right in the middle of the uplifting chorus from "Elijah," he had every voice suddenly hushed. All over the church sped the important information that Sister Jones was imparting to Sister Smithers: "I fry mine in lard!"

1397. I have come prepared to make two speeches—a short one and a long one. If you like the short one I will follow that up with the long one. The short one is "thank you," and seeing that you like that one I will give you the long one: "Thank you very much."

1398. Rabbi Stephen S. Wise, a dynamic speaker, opened a talk one day with: "When I make a speech, I actually make three speeches. The first is the one I prepare before I even see my audience, and let me tell you it's an excellent speech. Then I face the audience, and I somehow feel that this is not the right speech for this audience. So I tear up my first speech and deliver an impromptu one. There again it's a wonderful speech. Then comes the time for me to go home and think of what I *should* have said. That is the best speech of all. So, if you want to hear a good speech, walk home with me tonight."

1399. Mark Twain got off the train in a small town to find that his talk was poorly billed. Wondering if very many people knew about it, he stopped at the country store to feel out the proprietor.

"Good evening, friend," he said pleasantly. "Is there any entertainment in town tonight that would help a stranger while away the evening?"

The storekeeper straightened up from behind the counter and wiped the pickle brine off his hands. "I expect there's going to be a lecture tonight," he said. "I've been selling eggs all day."

1400. A famous speaker told this story after having been annoyed by a heckler: "When I was a boy on the farm, my father gave me a little donkey. 'This is a mighty fine animal,' he said, 'and I expect you to take good care of him. Always be sure to lock the barn door.'

"Well, one evening I forgot to lock the barn door; the donkey walked out and was run over by a truck. My father looked at the dead animal and said, 'Son, that animal will haunt you for the rest of your life.'

"And my father was right." The speaker pointed to the heckler and ended, "There sits that jackass now."

Punctuality

1401. It is never too late for a woman to keep an appointment.

1402. Strict punctuality is perhaps the cheapest virtue which can give force to an otherwise utterly insignificant character.

—F. J. BOYES

1403. I do think unpunctuality is a vile habit, and all my life I have been trying to break myself of it. The only straightforward course is to cut out one of two appointments and so catch up. But few men have the strength of mind to do this. It is better that one notability should be turned away expostulating from the doorstep, than that nine just deputations should each fume for ten minutes in a stuffy anteroom.

—Winston Churchill

Purpose, Singleness of

1404. The quickest way to do many things is to do only one thing at a time.

Quality—Qualities

1405. I have the simplest tastes. I am always satisfied with the best.

—Oscar Wilde

1406. Beautiful forms and compositions are not made by chance, nor can they, in any material, be made at small expense. A competition for cheapness and not excellence of workmanship is the most frequent and certain cause of the rapid decay and entire destruction of arts and manufactures.

—Josiah Wedgwood

1407. If a man has good corn, or wood, or boards, or pigs to sell, or can make better chairs or knives, crucibles, or church organs, than anybody else, you will find a broad, hard-beaten road to his house, though it be in the woods.

—Ralph Waldo Emerson

1408. When a customer buys a low-grade article, he feels pleased when he pays for it and displeased every time he uses it. But when he buys a well-made article, he feels extravagant when he pays for it and well pleased every time he uses it.

—Herbert N. Casson

Quarrel—Quarrels

1409. Two things, well considered, would prevent many quarrels: first, to have it well ascertained whether we are not disputing about terms, rather than things; secondly, to examine whether the thing on which we differ is worth contending about.

—CHARLES C. COLTON

Question—Answer—Questions—Answers

1410. It is a good answer which knows when to stop.

—Italian proverb

1411. It is better to ask some of the questions than to know all the answers.

—JAMES THURBER

1412. It isn't enough to ask intelligent questions; you have to listen thoughtfully to the answers.

Quotation—Quotations

1413. The words of great men do have a way of surviving in fragments fallen off the ruined structures of what were once whole speeches.

—MURRAY KEMPTON

1414. Whatever we may say against such collections of quotations, which present authors in disjointed form, they nevertheless bring about many excellent results. We are not always so composed, so full of wisdom, that we are able to take in at once the whole scope of a work according to its merits. Do we not mark in a book passages which seem to have a direct reference to ourselves? Young people especially, who have failed in acquiring a complete cultivation of mind, are roused in a praiseworthy way by brilliant passages.

—JOHANN WOLFGANG VON GOETHE

224

Race relations

1415. The rights for which the Negro is pressing are not things to be won. They already belong to him, morally and legally, and need only to be asserted.

1416. Integration is a moral imperative—the greatest moral imperative of our time. It is essential not so much for Negroes as for whites, who must learn to live in the great world in which they are the minority.

—Charles E. Silberman

1417. It is easy to see that racial discrimination undermines Negro children. But it's also true—though not as easily visible—that it is harmful to white children also. If they are told, for instance, that they must avoid Negroes because they are dirty or diseased or bad, they are really being taught that they must be afraid of them. This kind of fear also produces hate.

—Dr. Benjamin Spock

1418. Discrimination on the basis of race must be recognized as morally wrong, economically wasteful, and in many respects dangerous. . . . Every man and woman must have equal rights before the law, and an equal opportunity to vote and hold office, to be educated, to get a job and to be promoted when qualified, to buy a home, to participate fully in community affairs.

—Walter Norman May

1419. I am the inferior of any man whose rights I trample under my feet. Men are not superior by the accident of race or color; they are superior who have the best heart, the best brain. Superiority is born of honesty, of virtue, of charity, and above all, of the love of liberty. Of one thing you colored men can rest assured: the most intelligent, the grandest are on your side. The sympathies of the noblest are with you. Your enemies are also the enemies of liberty, of progress, and of justice.

—Julius Rosenwald

1420. A small Negro boy stood watching the balloon man at the country fair. Suddenly a red balloon broke loose and soared upward until it could scarcely be seen. So many people were attracted by the incident that the vendor thought it might be good business to let another go. So he slipped the string of a bright yellow balloon and, later, a white one. The little boy stood there, as if waiting for something. Finally he asked, "Mister, if you sent the black one up, would it go as high as the others?"

The balloon man, with an understanding smile, released the black balloon as he said, "Sonny, it isn't the color—it's the stuff inside that makes it rise."

1421. Many of us, in order to affirm our liberalism, declare that it requires us to be "color blind" wherever the equality of human beings is an issue. But the declaration is a barrier and a wall, not a guide and a bridge. For as a human trait, color-blindness is no virtue; color-blindness is a deficiency; color-blindness is a failure in seeing. To be realistically concerned about the status and well-being of humans whose skin-pigmentation is different from the actual pinkish-yellow that is called "white" is to be sensitive to the different pigmentation as it exists, to look upon the entire singularity of the individual of different color with sympathetic understanding of his struggles to make good his equal title to life, liberty, and the pursuit of happiness.

—Horace M. Kallen

1422. Long ago, a student of the American race question undertook a series of surveys. He asked representative American Negroes what their aspirations actually were. He asked a number of white Southerners what they thought Negro aspirations were. In the case of the Negroes, the No. 1 response was economic opportunity. At the very bottom of the Negroes' aspirations was that old bugaboo, social equality. In the case of the white Southerners, on the other hand, the results were precisely opposite: Economic opportunity was at the bottom of the list; social equality, at the top.

Here, very obviously, is one of the roots of the problem: There is a gross misunderstanding of what the Negro seeks. And the blindest, most irrational opposition to his efforts at self-expression comes from those who have the most wildly distorted notion of his goals.

Reading

1423. I would sooner read a timetable or a catalogue than nothing at all.

—W. Somerset Maugham

1424. To read merely for reading's sake, is almost as unprofitable as not reading at all.

—LEOPOLD H. GRINDON

1425. Sign in the Altanta Public Library: "Books do not pause to give a message from their sponsors."

—DON DORNBROOK

1426. The fuel for creative thinking comes from the thoughts of others, thoughts expressed in words and recorded in books.

—EDGAR S. ELLMAN

1427. There is a great deal of difference between the eager man who wants to read a book, and the tired man who wants a book to read.

—G. K. CHESTERTON

1428. If education did nothing more than to open the great and vital books, giving us the ability to read ourselves into and out of them, its worth were beyond all price.

—JOHN LANCASTER SPALDING

1429. Reading is magic. It makes the poorest man rich. It brings him wealth which no power can diminish, friends who never desert him, and pleasures that never end.

—EUGENE P. BERTIN

1430. If a man does not spend at least as much time in actively and definitely thinking about what he has read as he spent in reading, he is simply insulting his author.

—ARNOLD BENNETT

1431. The book which you read from a sense of duty, or because for any reason you must, does not commonly make friends with you. It may happen that it will yield you an unexpected delight, but this will be in its own unentreated way and in spite of your good intentions.

—WILLIAM DEAN HOWELLS

1432.   Our civilization is the sum of the knowledge and memories accumulated by the generations that have gone before us. We can only partake of it if we are able to make contact with ideas of these past generations.

The only way to do this—and so become a 'cultured' person—is by reading.

—ANDRE MAUROIS

1433.   Reading is one of the true pleasures of life. In our age of mass culture, when so much that we encounter is abridged, adapted, adulterated, shredded and boiled down, and commercialism's loud speakers are incessantly braying, it is mind-easing and mind-inspiring to sit down privately with a congenial book.

1434.   Have you ever rightly considered what the mere ability to read means? That it is the key which admits us to the whole world of thought and fancy and imagination, to the company of saint and sage, of the wisest and the wittiest at their wisest and wittiest moment? That it enables us to see with the keenest eyes, hear with the finest ears, and listen to the sweetest voices of all time? More than that, it annihilates time and space for us.

—JAMES RUSSELL LOWELL

Recreation

1435.   If I were a medical man, I would prescribe a holiday to any patient who considered his work important.

—BERTRAND RUSSELL

1436.   Recreation is not the highest kind of enjoyment; but in its time and place it is quite as proper as prayer.

—S. IRENAEUS PRIME

1437.   Recreation is intended to the mind as whetting is to the scythe, to sharpen the edge of it, which otherwise would grow dull and blunt.

—JOSEPH HALL

1438. The true purpose of recreation is not merely to amuse, not merely to afford pleasure, not merely to "kill time," but to increase our fitness, enhance our usefulness, spur achievement.

1439. You were intended not only to work, but to rest, laugh, play and have proper leisure and enjoyment. To develop an all-round personality you must have interest outside of your regular vocation that will serve to balance your business responsibilities.

—GRENVILLE KLEISER

1440. This is a tired age. People have not learned the blessed art of restful living and laboring. Everything they do is a burden to them. At work, at play, they are living tired, strained lives. People rush to their work and rush home. They rush to play and rush back. God did not mean for people to live in this manner. One of this generation's greatest needs is rest.

—REV. JAMES H. TAYLOR

Refusal

1441. Everybody knows how to say no, but it takes judgment to know when.

1442. There is something wanting in the man who does not hate himself whenever he is constrained to say no.

—ROBERT LOUIS STEVENSON

Religion

1443. Religion on earth is joy in heaven.

—WILLIAM S. DOWNEY

1444. Unless religion is free it is not religion.

—JOHANN GOTTFRIED ARNDT

1445. No man's religion ever survives his morals.

—ROBERT SOUTH, D. D.

1446. For the truly religious person, every day is Sunday.

1447. To neglect the church on the Sabbath is to break an appointment with God.
—Dr. William Arthur Ward

1448. Some people use religion like a bus—they ride on it only when it is going their way.
—Dale W. Campbell

1449. The upshot of all religion is to please God in order to make ourselves happy.
—Thomas Sherlock

1450. Since God suffers all religions to exist, it doth not become man to proscribe or persecute any.
—Theodoric

1451. Religion can be both steering wheel and brake; it can guide you along the right road and stop you at the wrong one.

1452. Our religion is our love affair with life, and no man who is not in love with life has a religion worthy of the name.
—Kenneth L. Patton

1453. Religion is not mere truth, gained by study, and retained by watchfulness in the soul. It is truth translated into actions, embodied in life.

1454. Nothing exposes religion more to the reproach of its enemies than the worldliness and hard-heartedness of the professors of it.
—Matthew Henry

1455. Let me always remember that it is not the amount of religious knowledge which I have, but the amount which I use, that determines my religious position and character.

—ALEXANDER MACLAREN

1456. The worst of errors is to believe that any one religion has the monopoly of goodness. For every man, that religion is good which makes him gentle, upright and kind.

—ERNEST RENAN

1457. The danger is not in the collapse of the churches, but in the preoccupation with the complexities of modern life. If religion is to be relevant, it must take into account the environment in which it lives.

—DR. CLARENCE E. LEMMON

1458. Religion is the answer to that cry of Reason which nothing can silence, that aspiration of the soul which no created thing can meet, that want of the heart which all creation cannot supply.

—ISAAC THOMAS HECKER

1459. Remove from the history of the past all those actions which have either sprung directly from the religious nature of man, or been modified by it, and you have the history of another world and of another race.

—MARK HOPKINS

1460. There are a good many pious people who are as careful of their religion as of their best service of china, only using it on holy occasions, for fear it should get chipped or flawed in working-day wear.

—DOUGLAS JERROLD

1461. Every religion has in common one element: faith! Faith is important, for it gives value to our word which makes it effective. Faith is the conscious realization that the thing we believe is so. We cannot reach out and draw faith to us, it is something within the self. It is an attitude of thought which is not subjectively denied.

1462. Religion is not an insurance policy promising the holder that he can surrender it for his salvation. Instead, it is a way of life that begins with faith in the heart and remains steadfast through the gauntlet of human frailties, gaining strength with each conquest. It is peace and compassion and the strength to forgive transgressions; silent, humble piety.

—Douglas Meador

1463. I believe in the proverb that any religion is better than no religion, because every man's conception of goodness and duty is an advance of his character; and when this conception is embodied in an object of worship, it becomes an elevating power upon his life that makes him capable of a certain degree of civilization.

—J. G. Holland

1464. Men use religion just as they use buoys and lifepreservers; they do not intend to navigate the vessel with them. but they keep just enough of them on hand to float into a safe harbor when a storm comes up and the vessel is shipwrecked; and it is only then that they intend to use them. I tell you, you will find air-holes in all such life-preservers as that.

—Noah Porter

1465. But when science, passing beyond its own limits, assumes to take the place of theology, and sets up its own conception of the order of nature as a sufficient account of its cause, it is invading a province of thought to which it has no claim, and not unreasonably provokes the hostility of its best friends.

—M. B. Carpenter

1466. It is only religion, the great bond of love and duty to God, that makes any existence valuable or even tolerable. Without this, to live were only to graze. Without this, the beauties of the world are but splendid gewgaws, the stars of heaven glittering orbs of ice, and, what is yet far worse and colder, the trials of existence profitless and unadulterated miseries.

—Horace Bushnell

1467. One may be as straight as a gun barrel theologically and as empty as a gun barrel spiritually. So often it turns out that fundamental and orthodox Christians become so severe in condemning false doctrine, gnashing their teeth at every sniff of heresy, that they end up without love. One may do a right thing in a wrong way. The same Paul who wrote, ". . . though we, or an angel from heaven, preach any other gospel . . . let him be accursed," also wrote the love chapter of Corinthians. Unless we can get that combination we shall be theological Hawkshaws and doctrinal detectives, religious bloodhounds looking for heretics, with hot heads and cold hearts.

—Vance Havner

1468. Religion does not consist in marble pillars, nor in costly vestments; it is not found in elegant churches or prettily bound books; robbing your neighbor six days in the week, and going to church on the seventh is not religion; devoting a lifetime to gathering pennies is not religion. Religion is that confidence in God which impels us always to trust in Him; marriage is religion; the love of husband and wife is religion; the affection of brother and sister is religion; the love of father and son, of mother and daughter, of mother and son—all these are religion.

—George G. Lippard

Reputation

1469. "I've heard so much about you. Now, let's hear your side of the story."

1470. He who has once the fame to be an early riser may sleep till noon.

—James Howell

1471. Some people pay so much attention to their reputation that they lose their character.

1472.   The rope is burned: Its twistings, still,
          The pallid ash retains.
     The man is dead: What good or ill
          He wrought in life remains.

—From the Chinese

Resourcefulness

1473. There is a service station operator in a southwestern state who gives a penny-a-gallon discount to drivers who pull up to the row of gasoline pumps closest to his office door—that's where he sits to keep cool in the summer and warm in the winter.

1474. A busy PTA room mother, inviting parents to a potluck supper, typed a letter with several carbons. But she made a mistake and put the carbon in backward. Not having time to do the job over, she just added a postscript: "If you want to know what this letter says, please hold it up to a mirror." They all came.

1475. A famed concert artist was asked about his feeling lonely during a tour of one-nighters. Not at all, he replied. He resorts to a never-failing trick to assure himself pleasant company. "After each concert," he said, "people line up backstage to congratulate me. When I see an attractive lady on the line, I rip a button off my vest. Then, when she congratulates me, I modestly say to her, 'What good is it all? I don't even have someone to sew this button on.' Invariably she volunteers, and stays."

—LEONARD LYONS

1476. Michelangelo was probably the world's greatest artist and sculptor. He was also a superb applied psychologist. At first, he was ignored and disdained by his own generation, Michelangelo, however, had faith in his ability and decided to use some psychology on his critics. Knowing that they were fascinated by excavating in old ruins to dig up supposedly priceless works of art, he tinted one of his masterpieces and then had it buried where an excavating party would be sure to find it. The critics were enraptured. They pronounced it an antique of rare value. The Cardinal of San Giorgio was so impressed that he paid a huge sum to add it to his art collection. Then, Michelangelo deftly let the cat out of the bag! Well, what could the art critics do? They were so far out on a limb that they had to admit that Michelangelo was an artistic genius. After that, Michelangelo was commissioned to do important work.

—DR. GEORGE W. CRANE

Retirement

1477. There's hardly a man alive who could not retire very comfortably in his old age if he could sell his experience for what it cost him.

1478.   Retirement is not the closing of an old door, but the opening of a new one. It is the exciting approach to an infinite variety of new testing of a man's ability, new stretchings of his mind, new releases for his energies and abilities. All that is required is that he must recognize new challenge when it presents itself, and accept it zestfully. If he has been doing this all his life, it will be easier for him in the later years, but in one form or another the opportunity awaits everyone, if he will only seek it.

—CLARENCE RANDALL

1479.   For most men there should come a time of shifting harness, of lightening the load one way and adjusting it for greater effectiveness in another. That is the time for the second career, time for the old dog to perform new tricks. The new career may bring in little money; it may be concerned only with good works. On the other hand, it may bring in much-needed support. It can be a delight to a man who comes at last to a well-earned job instead of a well-earned rest.

—DR. WILDER PENFIELD

1480.   ON MY RETIREMENT

What does one do? What does one say,
When finally comes that fateful day.
The news you've wanted long to hear
You're to be retired—sometime—next year.

What does one say? What does one do
When told his job at the Mill is through.
Does one shout hurrah or shed a tear?
Or is this the news you're glad to hear?

You joke and say that you've waited long
For this big day to come along.
When all your worries will be o'er
And it isn't your turn to keep the score.

The years roll by as they always do
And before you know it your day is through.
I like to think I've done my best
And that I deserve a well-earned rest.

More time for golf and time to fish
Or go on a cruise if I should wish.
More time to lend a helping hand
To all the needy in the land.

> I like to think that many folk
> Have found in me a friend.
> That I have helped them o'er life's way,
> And been loyal to the end.
>
> —DON BUCKRELL

Retraction—Retractions

1481. There is no indigestion worse than that which comes from having to eat your own words.

1482. There is nothing more tragic in life than the utter impossibility of changing what you have done.

—JOHN GALSWORTHY

Retrogression

1483. You can't sit on the lid of progress. If you do, you will be blown to pieces.

—HENRY KAISER

1484. Does the going seem to be a little easier lately? Better check to make sure you're not going downhill.

Retrospection

1485. It is the mark of a good action that it appears inevitable in retrospect.

—ROBERT LOUIS STEVENSON

1486. I want to do away with everything behind man, so that there is nothing to see when he looks back. I want to take him by the scruff of his neck and turn his face toward the future!

—LEONID ANDREYEV

1487. Probably no one alive hasn't at one time or another brooded over the possibility of going back to an earlier, ideal age in his existence and living a different kind of life. It is perhaps mankind's favorite daydream.

—HAL BOYLE

Revenge

1488. Who hath not courage to revenge will never find generosity to forgive.

—HENRY HOME

1489. Revenge is, of all satisfactions, the most costly and drawn-out; retributive persecution is, of all policies, the most pernicious.

—WINSTON CHURCHILL

1490. On him that takes revenge, revenge shall be taken, and by a real evil he shall dearly pay for the goods that are but airy and fantastical; it is like a rolling stone, which, when a man hath forced up a hill, will return upon him with a greater violence, and break those bones whose sinews gave it motion.

—JEREMY TAYLOR

1491. Certainly in taking revenge a man is but even with his enemy, but in passing it over he is superior, for it is a prince's part to pardon. And Solomon, I am sure, said "It is the glory of a man to pass by the offence." That which is past is gone and irrevocable and wise men have enough to do with things present and to come; therefore they do but trifle with themselves that labor in past matters.

—FRANCIS BACON

Romance

1492. A boy shouldn't ask for a girl's hand unless he is in a position to remove it from her father's pocket.

—HAL CHADWICK

1493. If you cannot inspire a woman with love of you, fill her above the brim with love of herself; all that runs over will be yours.

—CHARLES C. COLTON

1494. Sooner or later a man gives up trying to understand women and is satisfied just to marry one.

1495. Cavemen found June the most suitable month for acquiring a bride. Tradition says they had recovered from the rigors of winter and still had time to store food and furs before the next one. With time on their hands, they found the sunny month of June an ideal time to go forth and capture a bride.

Rumor—Rumors

1496. Rumors without a leg to stand on have a way of getting around anyway.

1497. It isn't hard to make a mountain out of a molehill. Just add a little dirt.

Sainthood

1498. Many people genuinely do not wish to be saints, and it is probable that some who achieve or aspire to sainthood have never felt much temptation to be human beings.

—GEORGE ORWELL

Salesmanship

1499. The power of suggestion is strong. People like to have it assumed that they can afford the best, even when they can't. A humble selling attitude leads to humble sales, and vice versa. It's much easier to trade down than up!

—FRANK W. GRAY

1500. Whether we know it or not, we're all engaged in selling something—if not our wares, then our personalities, our services, our ideas. As a matter of fact, all human relationships are based upon selling of one kind or another, and we all engage in it whenever we undertake to persuade others to our way of thinking.

—CALUDE BRISTON

1501. Ten Characteristics of a Master Salesman:

1. Persistence. Not insistence. The master salesman hangs on a little longer, works a little harder.

2. Imagination. He harnesses his imagination to practical plans that produce sales.

3. Vision. The present is just the beginning. He is impressed with the possibilities of the future.

4. Sincerity.

5. Integrity. He deserves the trust that others place in him.

6. Poise. He isn't overbearing, but is friendly, assured.

7. Thoughtfulness. He has his eye on the future.

8. Common sense. Good judgment based upon resaon.

9. Altruism. "Love thy neighbor as theyself."

10. Initiative. Try it and see—and do it now.

—ELMER G. LETERMAN

Science

1502. Every succeeding scientific discovery makes greater nonsense of old-time conceptions of sovereignty.

—ANTHONY EDEN

1503. The final test of science is not whether its accomplishments add to our comfort, knowledge, and power; but whether it adds to our dignity as men, our sense of truth and beauty. It is a test that science cannot pass alone and unaided.

—DAVID SARNOFF

1504. The aim of science is to seek the simplest explanations of complex facts. We are apt to fall into the error of thinking that the facts are simple because simplicity is the goal of our quest. The guiding motto in the life of every natural philosopher should be: Seek simplicity and distrust it.

—ALFRED NORTH WHITEHEAD

Science—Religion

1505. The intellectual content of religions has always finally adapted itself to scientific and social conditions after they have become clear. . . . For this reason I do not think that those who are concerned about the future of a religious attitude should trouble themselves with the conflict of science with traditional doctrines.

—JOHN DEWEY

Season—Seasons

1506. April prepares her green traffic light and all the world thinks GO!

1507. The first day of spring is one thing and the first spring day is another. The difference between them is sometimes as great as a month.

—HENRY VAN DYKE

Secret—Secrets—Secrecy

1508. A secret confided is no longer a secret.

1509. No one ever keeps a secret so well as a child.

—VICTOR HUGO

Security

1510. There is no security on this earth; there is only opportunity.

—GENERAL DOUGLAS MACARTHUR

1511. No one can build his security upon the nobleness of another person.

—WILLA CATHER

1512.   No one, from the beginning of time, has ever had security. When you leave your house you do not know what will happen on the other side of the door. Anything is possible. But we do not stay home on that account.

—ELEANOR ROOSEVELT

Self-appraisal

1513.   It is as hard to see one's self as to look backwards without turning around.

—HENRY DAVID THOREAU

1514.   Better a man who knows his own stupidities than a man who's too sure of everything.

—STEPHEN BECKER

1515.   It is always well to accept your own shortcomings with candor but to regard those of your friends with polite incredulity.

—RUSSELL LYNES

1516.   Neither human applause nor human censure is to be taken as the test of truth; but either should set us upon testing ourselves.

—RICHARD WHATELY

1517.   The clown is the symbol of the urge of men to laugh at fellow humans and of their need to laugh at themselves. Though he has often changed his dress, make-up, and antics, his contribution has always been essentially the same: to show the folly of taking oneself too seriously.

Self-confidence

1518.   Self-confidence is the first requisite to great undertakings.

—DR. SAMUEL JOHNSON

1519.   Self-confidence is a virtue that should never lead to a single life; it should be wedded to tireless energy.

—WILLIAM G. JORDAN

Self-control

1520. I have sometimes said the scarcest personal quality in our world today is genuine, deep, sustaining self-confidence. Look behind the behavior of the bully, the egotist, the show-off, the whiner, the dictator, and you will almost always find a lack of belief in self.

—Joe Batten

1521. The man who is smugly confident that he has arrived is ripe for the return trip. So is the business concern. A measure of self-confidence, even a large measure of self-confidence, is an asset when you are battling to forge your way to the top. But cocksureness is not an asset but a liability, a handicap.

—B. C. Forbes

1522. Any man who wants to succeed must begin by believing wholeheartedly in his own ability. He cannot expect others to believe in him unless he believes in himself, for it is a cardinal rule of life that the world takes a man at his own valuation.

Self-confidence begets the confidence in others that creates opportunity. Given that, a man has a chance to prove what he can do. Without confidence in himself, a man may never attract opportunity; and without opportunity, he cannot prove his worth.

Self-control

1523. To rule one's anger is well; to prevent it is better.

—Tryon Edwards

1524. To handle yourself, use your head; to handle others, use your heart.

1525. A real test of courtesy and restraint is to have an ailment just like the other fellow is describing and not mention it.

Self-importance

1526. About the smallest package there is, is a man all wrapped up in himself.

1527. Most of the trouble in the world is caused by people wanting to be important.

—T. S. Eliot

1528. When a person feels disposed to overestimate his own importance, let him remember that mankind got along very well before his birth, and that in all probability they will get along very well after his death.

—Charles Simmons

1529. A newly-appointed bishop, received by Pope John XXIII in a private audience, complained that the burden of his new office prevented him from sleeping. "Oh," said John kindly, "the very same thing happened to me in the first few weeks of my pontificate, but then one day my guardian angel appeared to me in a daydream and whispered, 'Giovanni, don't take yourself so seriously.' And ever since then I've been able to sleep."

1530. Sometimes a good story can do more to convey a pertinent truth than a well-written essay or a pointed sermon. Here is one that was recounted by John B. Reilly in an issue of *Rotarian Magazine*, in answer to the question: "How do you salvage a good man who gets a big head?"

The owner of a big gravel outfit had such a man. He called him in one day.

"Bill," he said, "you're the best superintendent we've had and I'm giving you a vacation on full pay."

Bill beamed, "How long?"

"There's no time limit. Stay away—well, till you're sure the business can get along as well without you as with you."

Bill grinned some more. Days and weeks passed. A month, no S. O. S. from the boss. Bill got the idea all right, and one day showed up— considerably humbled.

Self-interest

1531. He who cares only for himself in his youth will be a very niggard in manhood, and a wretched miser in old age.

—J. Hawes

1532. Man's main interest in life, the one subject that never bores him—is himself. Pen salesmen say that at least 97 out of every 100 people who try out a fountain pen, sign their own names. The three self-effacing souls merely make funny doodles.

Selfishness

1533.   Man seeks his own good at the whole world's cost.
—ROBERT BROWNING

1534.   The human being who lives only for himself finally reaps nothing but unhappiness. Selfishness corrodes. Unselfishness ennobles, satisfies. Don't put off the joy derivable from doing helpful, kindly things for others.

1535.   The selfish man cuts away the sand from under his own feet, he digs his own grave; and every time, from the beginning of the world until now, God Almighty pushes him into the grave and covers him up.
—C. H. FOWLER

Self-knowledge

1536.   It is the individual who knows how little he knows about himself who stands a reasonable chance of finding out something about himself before he dies.
—S. I. HAYAKAWA

1537.   To know oneself is, above all, to know what one lacks. It is to measure oneself against truth, and not the other way around. The first product of self-knowledge is humility.
—FLANNERY O'CONNOR

Self-respect

1538.   Without self-respect there can be no genuine success. Success won at the cost of self-respect is not success—for what shall it profit a man if he gain the whole world and lose his own self-respect?
—B. C. FORBES

1539. Self-respect cannot be hunted. It cannot be purchased. It is never for sale. . . . It comes to us when we are alone, in quiet moments, in quiet places, when we suddenly realize that, knowing the good, we have done it; knowing the beautiful, we have served it; knowing the truth, we have spoken it.

—A. WHITNEY GRISWOLD

Self-restraint

1540. A man's worst difficulties begin when he is able to do as he likes.

—THOMAS HUXLEY

1541. When you restrain yourself from relieving your feelings at the expense of somebody else, when you restrain yourself from making somebody else unhappy for the satisfaction of speaking your mind—you prove that you have advanced out of the hair-trigger stage of prehistoric days. Man's earliest ancestors didn't stop to think. Stopping to think is the true test of civilization.

—GROVER PATTERSON

Service

1542. Success satisfies but for a season; fame with a fearful finality; power passes with painful persistence; service to others abides without end.

1543. By rendering service men become taller. The more service one gives, the greater the growth. Through unselfish service even the smallest can become larger.

Sharing

1544. Men of the noblest dispositions think themselves happiest when others share their happiness with them.

—JEREMY TAYLOR

1545.   SHARING
I know not why God gave me bounteous store,
While others, worthy, beg around my door.
I know not why I should have more than they,
Unless He meant that I should give a part away.
                                        —RUTH SMELTZER

1546.   The greatest delight I take in what I learn is the teaching
of it to others; for there is no relish . . . in the possession of anything without a partner. . . . If wisdom itself were offered me upon condition only
of keeping it to myself, I should undoubtedly refuse it.
                                        —SENECA

1547.   The deepest experiences and satisfactions of human life come
ultimately because sooner or later we all learn to care for someone in particular and for others in general. Wealth, reputation, achievement, and
all else, sour, limit one's life, or become useless unless shared with or related
to other lives.
                                        —EDNA P. BRUNER

Shirking

1548.   It takes just as much effort to escape work as to do it.

1549.   Some people always grab the stool when there is a piano to
be moved.

Silence

1550.   There is nothing so like a wise man as a fool who holds his
tongue.

1551.   A good word is an easy obligation; but not to speak ill,
requires only our silence, which costs us nothing.
                                        —JOHN TILLOTSON

Sin—Sins

1552. A believer is far more apt to be burdened with a sense of sin, and to feel the fear of it in his own character than an unbeliever; because if we are carried along the stream we fear nothing, and it is only when we strive against it, that its progress and power are discernible.

—JOHN OWEN

1553. You cannot stay the shell in its flight; after it has left the mortar, it goes on to its mark, and there explodes, dealing destruction all around. Just as little can you stay the consequences of a sin after it has been committed. You may repent of it, you may even be forgiven for it, but still it goes on its deadly and desolating way. It has passed entirely beyond your reach; once done, it cannot be undone.

—WILLIAM M. TAYLOR

Sincerity

1554. Judge thyself with the judgment of sincerity, and thou wilt judge others with the judgment of charity.

—J. M. MASON

1555. Try how much of the word of God you can understand, and what is more, try how much you can practice. A sincere wish and purpose to *do* the will of God, will be your best way to know the mind of God.

—JOHN ANGEL JAMES

1556. The only guide to a man is his conscience; the only shield to his memory is the rectitude and sincerity of his actions. It is very imprudent to walk through life without this shield, because we are so often mocked by the failure of our hopes; but with this shield, however the Fates may play, we march always in the ranks of honor.

—WINSTON CHURCHILL

Singlehandedness

1557. When a man becomes convinced that he can achieve his ambition without regard for those around him, he can easily end in complete failure.

—GILBERT W. CHAPMAN

Skill

1558. In the fifteenth century, the art directors of the City of Florence wanted a new statue to adorn one of the local churches. They first thought of the well-known sculptor, Donatello, but he quoted a price of 50 *scudi* which the good directors thought was too much.

After consultation among themselves, they decided that a lesser-known artist ought to be able to produce a satisfactory statue at a considerable savings. So confident were they that Donatello's price was high, they hired one of his ex-pupils without even asking him what he would charge. To their astonishment, when the work was completed he demanded 80 *scudi*.

The indignant directors called upon Donatello to arbitrate the dispute with his one-time pupil. Donatello set the price at 70 *scudi*, a little less than the artist demanded but a lot more than the directors expected. One of them asked him why he would award 70 *scudi* for a statue he had offered to carve himself for only 50 *scudi*, especially since the work done was obviously inferior to what Donatello would have produced.

The renown artist replied: "Being a master of the art, I could have produced my work in a month and would have been fairly paid at 50 *scudi*. This fellow, with his talents and skill, took six months. Even at 70 *scudi* his wage each month was only one-fourth of mine."

Smoking

1559. Inscription on a cigarette lighter: "To my matchless wife."

1560. It is now proved beyond doubt that smoking is one of the leading causes of statistics.

1561. Those giving up cigarette smoking aren't the heroes. The real heroes are the rest of us—who have to listen to them.

1562. Pipesmokers are almost invariably solid, reliable citizens. They spend so much time cleaning, filling, and fooling with their pipes they don't have time to get into mischief.

1563. The fellow who now wishes he had quit smoking last New Year's Day and saved the money for this Christmas may get some consolation from the fellow who did quit to save money but hasn't the slightest idea where it went.

1564. An English housewife was determined to make her husband quit smoking. In her opinion smoking was a waste of money, saying, "You might as well toss it down the drain." So every time her husband lit a cigarette she did just that. She threw 2s. 6d. (about 35 cents) down the nearest sewer. He held out until she had thrown away about $50.00 and then gave up his cigarettes.

Socialism

1565. Socialism is the philosophy of failure, the creed of ignorance and the gospel of envy.

—WINSTON CHURCHILL

1566. What is the difference between capitalism and socialism? Capitalism makes social errors, but socialism makes capital errors.

1567. There are two places where Socialism will work: In Heaven where it is not needed, and in Hell where they already have it.

—WINSTON CHURCHILL

Solitude

1568. The strongest man is the one who stands most alone.

—HENRIK IBSEN

1569. Those beings only are fit for solitude, who like nobody, and are liked by nobody.

—JOHANN ZIMMERMAN

1570. Our language has wisely sensed the two sides of man's being alone. It has created the word "loneliness" to express the pain of being alone. And it has created the word "solitude" to express the glory of being alone.

—PAUL TILLICH

Sorrow—Sorrows

1571. Sorrows remembered sweeten present joys.

—R. POLLOK

1572. There is a joy in sorrow which none but a mourner can know.

—M. F. TUPPER

1573. That grief is the most durable which flows inward, and buries its streams with its fountain, in the depths of the heart.

—JANE PORTER

1574. The capacity of sorrow belongs to our grandeur; and the loftiest of our race are those who have had the profoundest grief, because they have had the profoundest sympathies.

—HENRY GILES

Soul, The

1575. Just as the sun draws water from nature's reservoir to nurture man's crops without the reservoir going dry, so also is it with man's reservoir of soul if he keeps open the inlet and outlet of his spiritual being. The waters of the Dead Sea turn to salt because, while it has an inlet, it has no outlet. Isn't that a parable of man? He has to feed his body by what he takes in but to nurture his soul he must have an outlet for his love and loyalty, service and sacrifice.

—HENRY H. SCHOOLEY

1576. Two things a master commits to his servant's care—the child and the child's clothes. It will be a poor excuse for the servant to say, at his master's return, "Sir, here are all the child's clothes, neat and clean, but the child is lost." Just so of the account that many will give to God of their souls and bodies at the great day. "Lord, here is my body; I am very grateful for it; I neglected nothing that belonged to its contents and welfare; but as for my soul, that is lost and cast away forever. I took little care and thought about it."

—JOHN FLAVEL

250

Specialization

1577. Specialists are called narrow. Well, an arrow is narrow, too.

Speech—Speeches

1578. The mouth of a wise man is in his heart; the heart of a fool is in his mouth, because what he knoweth or thinketh he uttereth.

—The Bible

1579. "It is always interesting to watch the wives of the men making the speeches," said a long-time observer. "Just about every shade of emotion is shown—pride, dismay, uncertainty, persevering loyalty, and patient endurance; once in a while a look that says, 'Now what did you say that for?'"

1580. The man who loses his temper often thinks he is doing something rather fine and majestic. On the contrary, so far is this from being the fact, he is merely making an ass of himself.

—Arnold Bennett

Spending

1581. To spend before earning is to rest before working, to teach before learning, to speak before thinking, and to build before planning.

—Dr. William Arthur Ward

1582. What a man does with his wealth depends upon his idea of happiness. Those who draw prizes in life are apt to spend tastelessly, if not viciously; not knowing that it requires as much talent to spend as to make.

—E. P. Whipple

Statistics

1583. Statistics are to a speech what lumps are to mashed potatoes: the fewer the better.

—J. Lewis Powell

Stature

1584. One hundred men went into the woods to cut logs. They took along two women to cook for them. Before the winter ended, two of the men married the women. This was normal. However, a statistician startled outsiders by reporting that two per cent of the men married 100 per cent of the women!

1585. On the basis of statistics, space travel is still a very safe form of travel. In recent years there have been no fatalities. In the same period there have been countless thousands of fatal accidents in the air, on the road and by rail and sea travel. (1968)

Stature

1586. When little men cast shadows, it is a sign that the sun is setting.

—WALTER SAVAGE LANDOR

Status

1587. Status: sitting on the platform so that you can look down on everybody.

1588. If all were determined to play the first violin we should never have a complete orchestra. Therefore respect every musician in his proper place.

—ROBERT SCHUMANN

Status quo

1589. Don't let your status become too quo.

1590. Freedom from anxiety is not the most important goal in life. The ideas, inventions and techniques that make for social progress usually have their origin in the minds of anxious or discontented persons.

The advances and improvements in the social complex generally come from those who are dissatisfied with its status, can see its shortcomings and have the inclination and ability to devise better methods, materials and equipment. These are the individuals who are alert and anxious about the status quo and who undertake to improve it. Anxiety is necessary for progress.

Stick-to-itiveness

1591. Who gives up when behind is cowardly. Who gives up when ahead is foolish.

—Dr. William Arthur Ward

1592. It's the steady, constant driving to the goal for which you're striving, not the speed with which you travel, that will make your victory sure; it's the everlasting gaining, without whimper or complaining at the burdens you are bearing or the woes you must endure.

It's the holding to a purpose, and never giving in; it's the cutting down the distance by the little that you win; it's the iron will to do it, and the steady sticking to it, so whate'er your task, go to it! Keep your grin and plug along.

Substitute—Substitutes

1593. Thomas K. Beecher was called upon unexpectedly to substitute for his famous brother, Henry Ward Beecher. People who had come to hear the noted preacher started to leave during the singing of the first hymn. Thomas stopped the hymn and announced, "Those who came to worship my brother may leave; but let those who came to worship God join me in singing the rest of the hymn."

—Robert W. Youngs

Success

1594. The successful person is the one who went ahead and did the thing I always intended to do.

—Ruth Smeltzer

1595. About the best way for a young fellow to become successful is to look for work after he gets a job.

1596. Perhaps, for worldly success, we need virtues that make us loved and faults that make us feared.

—Joseph Joubert

1597. The penalty of success is to be bored by the attentions of people who formerly snubbed you.

—Mary Wilson Little

1598. The secret of financial success is to spend what you have left after saving, instead of saving what is left after spending.

1599. Niccolo Paganini, the great violinist, was once asked to give the secret of his success. His reply was offered in three words: *Toil, solitude, prayer.*

1600. In many businesses, today will end at five o'clock. Those bent on success, however, make today last from yesterday right through tomorrow.

—Lawrence H. Martin

1601. To maintain that our successes are due to Providence and not to our own cleverness is a cunning way of increasing in our own eyes the importance of our successes.

—Cesare Pavese

1602. Nature gave men two ends—one to sit on and one to think with. Ever since then man's success or failure has been dependent on the one he used most.

—George R. Kirkpatrick

1603. Failure is part of success. . . .A man's success is made up of failures, because he experiments and ventures every day. . . .The power of persistence, of enduring defeat and of gaining victory by defeats, is one of those forces which never loses its charm.

—Ralph Waldo Emerson

1604. What is known as success assumes nearly as many aliases as there are those who seek it. Like love, it can come to commoners as well as courtiers. Like virtue, it is its own reward. Like the Holy Grail, it seldom appears to those who don't pursue it.

—Stephen Birmingham

1605. No amount of money got by questionable expedients can win success or bring happiness. The things that are most worthwhile in life are really those within reach of almost every normal human being who cares to seek them.

—B. C. Forbes

1606. It is no wisdom ever to commend or discommend the actions of men by their success; for oftentimes some enterprises attempted by good counsel end unfortunately, and others unadvisedly taken in hand have happy success.

—Sir Walter Raleigh

1607. The people cannot look to legislation generally for success. Industry, thrift, character are not conferred by act or resolve. Government cannot relieve from toil. It can provide no substitute for the rewards of service.

—Calvin Coolidge

1608. True success is never an end in itself. A man may call a million dollars a success, and sit down to ease with it. But a great artist, a great organizer, a great engineer, a great missionary, a great hero finds in success only a step toward more effort and achievement.

1609. Don't try to be the richest man in the world, for you will always have Rockefellers and Morgans. Don't try to be the strongest man in the world, for there will always be someone stronger. But have five minutes more patience than your opponent, and you will be the victor.

—Nicolas Risini

1610. Most of us know men who succeed in a big way, and yet who exhibit only an ordinary amount of intelligence and ability. If we analyze their success we shall generally find that they are conspicuous above other men, even above those of greater powers in one striking particular—they have implicit confidence in their ability to do whatever they attempt.

1611.   Success cannot be fairly judged by what we have, but by what we are doing with it. The successful person is not one who has accumulated much, but one who is participating in life in a useful, profitable way. Money that is hoarded is a greater responsibility than it is an asset, and causes more anxiety than it gives pleasure. Knowledge that is acquired without being used becomes meaningless. Intellectual achievements may inflate the ego, but they bring neither prosperity nor honor unless they are applied to constructive purposes. Success thrives on giving more than on getting.

1612.   Natural talent, intelligence, a wonderful education—none of these guarantees success. Something else is needed: The sensitivity to understand what other people want and the willingness to give it to them. Worldly success depends on pleasing others. No one is going to win fame, recognition, or advancement just because he thinks he deserves it. Someone else has to think so, too.

—JOHN LUTHER

1613.   Real success is not an outward show but an inward feeling. It begins inside, and probably its first inkling is the feeling, even the knowledge, that one is worth while. That's quite a discovery. Regardless of how the rest of the world may value us, there is no fooling the inner Bureau of Standards.

—HOWARD J. WHITMAN

1614.   Successful people rarely consider work as just so much labor; they regard it in the nature of an opportunity for service and find enjoyment in and derive success from it. Work brings compensations of greater value than the money it may pay. The person who makes money his sole object of labor is cheating himself and others. To be successful an individual's efforts must be supported by something more substantial than the desire to make money. They must have back of them the ideal and spirit of service. Success will come in proportion to the efficiency with which that ideal and that spirit are developed and expressed.

1615. There are six big reasons why men find their way into top management positions:

They know how to manage other men;

They know how to read what is behind the figures of the business;

They think simply;

Problems never take them by surprise;

They have imagination about the public;

They have faith in human nature.

—ROBERT R. UPDEGRAFF

1616. Success is not rare—it is common. Very few miss a measure of it. It is not a matter of luck, or contesting—for certainly no success can come from preventing the success of another. It is a matter of adjusting one's efforts to obstacles and one's abilities to a service needed by others. There is no other possible success. But most people think of it in terms of getting; success, however, begins in terms of giving.

—HENRY FORD, SR.

1617. The one outstanding trait of every successful man, whatever his business or profession may be, is confidence in himself. His opinions of others may vary, but one thing that never falters is the conviction he has about what he, himself, can do. He is certain that he can accomplish anything to which he puts his mind and skills. He not only has faith, but the courage to back it up. He wastes no time worrying about what others may think or say; nor does he listen long to the doubts and fears of the timid ones. He makes his own bold decisions, sets a mark for himself that is reasonable to attain, and never doubts his ability to reach it.

1618. You will attain true success when your efforts confer a direct and lasting benefit on your fellow men as well as on yourself; when you are actuated by a sincere desire to help others; when your standard of success is based on self-interest plus the interest of others; the greatest individual successes are always found to be those noble characters who have labored that others would benefit.

Again, true success is achieved when you have made the best use of your time for a worthy purpose, when you have studied, cultivated and developed your physical and mental equipment to the highest possible degree of efficiency. Health, contentment and happiness are the rewards of the right use of your equipment.

—DR. HAMILTON CAMERON

Suffering

1619. The great majority of conspicuously successful men are early risers. Many men of far-flung affairs have a half day's work done by ten o'clock. By the time other folks get around, these men are more or less free to receive visitors, hold consultations with their own associates, attend meetings, and so forth. An early start enables them to drive their business. Often, the late starter finds his business driving him; he is so busy striving to catch up with each day's duties that he has little time for thought, reflection, for initiative, for exercising foresight. Moral: To get up in the world, get up early in the morning.

—B. C. FORBES

1620. Here are ten rules for success that have been attributed to Thomas Jefferson:

1. Never put off until tomorrow what you can do today.
2. Never trouble another for what you can do yourself.
3. Never spend your money before you have earned it.
4. Never buy what you don't want because it is cheap.
5. Pride costs more than hunger, thirst, or cold.
6. We seldom repent of eating too little.
7. Nothing is troublesome that we do willingly.
8. Avoid worry. How much pain the evils have cost us that have never happened!
9. Take things always by the smooth handle.
10. When angry, count ten before you speak; if very angry, count a hundred.

Suffering

1621. It is easier to suffer in silence if you are sure someone is watching.

Suicide

1622. The coward sneaks to death; the brave live on.

—DR. GEORGE SEWELL

Sunday school

1623. The parent who gives his child 75 cents for a movie and a dime for Sunday School is teaching him a set of values that could carry through a lifetime.

258

Superstition—Superstitions

1624. Superstition is but the fear of belief; religion is the confidence.

—LADY BLESSINGTON

1625. Superstition is a senseless fear of God; religion the pious worship of God.

—CICERO

Survival

1626. What is fit to survive does survive and what is unfit perishes.

—D'ARCY W. THOMPSON

1627. If a thing is old, it is a sign that it was fit to live. Old families, old customs, old styles survive because they are fit to survive. The guarantee of continuity is quality. Submerge the good in a flood of the new, and the good will come back to join the good which the new brings with it. Old-fashioned hospitality, old-fashioned politeness, old-fashioned honor in business had qualities of survival. These will come back.

—CAPTAIN EDDIE RICKENBACKER

Suspicion—Suspicions

1628. What you don't know never hurts you—it's what you suspect that causes all the trouble.

1629. He that is never suspected is either very much esteemed or very much despised.

—GEORGE SAVILE (Marquis of Halifax)

1630. It would be well for all of us to remember that suspicion is far more apt to be wrong than right, and unfair and unjust than fair. It is a first cousin to prejudice and persecution and an unhealthy weed that grows with them.

—DR. FRANCIS J. BRACELAND and
MICHAEL STOCK, O. P.

Sympathy—Sympathies

1631. There'd be plenty of sympathy if people would spread it around instead of using it all on themselves.

1632. To commiserate is sometimes more than to give; for money is external to a man's self, but he who bestows compassion communicates his own soul.

—REV. W. MOUNTFORD

1633. We often do more good by our sympathy than by our labors. A man may lose position, influence, wealth, and even health, and yet live on in comfort, if with resignation; but there is one thing without which life becomes a burden—that is human sympathy.

—CANON FARRAR

1634. There is poetry and there is beauty in real sympathy; but there is more—there is *action*. The noblest and most powerful form of sympathy is not merely the responsive tear, the echoed sigh, the answering look; it is the embodiment of the sentiment in *actual help*.

—OCTAVIUS WINSLOW

Taciturnity

1635. An editor of a nationally known magazine once asked Calvin Coolidge, when he was President, how he had acquired the reputation for being a man of few words. "You talk freely enough to me; why do people think you taciturn?" was the question he put to the man sometimes called "Silent Cal."

Coolidge replied that he cultivated silence in order to have time to see all the people he had to see and do the tasks he had to do. He found that if he argued with visitors or expressed any opinion, they talked twice as long, and he was unable to end the interview politely. So he said nothing and visitors came and went fast.

Tact

1636. Tact fails the moment it is noticed.

—EDWARD LONGSTRETH

1637. Talent without tact is only half talent.

—Horace Greeley

1638. A man who has tact won't change his mind but will change the subject.

1639. Tact is the art of giving a person a shot in the arm without letting him feel the needle.

1640. It may be difficult to say the right thing at the right time, but it is far more difficult to leave unsaid the wrong thing at the tempting moment.

1641. Tact is the knack of keeping quiet at the right time; of being so agreeable yourself that no one can be disagreeable to you; of making inferiority feel like equality. The tactful person can pull the stinger from a bee without getting stung.

1642. Tact is a priceless quality in good human relations. Whenever you find anyone who is outstandingly successful and popular, you will find a person who is outstandingly tactful. Tact is merely doing things in the way the other person would like them done, rather than in the way you yourself would do them if you had only yourself to please.

—Donald A. Laird

1643. Talent is something, but tact is everything. Talent is serious, sober, grave and respectable; tact is all that, and more, too. It is not a seventh sense, but is the life of all the five. It is the open eye, the quick ear, the judging taste, the keen smell, and the lively touch; it is the interpreter of all riddles, the surmounter of all difficulties, the remover of all obstacles.

—W. P. Scargill

Tale-bearing

1644. Should someone speak ill of me he is not my friend who hastens to tell me.

—Ruth Smeltzer

Talent

1645. If the power to do hard work is not talent, it is the best possible substitute for it.

1646. There is no such thing as a born hard-worker, a born salesman or a born genius. We are all born ignorant, with innate underdeveloped abilities. One cannot afford to merely let things happen. If one seeks success, he will have to *make* things happen.

—MARK BRINKERHOFF

1647. What is talent but originality robed in resourcefulness; what is success but effort draped in determination; what is achievement but a dream dressed in work clothes; what is accomplishment but ability stripped of its doubts; what is life but a series of opportunities marked as difficulties.

—DR. WILLIAM ARTHUR WARD

Talkativeness

1648. The young man whose stock of knowledge is small, by talking when he should listen may miss of that intelligence which might be of great use to him.

—L. CARROLL JUDSON

Talking

1649. We talk for either one of two reasons: Some of us because we have something to say, but most of us just to say something.

Taxation

1650. There is no art which one government sooner learns of another than that of draining money from the pockets of the people.

—ADAM SMITH

1651. Research reveals that 57 per cent of all American adults gamble regularly. So what else but hypocrisy explains the opposition to my bill to set up a national lottery as a quick remedy for Uncle Sam's fiscal headaches?

A novel idea? Not at all. According to the Old Testament, Moses divided the land west of the Jordan among the Israelites "by lot."

Ancient Rome was rebuilt under Augustus with lottery revenue.

The Virginia Company financed its colonizing expeditions into America in the early 17th Century with lotteries.

Lottery revenue fed and clothed the army of George Washington, who bought the first ticket.

Many universities—Harvard, Yale, Princeton, Dartmouth—financed early building programs with lotteries.

The last national lottery was the World War II draft—and the stakes were death.

—Rep. Paul A. Fine

Taxes

1652.   Kings cut to shear, not skin their sheep.

—Robert Herrick

1653.   One businessman to another: "I wanted my son to share in the business, but the government beat him to it."

1654.   Taxes have their ups and downs; when one tax goes down, another goes up.

1655.   In levying taxes and in shearing sheep it is well to stop when you get down to the skin.

—Austin O'Malley

1656.   The men who collect taxes are working in one of the oldest professions known. Archaeological evidence dating from 1900 b.c. includes a clay tablet recording a tax for public works and a papyrus scroll which reveals that even 4,000 years ago, taxpayers had some complaints.

1657.   The taxes are indeed very heavy, and if those laid by the government were the only ones . . . we might easily discharge them. . . . We are taxed twice as much by our idleness, three times as much by our pride, and four times as much by our folly; and from these taxes the commissioners cannot ease or deliver us. . . .

—BENJAMIN FRANKLIN

Teacher—Teachers—Teaching

1658. Delight in teaching what you have learned.

—SENECA

1659. Those who educate children well are more to be honored than parents, for these only gave life, those the art of living well.

—ARISTOTLE

1660. Three reasons for entering a teaching career: June, July and August.

1661. The teacher is a power in proportion to the intelligence, skill, and fidelity with which the pupil is educated.

—J. W. BULKLEY

1662. A teacher who is attempting to teach without inspiring the pupil with a desire to learn is hammering on cold iron.

—HORACE MANN

1663. The mediocre teacher tells. The good teacher explains. The superior teacher demonstrates. The great teacher inspires.

—DR. WILLIAM ARTHUR WARD

1664. Thank goodness educators are having second thoughts about the value of teaching machines. Many a graduate has remembered a great teacher and expressed the debt he owed him. Can that ever be said about a teaching machine?

1665. If, in instructing a child, you are vexed with it for want of adroitness, try, if you have never tried before, to write with your left hand, and then remember that a child is all left hand.

—J. F. BOYES

1666. The teacher should carefully study the disposition and character of his pupils, that he may adapt his teaching to their peculiar needs. He has a garden to tend, in which are plants differing widely in nature, form, and development.

—Dr. Harry Edwards

1667. The teacher, like the artist, the philosopher, and the man of letters, can perform his work adequately only if he feels himself to be an individual directed by an inner creative impulse, not dominated and fettered by an outside authority.

—Bertrand Russell

1668. The teacher is like a switchman, who holds the key to the switches on the railroad; if he does his duty faithfully, the train will reach its destination; if he neglects it, disaster and ruin follow. A misplaced switch or a wrong signal may send hundreds into eternity unprepared.

—Elon Foster, D. D.

1669. Today the teacher no longer carries all knowledge within his brain. He does not transmit knowledge so much as feed it to each individual. He steps in to excite curiosity, to guide pupils towards knowledge, and to see that they have acquired it. It is up to the pupil to assume his responsibilities, to conquer knowledge independently and make use of his own initiative.

—Henri Dieuzeide

1670. Teaching, by its very nature, is a process sensitive to and dependent upon inspiration. Teaching is at once artistic and scientific. The teaching act thrives upon creativity and a high sense of calling or altruism. Teaching is participation in creation through the pupil's discovery and exploration of knowledge with the reward of self-realization. Teaching is selflessness in the service of others.

—Berlie J. Fallon

Teacher—Pupil

1671. A tutor should not be continually thundering instruction into the ears of his pupil, as if he were pouring it through a funnel, but, after having put the lad, like a young horse, on a trot, before him, to observe his paces, and see what he is able to perform, should according to the extent of his capacity, induce him to taste, to distinguish, and to find out things for himself; sometimes opening the way, at other times leaving it for him to open; and by abating or increasing his own pace, accommodate his precepts to the capacity of his pupil.

—MICHAEL E. DE MONTAIGNE

Teamwork

1672.   The point that most needs to be borne in mind is that the welfare of every business is dependent upon cooperation and teamwork on the part of its personnel. Proper cooperation cannot be secured between groups of men who are constantly quarreling among themselves over petty grievances.

—CHARLES GOW

Tear—Tears

1673.   The soul would have no rainbow had the eyes no tears.

—JOHN VANCE CHENEY

1674.   They that sow in tears shall reap in joy.

—THE BIBLE

1675.   Tears are the safety-valves of the heart, when too much pressure is laid on.

—ALBERT SMITH

1676.   God sometimes washes the eyes of His children with tears in order that they may read aright His providence and His commandments.

—T. L. CUYLER

Technocracy

1677.   One machine can do the work of 50 ordinary men, but no machine can do the work of one extra ordinary man.

—ELMER LETERMAN

Teenage—Teenager

1678. One way to keep your teenage daughter out of hot water is to put dirty dishes into it.

Television

1679. Many a child who watches television for hours will go down in history—not to mention arithmetic, English and geography.

Temper

1680. It pays to keep one's temper in tact.

1681. Bad temper is its own scourge. Few things are more bitter than to feel bitter. A man's venom poisons himself more than his victim.

1682. Once a Quaker, calm and poised after a volley of bitter abuse, was asked how he conquered his patience. He replied: "Friend, I will tell thee. I was naturally as hot and violent as thou art. Yet, when I observed that men in passion always speak loud, I thought if I could control my voice, I should repress my passion. I have therefore made it a rule never to let my voice rise above a certain key. By careful observance of this rule I have, by the blessing of God, mastered my tongue."

Temptation

1683. God is better served in resisting a temptation to evil than in many formal prayers.

1684. Opportunity has to knock, but it is enough for Temptation just to stand outside and whistle.

Tenacity

1685. The giant oak is an acorn that held its ground.

Ten Commandments

1686.　It seems incredible—thirty-five million laws, and no improvement on the Ten Commandments!

Tenderness

1687.　There never was any heart truly great and generous that was not also tender and compassionate.

—ROBERT SOUTH, D. D.

1688.　While we would have our young sisters imitate, as they cannot fail to love, the conduct of Ruth, will not their elders do well to ponder on, and imitate the tenderness of Naomi? Would we have our daughters Ruths, we must be Naomis.

—GRACE AGUILAR

Tension—Tensions

1689.　Tension is as important an element of living as hunger or thirst. Like fire, it can be invaluably useful when controlled; but, unharnessed, its effects can spell disaster. In business, as in every other aspect of life, tension furnishes interest and excitement, incentive and ambition, and promotes achievement and happiness.

Testimonial—Testimonials

1690.　"One of the tragedies of life," remarked a famous writer at a testimonial banquet for a newly successful colleague, "is the fact that no one ever gives you a dinner until you don't need it."

Texas—Alaska

1691.　An Alaskan who was getting tired of hearing a Texan complain about his state now being only the second largest said, "If you don't keep quiet we'll split in half and then you'll be number 3!"

1692.   A Texan sent an eight-pound cucumber to the editor of an Alaskan newspaper. "The big ones are too heavy," he wrote, "but I thought you would like to see the kind of gherkins we grow in Texas."

In a few days the editor responded with a forty-pound cabbage. "The same is true of our cabbages," he wrote to the Texan, "but I thought you would like to see an Alaskan brussels sprout!"

1693.   A Texan who got to brooding over the fact that he was living in only the second largest state, went up to Alaska and asked: "How do I get to be an Alaskan?" The bartender in the Last Chance Saloon, figuring on having a little fun with him, said: "Podnuh, you can't be a full-blooded Alaskan until you've downed a pint a whiskey at one gulp, danced with an Eskimo and shot a polar bear."

"That's for me," said the Texan and ordered the pint of whiskey. He got it down at one gulp, although his eyes were glazing slightly as he lurched from the saloon. The boys waited for him until almost midnight, when he stumbled through the doors all scratched and ripped and bloody.

"Okay," he said, "okay, I'm gonna be an Alaskan. Now where's that Eskimo I'm supposed to shoot?"

Thanksgiving Day

1694.   It is meet and proper that a nation should set apart an annual day for national giving of thanks. It is a public recognition of God as the Author of all prosperity. It is the erection of a memorial to the honor of Him who has led us through another year. The annual proclamations . . . of thanksgiving are calculated to remind the people of their indebtedness to God, to stir in their minds and hearts emotions of gratitude and praise and to call out thanks and sincere worship which otherwise might not find expression.

—Rev. Dr. J. R. Miller

1695.   O Lord our heavenly Father . . . We praise Thee that Thou has surrounded us with Thine infinite goodness, that Thou hast continually poured forth Thy benefits age after age, and that of Thy faithfulness there is no end. For the beauty of the earth, and the bounty it produces for our physical need, for the order and constancy of nature which brings us day and night, summer and winter, seed-time and harvest—for all gifts of Thy mercy—we are thankful.

—Rev. Donald A. Wenstrom

1696. We thank thee, O Lord, for the privilege for being a part of our United States. We thank Thee for our forefathers who established a nation in which there would be liberty and justice for all. We firmly believe that more people enjoy freedom and more people share in opportunities here than anywhere else on earth. We would be thankful for the gift of life wherever it was Your will that we live it. On this national Thanksgiving Day, we are doubly grateful that you gave us the privilege of being American.

—*Nuggets*

1697. As we approach this Thanksgiving let us pause to reflect upon the many blessings that are ours. Blessings that we accept as commonplace—things that we feel are owed to us. We enjoy the highest standard of living in the world and we expect it. In the United States we have more homes owned by families, more autos, more television sets, more washing machines, more bath tubs—more of anything we can name than any place else on the face of the earth . . . So now, this Thanksgiving, it behooves all of us, on bended knee, to give thanks to Almighty God, for all the multitude of blessings He has showered upon each and every one of us, and pray that He will help us preserve our way of life.

—H. S. Jackson

1698. A LOT OF THINGS

I'm thankful for a lot of things.
 I'm thankful, so I say;
I'm thankful for the big outdoors
 Where I can run and play.
I'm thankful for the things that grow—
 The apples—aren't they good!
Cornfield, where we played hide-and-seek,
 As in a little wood.
I'm thankful for the pumpkins round,
 Just like a golden ball;
And Jack-o'-lanterns, big and queer—
 They don't scare me at all.

I'm thankful for Thanksgiving Day—
 For pies all in a row;
I'm thankful Grandma made them sweet—
 She knows I like 'em so.
I'm thankful for the turkey, too,
 How brown it is, and nice!
And I'd be very thankful, please,
 For only one more slice!

1699.   Let Us Be Thankful

For the forefathers who established the good day of Thanksgiving, and for the nation which now shelters us in peace and plenty.

For the commonly overlooked wayside mercies; for the music of the dawn and the fires of sunset; for the light of the stars and the shifting beauty of the seasons; for the days of health and the nights of quiet sleep; for the laughter of little children and the counsels of the aged; for the poetry of the hearth and the converse with congenial friends; for all those countless gifts which join hands to make our hearts content.

For the discipline of sorrow, the trial of failure and the encouragement of success.

For the pressure of work and the responsibility which saves us from the allurements of a selfish ease, and for the stern retributions which strike us when we walk in the ways of impurity and dishonor.

For the sweetness of love, the inspiration of duty and the joys of self-sacrifice.

For the lives of our sacred dead, for the happy days we spent in their companionship, for the example of their faith and patience, and for our faith which sees them living, loving and waiting for our coming.

For ideals which chime and beckon from the heights; for the dignity and mystery of our humanity; for the comfort and security of our homes; for the principles on which fraternal benefit societies are founded; and for the privilege of living in this great land of ours. For these and all things else which bring us nearer to our true selves, nearer to our brothers, and nearer to our Father, let us be truly Thankful.

Thinking

1700.   The man who does the hard work may always have a job, but the one who does the thinking will be his boss.

Thoroughness

1701. The more a man thinks, the better adapted he becomes to thinking, and education is nothing if it is not the methodical creation of the habit of thinking.

—ERNEST DIMNET

1702. Albert Einstein was once asked what he would most like to say to the science students in American schools. Without hesitation he replied: "I would ask them to spend an hour every day rejecting the ideas of others and thinking things out for themselves. This will be a hard thing to do but it will be rewarding."

1703. There is a basic law that like attracts like. That which you mentally project reproduces in kind and negative thoughts definitely attract negative results. Conversely, if a person habitually thinks optimistically and hopefully he activates life around him positively and thereby attracts to himself positive results. His positive thinking sets in motion creative forces, and success instead of eluding him flows toward him.

—DR. NORMAN VINCENT PEALE

1704. A do-it-yourself enthusiast had read the instructions accompanying the newly-acquired gadget time and again, but just couldn't assemble it.

Gathering all the parts and instructions, he finally sought the help of the old handyman working in the garden. After looking at the gadget a few moments, the oldster soon had it in working condition.

"It's beyond me," said the do-it-yourselfer, "how you got it together so quickly without even reading the instructions."

"Fact is," was the reply, "I can't read—an' when a fellow can't read, he's got to think."

Thoroughness

1705. One worthwhile task carried to a successful conclusion is worth half-a-hundred half-finished tasks. On the football field you cannot score a goal unless and until you have forced the ball between the posts. It is the same in the business field. Concentrate. Be a finisher.

—B. C. FORBES

Thought—Thoughts

1706. Good thoughts are true wealth; they are fountains of living water; they are gems that always shine; they are impenetrable shields to protect the character; they are goodly apparel for the mind; they are right noble companions; they are fair angels of light; they are flowers of rich beauty and sweet fragrance; they are seeds of noble actions and noble institutions; they are moulds in which exalted characters are formed; they make good and great men; they are a nation's mightiest bulwarks. A good thought is a grand legacy to bequeath to the world.

1707.   GOOD THOUGHTS

As patriots let's take our stand
And hold good thoughts of our great
    land—
Good thoughts of neighbors, one and
    all—
Good thoughts of self so we won't fall;
Good thoughts of want we have to
    do—
Good thoughts so there'll be naught
    to rue;
Good thoughts e'er help us well to
plan—
Good thoughts are thoughts that make
    the man.

—ANONYMOUS

Thrift

1708. Economy is in itself a source of great revenue.

—SENECA

1709. If you want to know whether you are destined to be a success or a failure in life, you can easily find out. The test is simple and infallible. Are you able to save money? If not, drop out. You will lose.

—JAMES J. HILL

1710. It is not what men eat, but what they digest, that makes them strong; not what we gain, but what we save, that makes us rich; not what we read, but what we absorb, that makes us learned; not what we preach, but what we practice, that makes us lovable.

—FRANCIS BACON

1711. The principle of saving is the first great principle of all success. It creates independence, it gives a young man standing, it fills him with vigor, it stimluates him with the proper energy; in fact, it brings to him the best part of any success—happiness and contentment. If it were possible to inject the quality of saving into every boy, we would have a great many more real men.

—SIR THOMAS LIPTON

Time

1712. Time goes, you say? Ah no!
Alas, Time stays, we go.

—AUSTIN DOBSON

1713. One loses all the time which he might employ to better purpose.

—JEAN JACQUES ROUSSEAU

1714. Time heals all wounds but only you can keep the scars from showing.

1715. Time is so powerful a medicine that God has wisely given it to us only in small doses.

1716. Lose an hour in the morning and you will be looking for it the rest of the day.

—LORD CHESTERFIELD

1717. The great men of the past did not slide by any fortune into their high place. They have been selected by the severest of all judges, Time.

—RALPH WALDO EMERSON

1718. A sense of the value of time—that is, of the best way to divide one's time into one's various activities—is an essential preliminary to efficient work; it is the only method of avoiding hurry.

—ARNOLD BENNETT

1719. It has been said that time is money. That proverb understates the case. Time is a great deal more than money. It is the inexplicable raw material of everything. With it, all is possible; without it, nothing.

—ARNOLD BENNETT

1720. It is astonishing how much more anxious people are to lengthen life than to improve it. . . . Hypochondriacs squander large sums of time in search of nostrums by which they vainly hope they may get more time to squander.

—CHARLES C. COLTON

1721. It is possible for all of us to give the gift of time—the time it takes to do our work conscientiously. The time it takes to offer a sincere compliment. The time it takes to think twice before we say an unkind word, and then not say it at all.

1722. In the Bible there are two words for time. One is *"chronos"* from which we get chronological. This is the timetable measure we know so well. But the Bible has little to say about *"chronos."* . . . The Bible's interest is in the other kind of time, for which the word is *"kairos."* This is what we mean when we talk about "the right time" for doing something. It is the opportune moment, so defined not by its position on a time scale or in a datebook, but by its being in the center of the right conjunction of circumstances which together create the right time for this deed or that word. And when we, responding, act or speak, then the time is realized, filled full.

—N. BRUCE MCLEOD

Time-saving

1723. To choose time is to save time; and an unseasonable motion is but beating the air.

—FRANCIS BACON

Time-wasting

1724. Believe me when I tell you that thrift of time will repay you in after life, with a usury of profit beyond your most sanguine dreams; and that waste of it will make you dwindle, alike in intellectual and moral stature, beyond your darkest reckoning.

—WILLIAM E. GLADSTONE

Timing

1725. A smart politician needs a sense of timing—to know how soon to grab credit for a program if it succeeds without taking the blame if it fails.

1726. Timeliness is the weapon of the worldly wise. . . . After you know the what and the how of anything, you still must learn the when. The right thing, done at the wrong time, is the wrong thing to do.

—BALTASAR GRACIÁN

Tip—Tips—Tipping

1727. The head of a large company, whose business involves inevitable tipping, realized lately that the new employees didn't understand the fine art of extracting liberal gratuities from customers.

The boss had to harmonize his own interests with the selfishness of his men. He wanted satisfied customers, thus assuring repeat business. The men wanted tips.

The boss put it this way to the men: To insure a good tip dismiss all thought of a tip from your mind while you are giving the service. Do a good job and act as though you enjoyed your work. Let the customer worry about the tip, but give him no inkling that you are concerned about it. The result will be bigger tips than you have ever known.

A week later one of the men came to the boss and confessed, "Say, that theory of yours works."

1728. Tipping is evidently an ancient problem. There is a charming tale about Nasreddin Hoja, a 13th century Turkish philosopher, who once went to a public bath in a neighboring city.

276

The attendants, noticing his shabby costume, paid him little attention and brought him a torn towel and a tiny piece of soap. On leaving, Hoja gave a gold piece to each of the attendants, who mentally kicked themselves for having been deceived by his ragged appearance.

He returned to the same bath the following week, dressed as before, this time he was received with great deference—new towels, scented soap, much bowing and scraping with the anticipation of more gold pieces.

But, on leaving, he gave each attendant a nickel, replying to their startled looks:

"The gold pieces I gave you last week were for the way you treated me today; the nickels I've just given you are for the way you treated me last week."

Tit for tat

1729. An old farmer wrote to a mail order house as follows: "Please send me one of the gasoline engines you show on page 978, and if it's any good, I'll send you a check."

In time, he received the following reply: "Please send check. If it's any good, we'll send the engine."

1730. The Hungarian playwright Ferenc Molnar used to tell a story of Fürstenberg, a German banker, who telephoned another banker to make an appointment. The man said he would have to look through his engagement book first.

Fürstenberg could hear the surf of the pages being ruffled in the banker's book. No time free in January, February or March, the man reported. The third of April was his first free afternoon. "Oh April third," said Fürstenberg, "I have a funeral."

Toast—Toasts—Toasting

1731. May your death give nobody pleasure!

—from the Irish

1732. Here's to my wife! Thirty years ago I gazed into the depths of her eyes and I have never recovered from the spell of it.

Tolerance

1733. William Jennings Bryan was once asked to toast the British Navy. A teetotaler, he lifted a glass of water and said, "Gentlemen, I believe all your victories were won on water."

1734.
I drink to your health, when I'm with you.
I drink to your health when I'm alone.
I drink to your health so darned much,
I find that I'm ruining my own.

1735.
We wish you well, we cannot tell
How much, although we'd like to:
May your new year bring lots of cheer
And every day delight you.

1736.
We trim the tree for
Christmas night, and trim the
house with holly bright; but
poor old Dad—he gets
trimmed first, and what is
more, gets trimmed the worst;
but still, he never says a word;
so here's to Dad—a game
old bird.

Tolerance

1737. The trouble with being tolerant is that people think you don't understand the problem.

1738. Tolerance is the positive and cordial effort to understand another's beliefs, practices and habits without necessarily sharing or accepting them.

—JOSEPH L. LIEBMAN

1739. Tolerance is too often a weak-kneed rationalization of unsound views or prejudices. We hold on to a prejudice as though it were a conviction; keep it in abeyance chiefly to fight the friction its exposure might bring. What sometimes seems to be tolerance may sometimes be only a lack of conviction. . . . Tolerance may be a cloak which is hiding bigotry. Better to exercise a prejudice than to conceal it behind a screen labelled tolerance.

—Norman G. Shidle

Tomorrow

1740. The way to have a better tomorrow is to start working on it today.

1741.
I've shut the door on yesterday, its sorrows and mistakes,
I've looked within its gloomy walls past failures and
    mistakes,
And now I've thrown the key away to seek another room,
And furnish it with hope and smiles and every spring-like
    bloom.
No thought shall enter this abode that has a hint of pain,
And neither malice nor distrust shall therein reign.
I've shut the door on yesterday and thrown away the key,
Tomorrow holds no doubt for me, since I have found
    today.

—Author unknown

Traffic, Automobile

1742. The sad part about reckless driving is the mourning after.

1743. The cause of most traffic accidents: High hp. and low I.Q.

1744. Famous last words: "Well, if he won't dim his, I won't dim mine."

1745. Sign on the rear of a truck: "Many a man has carved his tombstone by chiseling in traffic."

1746. A woman driver was arrested for making an "O" turn. She began to make a "U" turn but changed her mind.

Travel

1747.   Tests show that women make better satellite pilots than men. This confirms the widely held opinion that women are excellent drivers, given plenty of space.

1748.   Scientists have computed that it takes a fifth of a second to blink an eye and that a person blinks twenty-five times a minute. Thus, a motorist who averages 55 mph on a ten-hour trip drives 33 miles with his eyes shut.

1749.   Men were critical of women drivers long before the invention of the automobile. In the horse-and-buggy age many women drove their own carriages. The streets of Paris in the 18th century were narrow and crowded. Naturally much of this crowding was blamed on the number of carriages being driven by women. To relieve the congestion, Louis XVI ordered one of his ministers to outlaw women drivers. Knowing the enmity of the ladies at the court could ruin him, the wily minister found a way out. He simply proclaimed an ordinance that only women over 30 years of age could drive a horse and carriage in Paris.

Travel

1750.   Each year it takes less time to fly around the world and more time to drive to work.

1751.   To travel is to possess the world. The traveler possesses the world more completely than those who own vast properties. Owners become the slaves of what they own.

—BURTON HOLMES

1752.   People expend vast sums of money in useless travel to visit the places of the world famous for beauty, many seeing less than the real nature lover who gazes with rapture on the sunset light on a range of hills or mountains. It is not the places seen, but a capacity for seeing and an appreciation of the beautiful that is really important.

Trouble—Troubles

1753.   The easiest way to get into trouble is to be right at the wrong time.

280

1754. Trouble is the structural steel that goes into the structural building of character.

—Douglas Meador

1755. The fleet-footed twins of trouble and misfortune may have the ability to outrun you in a short dash, but they are strangely short-winded when you challenge them to a marathon.

Trust, Mutual

1756. Every kind of peaceful cooperation among men is primarily based on mutual trust and only secondarily on institutions such as courts of justice and police.

—Albert Einstein

Truth

1757. The truth doesn't hurt unless it ought to.

—B. C. Forbes

1758. A judicious silence is always better than truth spoken without charity.

1759. I have discovered the art of fooling diplomats; I speak the truth and they never believe me.

—Benso di Vacour

1760. We must not let go manifest truths because we cannot answer all questions about them.

—Jeremy Collier

1761. Truth does not consist in minute accuracy of detail; but in conveying a right impression.

—Dean Alford

1762. If an offence comes out of the truth, better is it that the offence come, than the truth be concealed.

—St. Jerome

1763. The truth neither confuses the memory nor confounds the conscience, but the most cleverly fabricated lie does both.

1764. No truth can be said to be seen as *it is* until it is seen in its relation to all other truths. In this relation only is it true.

—Elizabeth Prentiss

1765. No one can open his mind to the truth without risking the entrance of falsehood; and no one can close his mind to falsehood without risking the exclusion of truth.

1766. Experience has shown, and a true philosophy will always show, that a vast, perhaps the larger, portion of the truth arises from the seeming irrelevant.

—Edgar Allen Poe

1767. Truth and telling the truth are about as much alike as moral philosophy and personal memoirs. Moreover, we often tell the truth as though that were equivalent to doing something about it.

—Louis Kronenberger

Type, Reversion to

1768. It is said that when Napoleon had a son, at the height of his career, the people of Paris gave the baby a gold cradle. It was symbolic of the luxury to which the youngster was born. One day when he was about three, Napoleon took him along for a review of the troops at the Champ de Mars. The emperor was apprehensive that the boy, held on the horse with him, might be frightened by the blare of trumpets and the roll of drums. Unseemly screams could mar a beautiful ceremony. His fears were groundless as the little fellow apparently enjoyed it.

When the review was over Napoleon wanted to reward his son for his good behaviour and told him he could have anything he wanted.

Pointing to a puddle left near the parade grounds by the recent rain, the little boy said, "May I go and paddle in the mud?"

Tyranny

1769. The tidal waves of tyranny always begin as tiny ripples of indifference.

—Dr. William Arthur Ward

1770. O, it is excellent
To have a giant's strength; but it is tyrannous
To use it like a giant.

—William Shakespeare

1771. Tyranny does not come with tanks and jack boots. Tyranny creeps in, like the fog, "on little cat feet." Tyranny carries a sign which says, "This is being done for the public good." Tyranny is sly. It says, "You and I know what is best to do. But those poor people over there are not as fortunate. They do not know that what we want is really for their own good." Tyranny puts its arm around your shoulder and says, "Let's you and I save them from themselves. Let us force them to make the right choice, and later, when they are wiser, they will thank us." Tyranny says, "Let us draw up rules to prevent ideas we know are wrong. Let us together curb evil."

—Tom Dillon

Understanding

1772. We do not learn to know men through their coming to us. To find out what sort of persons they are, we must go to them.

—Johann Wolfgang von Goethe

1773. I have sedulously endeavored not to laugh at human actions, not to lament them, nor to detest them, but to understand them.

—Benedict Spinoza

1774. If the cultivation of the understanding consists in one thing more than in another, it is surely in learning the grounds of one's own opinions.

—John Stuart Mill

Unemployment

1775. To understand another does not mean that one has to agree with all that he says or does. Understanding, however, is the basis for getting along with people in our daily contacts. Friction, bickering, and confusion in our environment cannot exist where there is understanding.

1776. Thoughtfulness contributes to understanding, for it helps us to be aware of the ambitions, the desires, the needs, and even the faults of those whom we seek to understand by knowing better.

Consideration contributes to understanding, for it helps us recognize that there are different forms of goodness. It helps us to see that the modest goals of one may be a mountain of achievement for another—that what satisfies one person may be only enough to whet the appetite of someone else.

Sympathy contributes to understanding, for it helps us feel the frustrations and sorrows of those whose legitimate desires seem always beyond their grasp.

Helpfulness contributes to understanding, for it is the tangible expression of thoughtfulness, consideration, and sympathy.

—Nuggets

Unemployment

1777. It is not inventions that put people out of work, but their own failure to change with the times.

—Donald A. Laird

Unhappiness

1778. The most unhappy of all men is he who believes himself to be so.

—Henry Home

Vacation—Vacations

1779. At today's prices, people don't take vacations—vacations take people.

1780. The trouble with vacations is you have to earn them before you go and make up for them when you come back. It's really more restful to just keep on working.

—HENRY ALLEN MOE

1781. From the size of the luggage some people take on vacations they're not getting away from it all, they're taking it with them.

Value—Values

1782. What we obtain too cheap, we esteem too lightly. 'Tis dearness only that gives everything its value.

—THOMAS PAINE

1783. The man who will use his skill and constructive imagination to see how much he can give for a dollar, instead of how little he can give for a dollar, is bound to succeed.

—HENRY FORD

Vanity

1784. A vain man can never be utterly ruthless; he wants to win applause and therefore he accommodates himself to others.

—JOHANN WOLFGANG VON GOETHE

Veterans' Day. See Armistice Day

Vigilance

1785. Eternal vigilance is the price of liberty.

—JOHN PHILPOT CURRAN

Virtue—Virtues

1786. Live virtuously and you cannot die too soon, nor live too long.

—LADY RACHEL RUSSELL

Vote—Votes—Voting

1787. Beware of the one whose virtue lies in the fear of God and not in the love of man.

—Dagobert D. Runes

Vote—Votes—Voting

1788. People vote their resentment, not their appreciation. The average man does not vote for anything; but rather he votes against something.

1789. The distinguishing monument of the western world is not an arch like those in the Roman Forum, nor a temple on a Greek hill, nor an automated factory, nor a towering skyscraper. It is a little booth, the polling booth in which free men and women declare their political will.

1790. In an election at St. Charles, Illinois, a proposal for a council-manager form of government was to be voted upon. The local League of Women Voters urged the population: "Vote Yes or No—But Vote!" When the ballots were counted, election officials found a flock of them marked: "Yes or No."

Vulnerability

1791. A person who buries his head in the sand offers an engaging target.

—Mabel A. Keenan

Wages. See Salary

War—Wars

1792. The tragedy of war is that it uses man's best to do man's worst.

—Harry Emerson Fosdick

286

1793. A few big bombs set off in the right places can destroy all living men, but a few big men set in the right places can destroy all killing bombs.

—J. GUSTAV WHITE

1794. War is a game with a good deal of chance in it, and, from the little I have seen of it, I should say that nothing in war ever goes right except by accident.

—WINSTON CHURCHILL

1795. Little men who want to be remembered start great wars; great men who wish to be forgotten are the architects of peace.

—DAGOBERT D. RUNES

1796. For national leaders it is sometimes easier to fight than to talk. Impatient cries for total victory are usually more popular than the patient tolerance required of a people whose leaders are seeking peaceful change down the intricate paths of diplomacy.

—HARLAN CLEVELAND

1797. We often say how impressive power is. But I do not find it impressive at all. The guns and bombs, the rockets and the warships, all are symbols of human failure. They are necessary symbols. They protect what we cherish. But they are witness to human folly.

—LYNDON B. JOHNSON

1798. War never shows who is wrong; it can only show who is strong. It is a superstition because people falsely believe that God will be on the side of the right. God has nothing to do with a hellish business like war. It is a superstition on a par with the burning of witches and trial by ordeal. The fallacy, the futility, and the fatality of force were manifested in the last war. We fought to destroy militarism and created a super-militarism. We fought to make the world safe for democracy and have created countless dictatorships.

—RABBI LOUIS L. MANN

Weakness—Weaknesses

1799. Two things indicate weakness—to be silent when it is proper to speak, and to speak when it is proper to be silent.

—PERSIAN PROVERB

1800. Knowing your strength makes you confident; forgetting your weakness makes you vulnerable.

1801. If you have a weakness, make it work for you as a strength—and if you have a strength, don't abuse it into a weakness.

—DORE SCHARY

Wealth

1802. There is nothing wrong with men possessing riches but the wrong comes when riches possess men.

—BILLY GRAHAM

1803. Worldly riches are like nuts; many clothes are torn getting them, many a tooth broken in cracking them, but never a belly filled with eating them.

—RALPH VENNING

1804. The use we make of our fortune determines its sufficiency. A little is enough if used wisely, and too much if expended foolishly.

—CHRISTIAN NEVELL BOVEE

1805. Wealth, after all, is a relative thing, since he that has little, and wants less, is richer than he who has much and wants more.

—CHARLES C. COLTON

1806. You can be rich in two ways: in the abundance of your possessions, or in the fewness of your wants. When your wants are reduced by simplicity, then you are rich.

—MELVIN J. EVANS

1807. All the world imagine they will be exceptional when they grow wealthy; but possession is debasing, new desires spring up; and the silly taste for ostenstation eats out the heart of pleasure.
—Robert Louis Stevenson

1808. Wealth is simply one of the greatest powers which can be entrusted to human hands: a power, not indeed to be envied, because it seldom makes us happy; but still less to be abdicated or despised.
—John Ruskin

1809. True riches can never be measured in terms of money or of things. No amount of material goods can ever compensate for the wealth of the spirit, because this is eternal. "Some day we are going to be rich," said a young wife, proud of her talented husband. But that wise man quickly corrected her by the response. "We are already rich. Some day we may have money."

1810. We become poor in the profoundest sense when we become afraid of modest circumstances, and rich when we come to value and enjoy all the marvelous things which do not have to be bought. We get so much for nothing . . . our enormous heritage of ideas, inventions, music and forms of government previous generations bled and died to create.
—F. Alexander Magoun

1811. Beware of the effect of wealth. It is usually least dangerous when it has been earned by painstaking effort over a long stretch of years. That process tends to make and keep a man level-headed. Wealth can make or unmake a personality. Its possession sometimes breeds vanity, offensive self-assurance, an overbearing attitude towards others. Many who come into wealth are tempted to draw away from ordinary mortals, to become aloof, isolated, suspicious that every person has designs on their pocket book. Happily, an abundance of money can bless as well as curse. The latter is to be vigilantly guarded against.

Weather

1812. When an American says it is raining "cats and dogs," the Englishman is satisfied just to call it beastly weather.

Wholeheartedness

1813. All animal life is endowed with mysterious instincts for its own well-being, and one of these is the ability to sense a change in the weather.

When swallows fly low, for example, rain may be expected. The insects which the swallows pursue in their flight are flying low to escape the coldness of the upper regions of the atmosphere.

Ducks and geese go to the water and dash it over their backs on the approach of rain. By wetting the outer coat of their feathers before the rain falls, by sudden dashes of water over the surface, they prevent the drops of rain from penetrating to their bodies through the open dry feathers.

Horses and cattle stretch out their necks and sniff the air on the approach of rain. They smell the natural perfumes which are diffused in the air by its increasing moisture.

Spiders busy themselves constructing their webs when fine weather is assured. Those insects are highly sensitive to the state of the atmosphere, and when it is setting fine, they seem to know instinctively that flies will be abroad and may be caught.

When owls scream during foul weather, it will change to fine. The birds are pleasurably excited by the favorable change in the atmosphere.

When bees wander far from their hives, fine weather will continue. Bees feel instinctively that they may go far in search of honey without danger of being overtaken by rain.

Moles throw up their hills when rain is coming. Moles seem to know that worms are moving in the ground on the approach of wet weather, and therefore become active themselves.

A magpie seen alone foretells bad weather. Magpies generally fly in company, but on the approach of rain or cold, one remains on the nest to take care of the young, while the other partner flies alone in search of food.

If birds cease to sing, wet weather, and perhaps a thunderstorm, may be expected. The birds are depressed by the change in the atmosphere, and lose those joyful spirits which give rise to their songs.

When cattle run around in the pastures, thunder may be expected. The electrical state of the atmosphere makes them feel uneasy and irritable, and they chase one another to relieve their irritability.

Wholeheartedness

1814. Never slap a king unless you intend to kill him.
—Ancient proverb

1815. There are important cases in which the difference between half a heart and a whole heart makes just the difference between signal defeat and a splendid victory.

—ANDREW K. BOYD

Will, Testamentary

1816. A Will is a legal instrument which becomes effective upon death. It is in effect a method by which an individual can speak with authority after he dies.

1817. Failure to make a Will may have unfortunate consequences. It can mean hardship and added expense for one's immediate family and benefit to some distant relative one has never seen.

Willpower

1818. A test of willpower is the opportunity to turn down something you want, to save money for something you need.

Wisdom

1819. If you realize you aren't so wise today as you thought you were yesterday, you're wiser today.

—OLIN MILLER

1820. Wisdom might be defined as having the means to make a fool of yourself and not doing it.

1821. Wisdom is the right use or exercise of knowledge, and differs from knowledge as the use which is made of a power or faculty differs from the power of faculty itself.

—WILLIAM FLEMING

1822. As nearly as I can make out, maturity is what used to be called wisdom. But wisdom obviously cannot be exactly defined, whereas maturity seems to be exact because it seems to be the same as biological and social maturity, only better, and maturity simply means "of age but not yet senile." Wisdom is a spiritual quality, and if there is one thing for which false science has less use than another, it is spirit, spirituality, the soul; *psyche* is the word, for you can add *ology* to it and sound as though you know exactly what you're talking about. Wisdom is mysterious and rare, and often a man's wisdom is patchy; but maturity sounds like maturity, a natural state of development which it is pathological not to attain. Wisdom is given we know not how or why. Maturity, like modern marriage, you work at; you strive for it; you surmount obstacles to attain it.

—GEORGE P. ELLIOTT

Wishfulness

1823.   Many of us spend half our time wishing for things we could have if we didn't spend half our time wishing.

—ALEXANDER WOOLLCOTT

1824.   WISHING

Do you wish the world were better?
    Let me tell you what to do,
Set a watch upon your actions, keep them
    always straight and true;
Rid your mind of self motives; let your
    thoughts be clean and high;
You can make a little Eden of the sphere
    you occupy.

Do you wish the world were wiser?
    Well, suppose you make a start
By accumulating wisdom in the scrap-
    book of your heart.
Do not waste one page on folly; live to
    learn and learn to live,
If you want to give men knowledge, you
    must get it ere you give.

Do you wish the world were happy?
    Then remember day by day
Just to scatter seeds of kindness as you
    pass along the way;

For the pleasure of the many may oft-
   times be traced to one,
As the hand that plants the acorn shelters
   armies from the sun.
                                    —ELLA WHEELER WILCOX

Wit and humor

1825.   Sharp wits, like sharp knives, do often cut their owner's fingers.

1826.   To place wit before good sense is to place the superfluous before the necessary.
                                    —M. DE MONTLOSIER

Woman—Women

1827.   Women have an unfair advantage over men: if they can't get what they want by being smart, they can get it by being dumb.

1828.   There is an old Jewish homily which undertakes to tell us why God made Eve from a rib of Adam. Here it is:
   "When creating Eve from the rib of Adam, God said to himself: 'I must not create her from the head that she should not carry herself haughtily; nor from the eye that she should not be too inquisitive; nor from the ear that she should not be an eavesdropper; nor from the mouth that she should not be too talkative; nor from the heart that she should not be too jealous; nor from the hand that she should not be too acquisitive; nor from the foot that she should not be a gadabout; but from a hidden part of the body that she should be modest!' "

1829.   Women are much tougher than men underneath. To call women the weaker sex is sheer nonsense. Beware those angel-faced types who always appear weak and helpless. They are the toughest of all.
   Talkative women should not be taken at their face value, either. Women who talk most, think least. To me, a particularly beautiful woman is a source of terror. As a rule, a beautiful woman is a terrible disappointment. Beautiful bodies and beautiful personalities rarely ever go together.

It is the same with men. The brain of a highly attractive man with a handsome physique becomes merely an appendage to his wonderful torso. On the other hand, you will often find that women who look a bit on the big side—too tall or too plump—are exceedingly kind and good-hearted.

—Dr. Carl Jung

Word—Words

1830. No man-made weapon has been devised so lethal, potent or dangerous as words wrongly used.

—Larry Dorst

1831. No one means all he says, and yet very few say all they mean, for words are slippery and thought is viscious.

—Henry Adams

1832. Why are materials sent in a ship called "cargo" and the goods sent in a car called a "shipment"?

1833. A Harvard classmate of Theodore Roosevelt asked TR to name him ambassador to France. Thereafter the man always boasted to his friends: "Only one little word kept me from becoming ambassador to France." He never revealed that the one little word was TR's "No."

—Charles E. Bohlen

1834. The words of a language resemble the strings of a musical instrument, which yield only uninteresting tones when struck by an ordinary hand, but from which a skilful performer draws forth the soul of harmony, awakening and captivating the passions of the mind.

—W. B. Clulow

1835. There are a number of words one encounters frequently—on the printed page if not in conversation—which are usually regarded as complete in themselves but which in reality are two words—a negative combined with a positive. We have reference to uncouth, unkempt, unruly, inept, immaculate, disgruntle and the like. Who today except the purist ever uses such words as couth, kempt, ruly, ept, maculate, or gruntle, ("To gruntle" means "To put in a good humor"), and yet at one time they were frequently seen and heard.

1836. New terminology and fresh twists on the old are constantly reshaping our mother tongue. Though we welcome the verve and vigor this implies, we cannot help bemoaning the fading away of many hearty "old soldiers" of our language. Some words are being retired by the same sort of occupational upgrading that seeks to replace *garage* with *lubritorium*. . . . Hairdresser into beautician, janitor into maintenance engineer, publicity agent into public relations counsel—the change goes on. Higher skills and broader responsibilities may be compassed by the classier designation. But also it's easier to spruce up an old occupation by giving it a new name than to spruce up an old name by improving the service it stands for.

1837. Words are funny. Did you know that:

"Blue Monday" was originally a day of revelry and pleasure? It was the last Monday before Lent, and the churches were decorated with blue hangings (hence its name). So excessive did the debauchery become on this pre-Lenten day of celebration that Blue Monday was finally abolished by law in the sixteenth century?

"Dunce" originally meant a scholar (or close to it)? The word comes from the middle name of a famous medieval scholar, Johannes Duns Scotus. When his philosophy became unpopular, the term was used in a sarcastic rather than a learned sense, and gradually came to mean "fool"?

"Sad" started as a cheerful word? It is derived from a similar sounding word meaning "full, contented"?

"Giddy," related to the word "God," used to mean "divinely possessed, enthusiastic"?

And "silly" at one time meant "blessed" or "happy," and "large" in early English referred to one's generous nature rather than big stature?

—CARROLL H. JONES

Work

1838. We work not only to produce but to give value to time.
—EUGENE DELACROIX

1839.　Work is of two kinds: first, altering the position of matter at or near the earth's surface relatively to other such matter; second, telling other people to do so. The first kind is unpleasant and ill paid; the second is pleasant and highly paid.

—Bertrand Russell

1840.　Napoleon described his reason for success: "Work," he said in 1816, "is my element. I am born and built for work. I have known the limitations of my legs, I have known the limitations of my eyes; I have never been able to know the limitations of my working capacity."

1841.　What is work? A way to make a living? A way to keep busy? A glue to hold life together? Work is all these things and more. As an activity and as a symbol, work has always pre-occupied us. We do it and we think about it. I go on working for the same reason that a hen goes on laying eggs.

—H. L. Mencken

1842.　Nature was a wise mother when she made it necessary for a man to work to live. In some parts of the wide world it is necessary to work harder than in other parts. There are intemperate climates where it is drudgery to scratch out a bare living, just as there are those idyllic places where food is plentiful and shelter scarcely needed. But in most parts of the world man needs shelter and must work to provide it, just as he must work to keep himself in food.

1843.　Of all work that produces results, nine-tenths must be drudgery. There is no work, from the highest to the lowest, which can be done well by any man who is unwilling to make that sacrifice. Part of the very nobility of the devotion of the true workman to his work consists in the fact that a man is not daunted by finding that drudgery must be done; and no man really succeeds in any walk of life without a good deal of what is called, in ordinary English, "pluck." That is the condition of all work whatever, and it is the condition of all success—and there is nothing which so truly repays itself as this very perseverance against weariness.

1844.　"I am the foundation of *all* prosperity. I am the fount from which all blessings flow. Everything that is of value in the world springs from me. I am the salt that gives life its savor.

"I am the sole support of the poor, and the rich who think they can do without me live futile lives and fill premature graves.

"I am the friend of every worthy youth. If he makes my acquaintance when he is young, and keeps me by his side throughout life, I can do more for him than the richest parent.

"I keep bodies clean and fit, minds alert. I am even the parent of genius itself.

"I am represented from every paper that flies from the press, in every loaf of bread that springs from the oven.

"Fools hate me, wise men love me. The man who shirks me, scorns my aid, never lives—*never really lives,* even though he may continue to breathe.

"Who am I? What am I?—

"My name is W-O-R-K!"

Worldliness

1845. Buying, possessing, accumulating—this is not worldliness. But doing this in the love of it, with no love of God paramount—doing it so that thoughts of eternity and God are an intrusion—doing it so that one's spirit is *secularized* in the process; this is worldliness.

—Herrick Johnson

1846. There is such a thing as a worldly spirit, and there is such a thing as an unworldly spirit—and according as we partake of the one or the other, the savor of the sacrifice of our lives is ordinary, common-place, poor, and base; or elevating, invigorating, useful, noble, and holy.

—Dean Stanley

1847. Worldliness consists in these three: attachment to the outward—attachment to the transitory—attachment to the unreal: in opposition to love for the inward, the eternal, the true: and the one of these affections is necessarily expelled by the other.

Unworldliness is this—to hold things from God in the perpetual conviction that they will not last; to have the world, and not let the world have us; to be the world's masters, and not the world's slaves.

—F. W. Robertson

World relations

1848. World politics takes on the appearance of a square dance. About the time all seems to be going smoothly, everybody changes partners.

1849. I do not see any way of realizing our hopes about world organization in five or six days. Even the Almighty took seven.
—Winston Churchill

1850. Preamble to the
Charter of the United Nations

WE THE PEOPLES OF
THE UNITED NATIONS
Determined

To save succeeding generations from the scourge of war, which twice in our lifetime has brought untold sorrow to mankind, and

To reaffirm faith in fundamental human rights, in the dignity and worth of the human person, in the equal right of men and women and of nations large and small, and

To establish conditions under which justice and respect for the obligations arising from treaties and other sources of international law can be maintained, and

To promote social progress and better standards of life in larger freedom, and for these ends

To practice tolerance and live together in peace with one another as good neighbors, and

To unite our strength to maintain international peace and security, and

To insure, by the acceptance of principles and the institution of methods, that armed force shall not be used, save in the common interest, and

To employ international machinery for the promotion of the economic and social advancement of all peoples, have resolved to combine our efforts to accomplish these aims . . . .

World, The

1851. One old farmer with a lot of wisdom said, "The best thing the Lord ever did was to leave the world to us unfinished so we would have something to do."

—REV. DAVID JOHNSON

1852. The world is divided into three groups—the small one, which makes things happen; the larger one, which watches things happen; and the multitude, which never knows what happens.

Worry—Worries

1853. Little minds have little worries, big minds have no time for worries.

—RALPH WALDO EMERSON

1854. One has two duties—to be worried and not to be worried.

—E. M. FORSTER

1855. Worry: a crime for which we punish ourselves by disturbing our own peace of mind.

1856. Worry is a small stream of fear running through the mind. If there were no fear, there would be no worry.

—CECIL A. POOLE

1857. Worry is a thin stream of fear trickling through the mind. If encouraged, it cuts a channel into which all other thoughts are drained.

—ARTHUR ROCHE

1858. Worry is a shadow on the snow which must pass when night falls, and the snow is but a passing thing; a blanket over flowers.

—DOUGLAS MEADOR

1859. "Don't worry" is the rather foolish advice that some people proffer on almost every occasion. One might as well say to the sun, "Don't rise." Any healthy, thoughtful, worthwhile person who is not utterly wrapped in selfishness cannot help worrying during troubled times. The thing he worries about may tell us what manner of man he is. A man who never worries either has not the character and the mentality necessary, or he just does not care. . . . Worry is merely a cue to do something about that which concerns us and requires action.

Worship

1860. Cut off from the worship of the divine, leisure becomes laziness and work inhuman.

—JOHN PIPER

1861. It is for the sake of man, not of God, that worship and prayers are required; not that God may be rendered more glorious, but that man may be made better—that he may be confirmed in a proper sense of his dependent state, and acquire those pious and virtuous dispositions in which his highest improvement consists.

—THE REV. DR. BLAIR

Youth

1862. Youth is the time to go flashing from one end of the world to the other both in mind and in body, to try the manners of different nations; to hear the chimes at midnight.

—ROBERT LOUIS STEVENSON

1863. The glory of the nation rests in the character of her men. And character comes from boyhood. Thus every boy is a challenge to his elders. It is for them that we must win wars—it is for them that we need a just and lasting peace. For the world of tomorrow, about which all of us are dreaming and planning, will be carried forward by the boys of today.

—HERBERT HOOVER

1864. Each new generation, where youth develops in a free society, has a tendency to act as if history, or life itself, makes a new start with it. In one sense this is healthy for forward-looking adolescents are the delight of their elders. Difficulty arises, however, when youth gets impatient and revolts against "old fashioned" restraints. They seem to be impediments to self-expression. Sometimes they are, but generally it is not so. Every pioneer has found out that pulling out old stumps is hard work.

1865. Regardless of age, you are still young at heart as long as you exclaim "Wow!" instead of "What's the use!" . . . when you say "Hot dog" instead of "Oh, well" . . . when you yell "Yippee" instead of "So what?" . . . when you contend "Everyone's important" instead of "You can't fight City Hall" . . . when you insist "Folks are swell" instead of "You can't trust people anymore" . . . when you greet others with "What a great day to be alive!" instead of "Ho hum" . . . when you believe "Things are looking up" instead of "The world is shot to pieces" . . . when you proclaim "What an opportunity" instead of "What a predicament."
　　　　　　　　　　　　　　　　　　—DR. WILLIAM ARTHUR WARD

1866. 1581—Seventeen-year-old Galileo startled the scientific world with a treatise on the pendulum, written while a student at the University of Pisa in Italy. He admitted making some of his experiments atop the celebrated Leaning Tower of Pisa, the first time that structure had been put to any practical use.

　　　　1751—Fifteen-year-old James Watt became curious about the steaming teakettle in the kitchen of his mother's house at Greenock, Scotland. "All that steam power shouldn't be going to waste," declared thrifty Jimmie. "If it could be harnessed, I might perfect a steam engine and become famous!"

　　　　1787—Twelve-year-old Alexander Anderson began engraving on copper and type in New York City. "No one instructed me how to do it," admitted Alex. "I just picked it up from watching jewelers at work."

　　　　1827—Eighteen-year-old Cyrus Hall McCormick experimented with an idea for speeding up the harvesting of America's grain crops. Within a half-dozen youthful years he expected to patent his reaping machine. It was hailed as one of the greatest advances in scientific farming and a boon to the economic life of the world.

　　　　1859—Twelve-year-old Thomas Alva Edison learned to operate the telegraph instrument while working for the Grand Trunk Railroad on the run between Detroit and Port Huron.

　　　　1861—Fifteen-year-old George Westinghouse designed a rotary engine while working in his father's machine shop at Schenectady, New York. Young George boasted that some day he would invent a safety device for stopping railroad trains—with compressed air.

Youth—Old age

1864—Seventeen-year-old Thomas Alva Edison had just taken out a patent on an automatic telegraph repeater. This was just the first of a promised twelve hundred patents to be secured in what looked like a busy lifetime ahead of Tom Edison.

Youth—Old age

1867. The young are slaves to dreams; the old, servants of regrets.

—HERVEY ALLEN

1868. The error of youth is to believe that intelligence is a substitute for experience, while the error of age is to believe that experience is a substitute for intelligence.

—LYMAN BRYSON

Zeal

1869. Zeal is very blind, or badly regulated, when it encroaches upon the rights of others.

—PASQUIER QUESNEL

1870. Perfectly truthful men of very vivid imagination and great force of sentiment often feel so warmly, and express themselves so strongly, as to give to what they say and write a disagreeable air of exaggeration, and almost of falsehood.

—J. F. BOYES

SUBJECT INDEX

(Numbers in the index refer to selections in the text, not to page numbers.)

Subject Index

Aim—Aims, 17
Aimlessness, 24
Air, 711, 1324
Air accident—Air accidents, 1585
Air brake—Air brakes, 1866
Aircraft, 171
Air hole—Air holes, 1464
Airplane—Airplanes, 580
Airplane ride, 1140
Alabama, State of, 94
Alaskan—Alaskans, 1691
Alcohol, 506
Alertness, 77–79
Alias—Aliases, 1604
Alibi—Alibis, 80
Alimony, 81, 82
Ally—Allies, 83
Alms, 712
Aloofness, 1811
Altar—Altars, 153
Alteration—Alterations, 446, 1012
Altruism, 1501
Amateurism, 144
Ambassador—Ambassadors, 1833
Ambiguity—Ambiguities, 832, 1104
Ambition—Ambitions, 84–88, 251, 284, 558, 561, 706, 987, 1194, 1314, 1557, 1689, 1776
America—American—Americanism, 89–95, 145, 198, 252, 268, 345, 478, 488, 561, 653, 739, 915, 1161, 1267, 1651, 1696, 1812, 1866
American history, 602
America, 622
Amusement—Amusements, 96, 97, 163, 204, 1289, 1438
Analogy—Analogies, 648
Anarchy, 649
Ancestor—Ancestors, 101, 156, 1541
Ancestry, 98–101
Andrews Methodist Church, 1162
Angel—Angels, 336, 710, 770, 1467
Angel, Guardian, 1529
Anger, 102–112, 116, 532, 1159, 1357, 1523, 1620
Animal—Animals, 795, 840, 993, 1400
Animal life, 1813
Animosity—Animosities, 510
Annihilation, 1070
Anniversary—Anniversaries, 1159
Annoyance—Annoyances, 1083, 1146
Answer—Answers—Answering, 730, 1386
Ant—Ants, 1032
Antagonism, 25, 113
Anteroom—Anterooms, 1403
Anthem—Anthems, 1396
Anthem, National, 449

Anthropologist—Anthropologists, 739
Anticlimax—Anticlimactic, 165
Antietam Creek, 369
Antipathy—Antipathies, 59
Antique—Antiques, 114, 115, 1476
Antiquarian—Antiquarians, 115
Anvil—Anvils, 464
Anxiety—Anxieties, 331, 386, 557, 777, 1135, 1250, 1290, 1590, 1611
Anxiousness, 1720
Apathy, Public, 1391
Ape—Apes, 568, 569
Apology—Apologies, 116, 117
Apparel, 118–120, 357, 1159
Appearance—Appearances, 56, 222
Appetite—Appetites, 1776
Applause, 441, 1034, 1516, 1784
Apple—Apples, 1081, 1698
Apple seed—Apple seeds, 1212
Application, Job, 541
Appointment—Appointments, 1401, 1403, 1447, 1730
Appreciation, 121–124, 152, 183, 519, 622, 1034, 1145, 1222, 1788
Apprehension—Apprehensions, 187, 1258
Apprenticeship, 1162
Approval, 987
Approval, Popular, 426
April, Month of, 1506, 1730
Apron—Aprons, 1159
Aqueduct—Aqueducts, 425
Arab—Arabs, 481
Arbitration, 1558
Arch—Arches, 1789
Archaeology, 1656
Architect—Architecture, 125, 618
Argument—Arguments, 126–133, 443, 499, 655, 1099, 1635
Argumentativeness, 1346
Arithmetic, 1346, 1679
Arkansas, State of, 94
Arm, Shot in, 1639
Armed forces, 1850
Armenian, 337
Armistice Day, 134, 135
Army—Armies, 631, 1824
Arrogance, 133, 136, 137, 258, 427
Arrow—Arrows, 1577
Art—Arts, 138–142, 933, 1045
Art collection—Art collections, 1476
Art exhibition, 145
Art gallery—Art galleries, 1274
Artist—Artists, 138, 143–145, 1274, 1476, 1558, 1608, 1667
Ash—Ashes, 1472
Aspiration, 284, 1422
Ass—Asses, 1580, 1805

Subject Index

Bellows, Blacksmith's, 691
Beneficence, 758
Benefit—Benefits, 660, 1267, 1618, 1817
Bequest—Bequests, *191, 192,* 1706
Bereavement, 200, 1062
Bet—Bets—Betting, 716
Bethlehem, 206, 336
Betray—Betrayal, 161, *193*
Bible, The, *194–206,* 357, 510, 601, 720, 915, 1316, 1578, 1674, 1722
Bickering, 1775
Bigness, 420, 432, 474, 1853
Bigot—Bigots, *207*
Bigotry, 207, 231, 1739
Bigshot—Bigshots, 1140
Bill of Rights, 364
Biology, 1158
Bird—Birds, 365, 795, 1030, 1813
Birth, 209, 230, 870, 964, 1528
Birth control, *209*
Birthday—Birthdays, 67, 69, 192, *208,* 1159, 1194
Bishop—Bishops, 1529
Bitter—Bitterness, 1007, 1681
Black lie—Black lies, 1004
Blacksmith—Blacksmiths, 710
Blame, *210,* 319, 984, 1725
Blanket—Blankets, 1858
Blank-filling, 401
Blessing—Blessings, 18, 176, *211,* 259, 353, 358, 496, 1069, 1112, 1329, 1697, 1811, 1844
Blindness, 1869
Blizzard—Blizzards, 537
Blood, 362
Bloom—Blooms, 1030
Blossom—Blossoms, 530
Blue Monday, 1837
Blunder—Blunders, 1130, 1258
Bluntness, 16
Boastfulness, 1146, 1692
Body, Human, 458, 999, 1177
Body politic, 1391
Bogey—Bogies, 1190
Bohemian, 337
Boldness, 1183, 1349, 1617
Bomb—Bombs, 1793, 1797
Bond—Bonds, 303
Bone—Bones, 440, 1490
Book—Books, 78, 154, 195, 196, *212–218,* 315, 440, 527, 698, 992, 995, 1102, 1174, 1414, 1425–1427, 1431, 1468
Book case—Book cases, 317
Book cover—Book covers, 430
Bookkeeping, 178, 648
Book learning, 958

Book review—Book reviews, 430
Book title—Book titles, 167
Books, Balance of, 648
Boot, Jack—Boots, Jack 1771
Bore—Bores, *219*
Boredom, *219,* 998, 1597
Borrow—Borrower—Borrowing, *220, 221*
Boss—Bosses, 281, 533, 863, 984, 1700
Boss rule, 1099
Bottle, Empty—Bottles, Empty, 998
Bounty—Bounties, 706, 1001
Bow tie—Bow ties, 161
Boy—Boys, 1337
Boyhood, 1863
Box, Painting—Boxes, Painting, 144
Boxing Day, 336
Brag—Bragging, 1087
Brain—Brains, 15, 143, 171, 782, 1419, 1669, 1829
Brain power, 172
Brake—Brakes, 1451
Branch—Branches, 530
Brandy, 508
Bravery, *222,* 313, 428, 827, 1183, 1268, 1622
Bread, 42, 94, 519, 537, 909, 1002, 1334, 1844
Breadth, 1394
Breakfast food, 42
Breath—Breathing, 669, 691, 1844
Breeze—Breezes, 97, 711
Brevity, *223–225,* 1397
Bribery, *226,* 1312
Brick—Bricks, 446
Bride—Brides, 370, 448, 1495
Bride—Bridegroom, 450
Bridegroom—Bridegrooms, 450
Bridal costume—Bridal costumes, 450
Bridal veil—Bridal veils, 450
Bridge—Bridges, 1167, 1421
Bridge party—Bridge parties, 754
Brimstone fire—Brimstone fires, 820
Brine, Pickle, 1399
British navy, 1202, 1733
Broad-mindedness, 793
Brood—Brooding, 22
Brother—Brothers, 230, 716, 1468
Brotherhood, *227–231,* 428, 622
Brow—Brows, 72, 909
Brush, Artist's, 140
Brush, Paint—Brushes, Paint, 144
Brussels sprout—Brussels sprouts, 1692
Brutality, 560
Bucket—Buckets, 142, 489, 1042, 1284
Budget—Budgets, *232, 233,* 1100
Build—Building, 40

Cynicism, *451*
Czech, 337

D

Dancer, Ballet—Dancers, Ballet, 79
Dandruff, 376
Danger, 21, 156, 164, 169, 369, 418, 446, 509, 614, 628, 827, 1212
Danish, 337
Dare—Dares, 474
Dark glasses, 1295
Darkness, 204, 217, 547, 722, 1043, 1386
Darkroom—Darkrooms, 625
Date—Dates, 481
Datebook—Datebooks, 1722, 1730
Daughter—Daughters, 47, 1688
Dawn, 1386, 1699
Day—Days, 419
Daydream—Daydreams, 1487, 1529
Daydreaming, 909
Dead end, 832
Dead Sea, 1575
Deaf—Deafness, 257
Defeat, 1300
Deal, Political—Deals, Political, 1312
Death, 27, 107, 153, 191, 192, 204, 230, *452–458*, 638, 798, 1028, 1054, 1071, 1096, 1153, 1193, 1211, 1236, 1472, 1528, 1622, 1731, 1805, 1816
Debasement, 319
Debate—Debates—Debating, *459, 460*
Debauchery, 1837
Debt—Debts, 512, 1048
Debt repayment, 220, 221, 462
Debtor—Debtors, 707
Debtor-Creditor—Debtors-Creditors, *461–463*
Decay, 1406
Deceit, 274, 428
Decency, 319
Deception, 230, 392, 902
Decision—Decisions, 52, 111, 150, 327, 331, 442, *464–471*, 536, 903, 940, 1617
Decision, Court—Decisions, Court, 967
Decision, Freedom of, 469
Decision-making, 466
Decisiveness, 161
Dedication, 284, 377
Deductability, 701
Deduction, Tax—Deductions, Tax, 309
Deed—Deeds, 255, 1002
Deed, Good—Deeds, Good, 831
Deed, Great—Deeds, Great, 831
Deed, Heroic—Deeds, Heroic, 603
De-education, 372

Defeat—Defeats, *472, 473,* 626, 678, 770, 1050, 1065, 1105, 1183, 1187, 1603, 1813
Defeatism, *474,* 817
Defect—Defects, 300, 1350
Defense—Defenses, 110, 331
Defense, Mutual, 230
Defenselessness, 938
Deference, 463, 622, 1728
Defiance, 9, 1269
Deficiency—Deficiencies, 911, 1421
Definition—Definitions, 132, 315
Degradation, 363, 522
Degree—Degrees, 1144
Degree, College—Degrees, College, 15, 526
Degree, Honorary—Degrees, Honorary, 1334
Deity, 153
Dejection, 428
Delay—Delays, 108, 377, 465, 829, 1135, 1262, 1620
Delinquency, Juvenile, 1231
Delusion—Delusions, *475, 476,* 847
Demagoguery, 480
Democracy, 231, 319, 470, *477–480,* 1223, 1391, 1798
Demonstration—Demonstrations, 1663
Denial—Denials, 1262
Denunciation, 532
Department store—Department stores, 498, 539
Dependability, 23
Deposit, Bank—Deposits, Bank, 178
Depositor, Bank—Depositors, Bank, 178
Depreciation, Automobile, 175
Deprivation—Deprivations, 32, 192
Depth—Depths, 507, 1394
Deputation—Deputations, 1403
Derailment, 130
Derision, 895
Desecration, 1099
Deserve—Deserving, 405
Design—Designs, 125
Design, Product, 384
Desire—Desires, 495, 799, 847, 887, 1076, 1272, 1325, 1776, 1807
Desolation, 1553
Despair, 60, 131, 204
Desperation, *481*
Despicability, 88
Destination—Destinations, 978, 1139, 1188, 1668
Destiny, 295, 1382
Destitution, 1148
Destruction, 136, 446, 553, 658, 1553
Destructiveness, 439, 885
Detail—Details, 161, 219, 1039, 1761

Subject Index

Moral philosophy, 1767
Moral principle—Moral principles, 93
Moral sickness, 759
Moral theory—Moral theories, 968
Morality, 1382
Morality, Negative, 330
Morals, 1445
Mortar—Mortars, 1153, 1553
Moscow, USSR, 367, 631
Mother—Mothers—Motherhood, 47, 619, *1154–1159*, 1160, 1162
Mother-Daughter—Mothers-Daughters, 47, 1468
Mother—Son—Mothers—Sons, 155, 1093
Mother tongue, 1836
Mother's Day, *1160–1162*
Motion, 1387
Motion picture—Motion pictures, 31, 357
Motive—Motives, *1163, 1164*
Motor—Motors, 406
Motorist—Motorists, 176
Motoring public, 176
Motto—Mottoes, 1504
Mountain—Mountains, 34, 95, 231, 1392, 1497, 1752
Mountain-climbing, 588
Mountain path, 329
Mourn—Mourning, 448, 1742
Mourner—Mourners, 1572
Mouth—Mouths, 1578, 1828
Movie—Movies, 31, 357, 1623
Moving sidewalk, 531
Mud, 96, 402, 1768
Mugwump, John X., 42
Mulberry leaf, 1260
Multitude—Multitudes, 43
Multiply—Multiplies—Multiplication, 800
Muscle—Muscles, 909
Muscle, Human, 172
Music, 37, 679, 986, 1102, *1165–1168*, 1810
Music teacher—Music teachers, 442
Musical instrument—Musical instruments, 1834
Musician—Musicians, 1167, 1588
Mutual concern, 439
Mutual friend—Mutual friends, 753
Mutual help, 822
Mutual trust, 1756
Mutual understanding, 622
Mystery—Mysteries, 505
Myth—Myths, 336

N

Nag—Nagging, 1099
Nahuan Indians, 1162

Nail—Nails, 1046
Naked eye—Naked eyes, 1207
Nakedness, 27
Name—Names, 6, *1169, 1170,* 1213, 1836
Narrowness, 816, 1577
Nation—Nations, 217, 260, 315, *1171*
National anthem, 449
National economy, 602
National lottery, 1651
Native tribe—Native tribes, 739
Natural law, 230, 908, 922
Naturalness, 866
Natural right—Natural rights, 363
Nature, 138, 156, 202, 397, 444, 458, 908, 909, 993, *1172–1174,* 1465, 1575, 1602, 1842
Nature, Law of 1395
Nature lover—Nature lovers, 1752
Navigation, 1464
Nearness, 1255
Neatness, 161
Necktie—Neckties, 161
Need—Needs, 829, 1386
Needle—Needles, 1639
Needlessness, 38
Negative—Negatives, 625, 1212
Negative morality, 330
Negative thought—Negative thoughts, 1703
Negative words, 1835
Neglect, 166, 321, 831, 1039, *1175,* 1255, 1447
Neglect, Parental, 1230
Negro—Negroes, 1415, 1420, 1422
Neighbor—Neighbors, 214, 408, 714, 718, 770, 843, 853, 1135, 1183, 1320, 1468, 1501, 1707
Neighborhood—Neighborhoods, 228
Nerve—Nerves, 450, 1142
Neutrality, 1216
Newly-wed—Newly-weds, 425
Newness, *1176, 1177*
News, 225, 752
Newspaper—Newspapers, 319, 1071, 1844
Newspaper, Alaskan, 1692
Newspaper publishing, 40
New Chicago, Wisconsin, 1170
New England, 94
New Testament, 194
New World, The, 425
New Year, The, 447, *1178–1184*
New Year's Day, 1563
New Year's Eve, 447
New Year's resolution—New Year's resolutions, 1179
New York, N.Y., 606
Night—Nights, 419

"Night and Day," 115
Nobleness, 1511
Nobility, 480, 790
"No Drums, No Bugles," 167
Noise, 842
Nomenclature, 6
Nonconformity, *1185–1187*
Nondiscipline, 322
Noninterference, 763
Nonsense, 1502
Normal—Normalcy, 4, 238
Norse gods, 336
North America, 1307
Northwestern University, 719
Norwegian, 337, 448
Nose—Noses, 182
Nostrum—Nostrums, 1720
Novel—Novels, 167, 1291
Novelty—Novelties, 1177
Nudity, 27
Nuisance—Nuisances, 1232
Number—Numbers, 244, 417
Nursery—Nurseries, 608, 609
Nursing, 870
Nut—Nuts, 1803

O

Oak tree—Oak trees, 1685
Oath, Official, 1345
Obedience, 622, 1031
Objective—Objectives, 825, 1315
Obituary—Obituaries, 294
Obligation—Obligations, 987, 1041, 1295
Oblivion, 1153
Observation—Observations, 28, 1045
Obstacle—Obstacles, 264, 552, *1188, 1189,*
    1616, 1643, 1822
Occasion—Occasions, 826
Ocean—Oceans, 1278
Offense—Offensiveness, 331, 821, 1214,
    1762
Official—Officials, 237
Official, Government, 580
Official, Public—Officials, Public, 364
Office—Offices, 996
Ogre—Ogres, 770
Oil, 424
Oka River, 631
Old age, 55, 69, 259, 293, 456, 548, 560,
    842, 990, 1054, 1085, *1190–1194*, 1257,
    1477, 1531, 1627
Old-fashioned, 1627, 1864
Old shoe—Old shoes, 450
Old Testament, 194, 1651

Olympia, 137
One-night stop—One-night stops, 1475
Open house custom, 447
Openmindedness, 247, 471, *1195*
Opiate—Opiates, 376
Opinion—Opinions, 183, 442, 485, 598,
    1036, 1037, 1066, *1196, 1197,* 1324, 1353,
    1617, 1635, 1774
Opinion, Collective—Opinions, Collective,
    1196
Opponent—Opponents, 133, 736, 741, 1187,
    1609
Opportune—Opportunism, *1198,* 1722, 1725
Opportunity—Opportunities, 15, 29, 150,
    243, 428, 496, 514, 811, 881, 909, 1135,
    1182, 1198, *1199–1202,* 1255, 1478, 1510,
    1522, 1614, 1647, 1684, 1865
Opportunity, Economic—Opportunities,
    Economic, 1422
Opportunity, Equality of, 561
Opposite—Opposites, 39, 914
Opposition, 133, 166, 552, *1203*
Oppression, 854, *1204*
Optimism, 69, 601, *1205–1207,* 1703
Optimist—Optimists, 1198, 1206, 1208, 1209
Optimism—Pessimism, *1208–1212*
Orator—Orators, 1395
Orbit—Orbits, 1089
Orchestra—Orchestras, 1588
Orchid—Orchids, 1320
Ordeal, Trial by, 1798
Orderliness, 446
Ordinariness, 1610
Organization—Organizations, 1361
Organization, Beaten—Organizations,
    Beaten, 394
Organizer—Organizers, 1608
Origin—Origins, 1590
Originality, 693, 889, 1647
Ornament—Ornaments, 856
Orphan—Orphans, 1038
Orthography, 797
Ostara (Easter), 510
Ostentation, 706, 1807, *1213, 1214*
Other—Others, 18, 254, 554, 792, 800, 810,
    1201, 1341, 1385, 1428, 1618, 1702
Ounce—Ounces, 259
Outdoors, 1698
Outer space, *1215*
Outlet—Outlets, 1575
Oven—Ovens, 1844
Overbearing, 1501
Overconfidence, 393, 1332
Overprotectiveness, 326
Overstatement, 1138
Overestimation, 1528

Subject Index

Subject Index

Watch dial, 173
Watchword—Watchwords, 927
Water, 96, 402, 489, 711, 1575, 1733
Water, Cold, 869
Water, Glass of, 1733
Water, Still, 225
Waterfall—Waterfalls, 913
Wave—Waves, 1115
Weaker Sex, 1829
Weakness—Weaknesses, 131, 333, 419, 560, 668, 764, 938, *1799, 1801,* 1829
Wealth, 27, 77, 114, 155, 303, 310, 357, 480, 488, 514, 552, 559, 654, 660, 764, 838, 933, 1039, 1094, 1308, 1320, 1321, 1324, 1429, 1547, 1582, 1609, 1633, 1706, 1710, *1802–1811*
Weapon—Weapons, 276, 1726, 1830
Weariness, 1159, 1166, 1234, 1843
Weather, 785, 1170, *1812, 1813*
Wedding—Weddings, 1099
Wedding cake—Wedding cakes, 450
Wedding customer, 448
Wedding, Japanese, 341
Wedding ring—Wedding rings, 450
Weed—Weeds, 1210, 1630
Weep—Weeping, 963
Weight, 235
Welfare, Intellectual, 561
Well-dressed, 159
Well-heeled, 77
Well-wishing, 1735
Wheat field, 1141
Wheel—Wheels, 234
Whip—Whips—Whipping, 1329
Whiskey, 1693
Whistle—Whistling, 442, 1684
Whistler's father, 1175
White lie—White lies, 1004
Whittle—Whittling, 362
Wholeheartedness, 91, *1814, 1815*
Wickedness, 821, 1328
Wife—Wives, 542, 862, 864, 1313, 1579, 1732
Wild—Wildness, 179
Willingness, 1620
Will power, 299, 474, 1037, 1592, *1818*
Will, Testamentary, *1816, 1817*
Wilt—Wilting, 698
Wind, 442, 723
Window—Windows, 442
Window-box, 689
Wine, 892
Winner—Winners, 312
Winter, 156, 456, 510, 559, 1386, 1473, 1696
Wisconsin, State of, 94

Wisconsin Supreme Court, 940
Wisdom, 20, 57, 66, 68, 75, 109, 215, 225, 250, 318, 374, 488, 521, 578, 579, 592, 770, 813, 893, 952, 958, 959, 973, 1134, 1153, 1182, 1183, 1201, 1248, 1293, 1312, 1347, 1414, 1434, 1546, 1606, *1819–1822*
Wishfulness, *1823, 1824*
Wit and wisdom, 1434, *1825, 1826*
Witch-burning, 1798
Witness—Witnesses, 1343, 1797
Wolf—Wolves, 411, 1198
Woman—Women, 59, 62, 118–120, 155, 249, 293, 326, 644, 1003, 1401, *1827–1829*
Wood-chopping, 489
Word—Words, 126, 132, 255, 303, 416, 488, 614, 1167, 1168, 1265, 1387, 1426, 1481, 1722, *1830–1837*
Word, Indivisible, 654
Word misuse, 1830
Words, Negative, 1835
Words, Positive, 1835
Wordless language, 1167
Work, 15, 236, 244, 333, 379, 532, 622, 984, 1030, 1049, 1439, 1548, 1581, 1595, 1614, *1838–1844*
Work clothes, 1647
Workhouse—Workhouses, 1032
Working people, 269
Workmanship, 1406
World, The, 12, 188, 228, 289, 301, 324, 598, 838, 873, 1082, 1378, 1750, 1751, 1824, 1847, *1851, 1852*
World, Changing, 29
World discovery, 598
World history, 182
World Organization—World Organizations, 1849
World politics, 1848
World relations, *1848–1850*
Worldliness, 1454, *1845–1847*
Worldly spirit, 1846
World War II, 580
Worm—Worms, 481, 687
Worry—Worries, 247, 461, 696, 871, 1093, 1135, 1149, 1198, 1250, 1321, 1480, 1617, 1620, *1853–1859*
Worship, 333, 1463, 1593, 1625, *1860, 1861*
Worship, Freedom of, 364
Worth—Worthiness, 22, 1358
Worthwhileness, 1020
Wound—Wounds, 203, 505, 1261, 1714
Wrapping, 699
Wrath, 103, 104
Wrinkle—Wrinkles, 72, 74, 293
Wristwatch—Wristwatches, 173

340

AUTHOR AND SOURCE INDEX

(Numbers in the index refer to selections
in the text, not to page numbers.)

Author and Source Index

Disraeli, Benjamin, 212, 991, 1281
Dobson, Austin, 1712
Dornbrook, Don, 1425
Dorsey, John M , 1028
Dorst, Larry, 1830
Dowell, Dudley, 29
Downey, William Scott, 819, 1443
Drier, Thomas, 560
Drummond, William, 207
Duggan, Alfred, 9, 269
Dunning, A.E., 930
Dunsany, Lord, 684
Durant, Will, 362
Dwelley, Charles M., 1249

E

Eden, Anthony, 1502
Edwards, Harry, 1666
Edwards, Tryon, 1523
Eibling, Harold H., 833
Eilers, Tom D., 1251
Einstein, Albert, 1072, 1756
Eisenhower, Dwight D., 93
Eliot, George, 700
Eliot, T.S., 1527
Elliott, Eroll T., 648
Elliott, George P., 1822
Ellis, Michael Franklin, 61
Ellman, Edgar S., 1426
Emerson, Ralph Waldo, 213, 216, 413, 435, 501, 555, 764, 904, 1010, 1268, 1293, 1407, 1603, 1719, 1853
Erskine, John, 978
Ervine, St. John, 128
Evans, Louis H., 1092
Evans, Melvin J., 1806
Evans, Richard L., 23, 494

F

Faber, F.W., 942
Fallon, Berlie J., 1670
Farrar, Canon, 1633
Faye, Elizabeth, 770
Feather, William, 183
Felknor, Bruce L., 391
Fichte, Immanuel, 22
Field, Franklin, 1395
Fielding, Henry, 310
Fields, R. McClain, 313
Fife, Shannon, 1081
Fine, Paul A., 1651
Flavel, John, 1576
Fleming, William, 1821

Flynn, Clarence Edwin, 1386
Forbes, B.C., 88, 124, 254, 441, 600, 844, 1274, 1521, 1538, 1605, 1619, 1705, 1757
Ford, Henry, 1039, 1616, 1783
Ford, Henry II., 535
Forster, E.M., 142, 1854
Fosdick, Harry Emerson, 451, 1792
Foster, Elon, 1668
Fowler, C.H., 1535
France, Anatole, 291
Franklin, Benjamin, 133, 273, 1016, 1128, 1657
Frost, Robert, 17, 482, 801
Fry, Christopher, 888
Fuller, Thomas, 187, 423, 669, 780, 1330
Furlong, William Barry, 741

G

Gaines, Francis P., 511
Galsworthy, John, 1482
Garfield, James, 72
Garsek, Isadore, 839
Giles, Henry, 1574
Gill, Gertrude, 215
Gilmer, Ben S., 987
Girardin, Mme. de., 160
Gladstone, William E., 1724
Glasgow, Ellen, 1008
Glasow, Arnold H., 429, 484, 664
Goeser, Alvin H., 893
Goethe, Johann Wolfgang von, 1053, 1414, 1784
Golding, William, 588
Gompers, Samuel L., 269
Goodwin, Lucy R., 172
Goodman, Ralph Lee, 917
Gordon, Julia Weber, 415
Gow, Charles, 1672
Gracián, Baltasar, 12, 150, 468, 557, 617, 790, 793, 1068, 1214, 1277, 1329, 1352, 1369, 1726
Graham, Billy, 1802
Gray, Frank W., 1499
Grayson, David, 263
Greeley, Horace, 1637
Grenfell, Wilfred T., 331
Greville, Lord, 392
Grindon, Leopold H., 1424
Griswold, A. Whitney, 1311, 1539
Grun, Francis J., 252
Guffin, Gilbert L., 1070
Guilliam, Robert, 1276
Gunston, David, 797
Gurnall, W., 1349

Author and Source Index

King, Martin Luther, 228
Kingsley, Charles, 1027
Kirk, Grayson, 324
Kirkpatrick, George R., 1602
Kittredge, A.E., 206
Kleiser, Grenville, 1439
Koestler, Arthur, 193, 1177
Komaiko, Jean R. 1038
Krasteff, Krastyu, 998
Kronenberger, Louis, 219, 383, 1139, 1767

L

Laberius, Decimus, 667
La Bruyère, Jean de., 455
Lachar, Rhoda, 3
Lactantius, Lucius, 821
Laird, Donald A., 1642, 1777
Landor, Walter Savage, 84, 158
Lapp, Charles L., 130
La Rochefoucauld, François de., 476, 666, 773
Lavater, Johann Kaspar, 186
Lawrence, D.H., 1133
Leacock, Stephen, 293
Leclos, Ninon de., 181
Lee, Harper, 398
Lee, Robert, 999
Leighton, Robert, 1357
Lemmon, Clarence E., 1457
Lennon, Joseph L., 373
L'Estrange, Roger, 578
Leterman, Elmer G., 1501, 1677
Lewis, Clive S., 1052
Liebman, Joseph L., 1738
Lincoln, Abraham, 763
Lindop, Boyd, 983
Lipschitz, Jacques, 138
Lippard, George G., 1468
Lipton, Sir Thomas, 1711
Little, Mary Wilson, 1597
Litsey, Edwin Carlile, 1320
Liverdale, Lord, 913
Lockyer, Charles W., 174
Lodge, Henry Cabot, 91
Long, Haniel, 522
Longfellow, Henry Wadsworth, 546, 603, 618
Longstreth, Edward, 1636
Lowell, James Russell, 477, 1120, 1124, 1305, 1434
Lucas, Charles L., 361
Lucas, E.V., 697
Lucas, Richard, 835
Luce, Clare Booth, 376, 1242
Luther, Martin, 845, 1612

Lynd, Robert, 46
Lynes, Russell, 1515
Lyons, Leonard, 1475
Lytton, Edward Bulwer, 503, 597, 605, 673

M

MacArthur, Douglas, 1510
Macartney, Clarence Edward, 1252
Macdonald, George, 96, 1006, 1253
Macduff, J.R., 730
MacIver, Robert J., 854
Maclaren, Alexander, 733, 955, 1455
MacLeish, Archibald, 994
MacNeil, Malcom F., 529
Madariaga, Salvador de, 467
Madison, Orin E., 385
Maeterlinck, Maurice, 746
Magoon, E.L., 25, 1344
Magoun, F. Alexander, 1060, 1063, 1064, 1810
Malchi, Eliezer, 969
Manion, Clarence, 759
Mann, Horace, 692, 787, 1662
Mann, Louis L., 1798
Mant, Richard, 843
Manton, Thomas, 1110
Marchault, Franz, 1163, 1223
Marcus Antonius, 1243
Marryat, Frederick, 1004
Martial, 744
Martin, Joseph W. Jr., 944
Martin, Lawrence H., 1600
Martineau, James, 894
Masterson, Bat, 559
Mason, J.M., 1554
Matthew, Henry, 1454
Maugham, W. Somerset, 1423
Maurois, Andre, 1432
May, Walter Norman, 1418
Meador, Douglas, 71, 87, 1115, 1462, 1754, 1858
Menander, 822
Mencken, H.L., 1841
Meredith, R.R., 203
Meyer, Paul J., 1042
Mill, John Stuart, 1196, 1774
Miller, J.R., 1694
Miller, Olin, 1819
Mills, C. Wright, 956
Mirabeau, Honoré, 898
Mitchell, R. Bryant, 1250
Mitchell, S. Weir, 663
Moe, Henry Allen, 1780
Monnet, Jean, 1365
Monroe, Vaughn, 1264

Author and Source Index

Thomas, David, 97
Thomas, Augustus, 674
Thompson, C.L., 227
Thompson, D'Arcy W., 1626
Thompson, Dorothy, 375, 418
Thoreau, Henry David, 548, 1152, 1513
Thurber, James, 828, 857, 1411
Tillich, Paul, 1104, 1570
Tillotson, John, 1551
Todd, Mike, 1322
Tournier, Paul, 1088
Trueblood, D. Elton, 1138
Tupper, Martin Farquhar, 1137, 1572
Turgot, A. Robert, 598
Twain, Mark, 485, 581, 859, 883

U

Updegraff, Robert R., 1615

V

Vacour, Benso di, 1759
Vanderpoel, Robert P., 1376
Van Dyke, Henry, 85, 1507
Van Gogh, Vincent, 726
Vauvenargues, Luc de Clapiers, 884
Venning, Ralph, 1384, 1803
Voltaire, 121, 889, 1125

W

Walker, Harold Blake, 682, 1094
Walker, Walter, 504
Warburton, William, 549
Ward, Dr. William Arthur, 34, 110, 128, 136, 149, 197, 283, 286, 497, 693, 709, 731, 776, 789, 837, 848, 861, 938, 1030, 1105, 1135, 1200, 1206, 1209, 1212, 1354, 1447, 1581, 1591, 1647, 1663, 1769, 1866
Washington, Booker T., 1204

Waterman, Nixon, 1372
Watson, Thomas J. Sr., 591, 1187
Watson-Watt, Robert, 951
Waugh, Evelyn, 566
Wedgwood, Josiah, 1406
Weiss, Edward H., 169
Wells, E.F., 264
Wenstrom, Donald A., 1695
Wesberry, Jim Jr., 1310
West, Jessamyn, 646
Whately, Richard, 1516
Whewell, William, 593
Whipple, E.P., 1582
White, E.B., 478
White, John, 981
White, J. Gustav, 1793
Whitehead, Alfred North, 1373, 1504
Whitman, Howard J., 1613
Wilcox, Carlos, 453
Wilcox, Ella Wheeler, 1824
Wilde, Oscar, 1011, 1405
Wilkinson, Edith, 318
Willkie, Wendell, 654
Windham, Ralph, 490
Winslow, Octavius, 1634
Wolfe, Harry K., 531
Wolfson, Louis E., 246, 257
Woolcott, Alexander, 1823
Woulfe, Louis Varnum, 428
Wrigley, William Jr., 242

Y

Young, Edward, 779
Young, Owen D., 245
Youngs, Robert W., 714, 1593
Yutang, Lin, 120

Z

Zimmerman, Johann, 1569

349

INDEX TO NAMES AND PERSONALITIES REFERRED TO IN THE TEXT

(Numbers in the index refer to selections in the text, not to page numbers.)

Index to Names and Personalities Referred to in the Text